C-4946 CAREER EXAMINATION SERIES

This is your PASSBOOK for...

Accounting Paraprofessional Test (APT)

Test Preparation Study Guide
Questions & Answers

COPYRIGHT NOTICE

This book is SOLELY intended for, is sold ONLY to, and its use is RESTRICTED to individual, bona fide applicants or candidates who qualify by virtue of having seriously filed applications for appropriate license, certificate, professional and/or promotional advancement, higher school matriculation, scholarship, or other legitimate requirements of education and/or governmental authorities.

This book is NOT intended for use, class instruction, tutoring, training, duplication, copying, reprinting, excerption, or adaptation, etc., by:

1) Other publishers
2) Proprietors and/or Instructors of "Coaching" and/or Preparatory Courses
3) Personnel and/or Training Divisions of commercial, industrial, and governmental organizations
4) Schools, colleges, or universities and/or their departments and staffs, including teachers and other personnel
5) Testing Agencies or Bureaus
6) Study groups which seek by the purchase of a single volume to copy and/or duplicate and/or adapt this material for use by the group as a whole without having purchased individual volumes for each of the members of the group
7) Et al.

Such persons would be in violation of appropriate Federal and State statutes.

PROVISION OF LICENSING AGREEMENTS – Recognized educational, commercial, industrial, and governmental institutions and organizations, and others legitimately engaged in educational pursuits, including training, testing, and measurement activities, may address request for a licensing agreement to the copyright owners, who will determine whether, and under what conditions, including fees and charges, the materials in this book may be used them. In other words, a licensing facility exists for the legitimate use of the material in this book on other than an individual basis. However, it is asseverated and affirmed here that the material in this book CANNOT be used without the receipt of the express permission of such a licensing agreement from the Publishers. Inquiries re licensing should be addressed to the company, attention rights and permissions department.

All rights reserved, including the right of reproduction in whole or in part, in any form or by any means, electronic or mechanical, including photocopying, recording, or by any information storage and retrieval system, without permission in writing from the Publisher.

Copyright © 2025 by
National Learning Corporation

212 Michael Drive, Syosset, NY 11791
(516) 921-8888 • www.passbooks.com
E-mail: info@passbooks.com

PASSBOOK® SERIES

THE *PASSBOOK® SERIES* has been created to prepare applicants and candidates for the ultimate academic battlefield – the examination room.

At some time in our lives, each and every one of us may be required to take an examination – for validation, matriculation, admission, qualification, registration, certification, or licensure.

Based on the assumption that every applicant or candidate has met the basic formal educational standards, has taken the required number of courses, and read the necessary texts, the *PASSBOOK® SERIES* furnishes the one special preparation which may assure passing with confidence, instead of failing with insecurity. Examination questions – together with answers – are furnished as the basic vehicle for study so that the mysteries of the examination and its compounding difficulties may be eliminated or diminished by a sure method.

This book is meant to help you pass your examination provided that you qualify and are serious in your objective.

The entire field is reviewed through the huge store of content information which is succinctly presented through a provocative and challenging approach – the question-and-answer method.

A climate of success is established by furnishing the correct answers at the end of each test.

You soon learn to recognize types of questions, forms of questions, and patterns of questioning. You may even begin to anticipate expected outcomes.

You perceive that many questions are repeated or adapted so that you can gain acute insights, which may enable you to score many sure points.

You learn how to confront new questions, or types of questions, and to attack them confidently and work out the correct answers.

You note objectives and emphases, and recognize pitfalls and dangers, so that you may make positive educational adjustments.

Moreover, you are kept fully informed in relation to new concepts, methods, practices, and directions in the field.

You discover that you are actually taking the examination all the time: you are preparing for the examination by "taking" an examination, not by reading extraneous and/or supererogatory textbooks.

In short, this PASSBOOK®, used directedly, should be an important factor in helping you to pass your test.

Sample Questions for Accounting Paraprofessional Test (APT)

Preparing for the Accounting Paraprofessional Test

Accounting Paraprofessional Test (APT)

What is this test?

The Accounting Paraprofessional Test (APT) is a written exam given to all applicants for accounting paraprofessional jobs.

What kinds of questions are on the test?

The test measures the basic abilities common to accounting paraprofessional jobs. There are sixty items on this test. The test questions are not divided into sections. The areas covered by the test questions are described below:

BOOKKEEPING AND ACCOUNTING PROBLEMS: 20 questions

These questions are designed to assess your ability to work bookkeeping and accounting problems.

MATH: 15 questions

These questions test your ability to compute the answer for basic mathematical word problems. You will be asked to make addition, subtraction, division and multiplication computations. You will also be asked to compute percentages and averages.

JOURNAL PROBLEMS: 15 questions

These questions are designed to assess your ability to decide the correct journal entry for specific transactions.

ACCOUNTING TERMS: 10 questions

These questions are designed to assess your knowledge of accounting term meanings.

How do I use this booklet?

This booklet contains a sample of the different types of questions on the test. None of the sample questions will actually be on the test, but they are very similar to the actual questions.

After the end of the sample question section, you are given the correct answers. You should carefully study each sample question to become familiar with questions of the same type on the test. Do not be discouraged if you are unable to answer some of the sample questions correctly.

Tips for taking the test

1. To avoid the risk of arriving too late to be admitted to the test, allow extra time for traveling to the test center. **Notify State Civil Service in advance, if you will require special testing accommodations due to a disability.**
2. Pay close attention to the instructions given by the monitor at the beginning of the test session.
3. Read the instructions included in the written test booklet carefully. These instructions are given to help you and should be followed very closely.
4. Use your watch or clock to keep track of the time.
5. Read each question carefully. Then read all of the answers to each question before deciding which answer is correct.
6. If you are having a hard time answering a question, skip that one and come back to it later if you have the time.
7. Try to answer each question even if you must guess at the answer. The final grade will be based only on the number of correct answers. There is no penalty for guessing.
8. Be sure to mark your answer properly on your answer sheet and not in the test booklet. You will only be given credit for answers you mark on the answer sheet.

Sample Questions

BOOKKEEPING AND ACCOUNTING PROBLEMS

Use the following information to answer questions 1-3: The table shown below has positive and negative numbers entered in the rows and columns. Use this table to answer questions 1 through 3.

582.76	321.54	-439.07
159.35	-647.28	-271.99
467.15	722.63	-951.63

1. The total of the second column is:
    1. -759.92
    2. -399.89
    3. 396.89
    4. 759.92

2. The total of the first row is:
    1. 465.23

2. 1209.26
3. 1343.37
4. -871.63

3. The total of the third column is:
    1. 845.95
    2. 238.15
    3. -356.29
    4. -1662.69

Use the following information for questions 4-6: The table below indicates the gross wages, insurance payment and net pay for each of three employees. Use this table to answer questions 4 through 6.

Employee Name	Gross Wages	Insurance Payment	Net Pay
Chris Taylor	$ 840.00	50.00	714.00
Pat Jones	1445.00	176.50	1068.50
Peter Spence	950.00	95.00	783.00

4. What percentage of gross wages from Peter Spence's check is being paid for insurance?
    1. 10%
    2. 15%
    3. 20%
    4. 22%

5. What percentages of gross wages is Chris Taylor receiving as net pay?
    1. 35%
    2. 54%
    3. 67%
    4. 85%

6. What would 12 percent of Pat Jones' gross wages be?
    1. $157.50
    2. $173.40
    3. $361.25
    4. $433.50

ACCOUNTING TERMS

7. A credit to a revenue account:
    1. decreases revenues.

2. increases equity.
3. decreases equity.
4. increases assets.

8. An amount, payable in money, goods, or service, owed by a business to a creditor is known as a/n:
   1. equity.
   2. debt.
   3. liability.
   4. asset.

9. The "straight-line" method of depreciation assumes that:
   1. the amount charged to operations, if placed on interest, will accumulate to more than the amount to be depreciated.
   2. the asset being depreciated will usually require heavier repairs in the later periods.
   3. the rate of return of an asset depreciated decreases with the age of the asset.
   4. the depreciation of an asset is a uniform function of time.

10. An accounting system that records income when earned and expenditures when the liability is incurred operates on the:
    1. cash basis.
    2. cumulative basis.
    3. deferred basis.
    4. accrual basis.

JOURNALIZING

Use the following passage to answer questions 11 through 14. Transactions take place during the current accounting period. Choose the correct journal entry for the transaction listed. Use the accounts listed below in formulating your journal entry.

Mage, Incorporated is a major department store in this area. A partial list of accounts used in the business is listed below.

Accounts Payable	Interest Receivable
Accounts Receivable	Notes Payable
Allowance for Bad Debt	Prepaid Taxes
Bad Debt Expense	Tax Expenses
Cash	Purchases
Cash Dividend	Purchase Returns and Allowances
Common Stock	Retained Earnings
Insurance Expense	Sales

| Interest Expense | Sales Returns and Allowances |
| Interest Income | Taxes Payable |

11. The company bought merchandise totaling $5000 on account.
    1. Debit Accounts Payable; credit Cash.
    2. Debit Purchases; credit Accounts Payable.
    3. Debit cash; credit Sales.
    4. Debit Accounts Payable; credit Purchases.

12. A customer returned merchandise that he had previously purchased on account.
    1. Debit Sales Returned and Allowances; credit Accounts Receivable.
    2. Debit Sales Returns and Allowances; credit Cash.
    3. Debit Cash; credit Accounts Receivable.
    4. Debit Sales Returns and Allowances; credit Accounts Receivable, Sales.

13. Received payment from a customer account; the payment included interest charges.
    1. Debit Interest Income; credit Cash.
    2. Debit Notes Payable, Cash; credit Interest Income, Accounts Receivable.
    3. Debit Cash; credit Cash, interest Income.
    4. Debit Cash; credit Accounts Receivable, Interest Income.

14. The accountant recorded the taxes accrued at the end of the period.
    1. Debit Tax Expense; credit Cash.
    2. Debit Taxes Payable; credit Tax Expense.
    3. Debit Tax Expense; credit Taxes Payable.
    4. Debit Prepaid Taxes; credit Cash.

MATH

15. Pat Wilmont processed 300 purchase agreements during the month of June. During the month of July, she processed 10 percent fewer purchase agreements. How many purchase agreements did she process in July?
    1. 220
    2. 240
    3. 270
    4. 280

16. A state employee drove from Lake Charles to a conference in Baton Rouge. A total distance from the round trip was 240 miles. The time required to travel one way to Baton Rouge was two hours. Due to heavy traffic during the return trip to Lake Charles, an extra hour was required. How much slower was the state employee traveling on the return trip?
    1. 20 mph slower

2. 15 mph slower
3. 10 mph slower
4. None of the above.

17. Yellow Marker Pens   5 boxes @ $4.37 a box
    Lined Legal Sized Tablets 8 tablets @ $1.49 a tablet
    Letter-Sized Binders   12 boxes of 24 @ $6.92 a box

What will the cost of these supplies be, if a 10 percent discount is given to the total cost?
1. $ 83.04
2. $ 94.89
3. $ 105.13
4. $ 115.81

18. The estimated completion time for a particular 100 item test is 3 1/3 hours. Ten applicants actually took the test and completed it in 3 hours. What is the difference between the actual and estimated rate of completion per item?

1. 10 seconds per item
2. 12 seconds per item
3. 14 seconds per item
4. 16 seconds per item

Answers to Sample Test Questions

Bookkeeping and Accounting Problems

1. 3
2. 1
3. 4
4. 1
5. 4
6. 2

Accounting Terms

7. 2
8. 3
9. 4
10. 4

Journalizing

11. 2
12. 1
13. 4
14. 3

Math

15. 3
16. 1
17. 3
18. 2

HOW TO TAKE A TEST

I. YOU MUST PASS AN EXAMINATION

A. WHAT EVERY CANDIDATE SHOULD KNOW

Examination applicants often ask us for help in preparing for the written test. What can I study in advance? What kinds of questions will be asked? How will the test be given? How will the papers be graded?

As an applicant for a civil service examination, you may be wondering about some of these things. Our purpose here is to suggest effective methods of advance study and to describe civil service examinations.

Your chances for success on this examination can be increased if you know how to prepare. Those "pre-examination jitters" can be reduced if you know what to expect. You can even experience an adventure in good citizenship if you know why civil service exams are given.

B. WHY ARE CIVIL SERVICE EXAMINATIONS GIVEN?

Civil service examinations are important to you in two ways. As a citizen, you want public jobs filled by employees who know how to do their work. As a job seeker, you want a fair chance to compete for that job on an equal footing with other candidates. The best-known means of accomplishing this two-fold goal is the competitive examination.

Exams are widely publicized throughout the nation. They may be administered for jobs in federal, state, city, municipal, town or village governments or agencies.

Any citizen may apply, with some limitations, such as the age or residence of applicants. Your experience and education may be reviewed to see whether you meet the requirements for the particular examination. When these requirements exist, they are reasonable and applied consistently to all applicants. Thus, a competitive examination may cause you some uneasiness now, but it is your privilege and safeguard.

C. HOW ARE CIVIL SERVICE EXAMS DEVELOPED?

Examinations are carefully written by trained technicians who are specialists in the field known as "psychological measurement," in consultation with recognized authorities in the field of work that the test will cover. These experts recommend the subject matter areas or skills to be tested; only those knowledges or skills important to your success on the job are included. The most reliable books and source materials available are used as references. Together, the experts and technicians judge the difficulty level of the questions.

Test technicians know how to phrase questions so that the problem is clearly stated. Their ethics do not permit "trick" or "catch" questions. Questions may have been tried out on sample groups, or subjected to statistical analysis, to determine their usefulness.

Written tests are often used in combination with performance tests, ratings of training and experience, and oral interviews. All of these measures combine to form the best-known means of finding the right person for the right job.

II. HOW TO PASS THE WRITTEN TEST

A. NATURE OF THE EXAMINATION

To prepare intelligently for civil service examinations, you should know how they differ from school examinations you have taken. In school you were assigned certain definite pages to read or subjects to cover. The examination questions were quite detailed and usually emphasized memory. Civil service exams, on the other hand, try to discover your present ability to perform the duties of a position, plus your potentiality to learn these duties. In other words, a civil service exam attempts to predict how successful you will be. Questions cover such a broad area that they cannot be as minute and detailed as school exam questions.

In the public service similar kinds of work, or positions, are grouped together in one "class." This process is known as *position-classification*. All the positions in a class are paid according to the salary range for that class. One class title covers all of these positions, and they are all tested by the same examination.

B. FOUR BASIC STEPS

1) Study the announcement

How, then, can you know what subjects to study? Our best answer is: "Learn as much as possible about the class of positions for which you've applied." The exam will test the knowledge, skills and abilities needed to do the work.

Your most valuable source of information about the position you want is the official exam announcement. This announcement lists the training and experience qualifications. Check these standards and apply only if you come reasonably close to meeting them.

The brief description of the position in the examination announcement offers some clues to the subjects which will be tested. Think about the job itself. Review the duties in your mind. Can you perform them, or are there some in which you are rusty? Fill in the blank spots in your preparation.

Many jurisdictions preview the written test in the exam announcement by including a section called "Knowledge and Abilities Required," "Scope of the Examination," or some similar heading. Here you will find out specifically what fields will be tested.

2) Review your own background

Once you learn in general what the position is all about, and what you need to know to do the work, ask yourself which subjects you already know fairly well and which need improvement. You may wonder whether to concentrate on improving your strong areas or on building some background in your fields of weakness. When the announcement has specified "some knowledge" or "considerable knowledge," or has used adjectives like "beginning principles of…" or "advanced … methods," you can get a clue as to the number and difficulty of questions to be asked in any given field. More questions, and hence broader coverage, would be included for those subjects which are more important in the work. Now weigh your strengths and weaknesses against the job requirements and prepare accordingly.

3) Determine the level of the position

Another way to tell how intensively you should prepare is to understand the level of the job for which you are applying. Is it the entering level? In other words, is this the position in which beginners in a field of work are hired? Or is it an intermediate or advanced level? Sometimes this is indicated by such words as "Junior" or "Senior" in the class title. Other jurisdictions use Roman numerals to designate the level – Clerk I, Clerk II, for example. The word "Supervisor" sometimes appears in the title. If the level is not indicated by the title, check the description of duties. Will you be working under very close supervision, or will you have responsibility for independent decisions in this work?

4) Choose appropriate study materials

Now that you know the subjects to be examined and the relative amount of each subject to be covered, you can choose suitable study materials. For beginning level jobs, or even advanced ones, if you have a pronounced weakness in some aspect of your training, read a modern, standard textbook in that field. Be sure it is up to date and has general coverage. Such books are normally available at your library, and the librarian will be glad to help you locate one. For entry-level positions, questions of appropriate difficulty are chosen – neither highly advanced questions, nor those too simple. Such questions require careful thought but not advanced training.

If the position for which you are applying is technical or advanced, you will read more advanced, specialized material. If you are already familiar with the basic principles of your field, elementary textbooks would waste your time. Concentrate on advanced textbooks and technical periodicals. Think through the concepts and review difficult problems in your field.

These are all general sources. You can get more ideas on your own initiative, following these leads. For example, training manuals and publications of the government agency which employs workers in your field can be useful, particularly for technical and professional positions. A letter or visit to the government department involved may result in more specific study suggestions, and certainly will provide you with a more definite idea of the exact nature of the position you are seeking.

III. KINDS OF TESTS

Tests are used for purposes other than measuring knowledge and ability to perform specified duties. For some positions, it is equally important to test ability to make adjustments to new situations or to profit from training. In others, basic mental abilities not dependent on information are essential. Questions which test these things may not appear as pertinent to the duties of the position as those which test for knowledge and information. Yet they are often highly important parts of a fair examination. For very general questions, it is almost impossible to help you direct your study efforts. What we can do is to point out some of the more common of these general abilities needed in public service positions and describe some typical questions.

1) General information

Broad, general information has been found useful for predicting job success in some kinds of work. This is tested in a variety of ways, from vocabulary lists to questions about current events. Basic background in some field of work, such as sociology or economics, may be sampled in a group of questions. Often these are principles which have become familiar to most persons through exposure rather than through formal training. It is difficult to advise you how to study for these questions; being alert to the world around you is our best suggestion.

2) Verbal ability

An example of an ability needed in many positions is verbal or language ability. Verbal ability is, in brief, the ability to use and understand words. Vocabulary and grammar tests are typical measures of this ability. Reading comprehension or paragraph interpretation questions are common in many kinds of civil service tests. You are given a paragraph of written material and asked to find its central meaning.

3) Numerical ability

Number skills can be tested by the familiar arithmetic problem, by checking paired lists of numbers to see which are alike and which are different, or by interpreting charts and graphs. In the latter test, a graph may be printed in the test booklet which you are asked to use as the basis for answering questions.

4) Observation

A popular test for law-enforcement positions is the observation test. A picture is shown to you for several minutes, then taken away. Questions about the picture test your ability to observe both details and larger elements.

5) Following directions

In many positions in the public service, the employee must be able to carry out written instructions dependably and accurately. You may be given a chart with several columns, each column listing a variety of information. The questions require you to carry out directions involving the information given in the chart.

6) Skills and aptitudes

Performance tests effectively measure some manual skills and aptitudes. When the skill is one in which you are trained, such as typing or shorthand, you can practice. These tests are often very much like those given in business school or high school courses. For many of the other skills and aptitudes, however, no short-time preparation can be made. Skills and abilities natural to you or that you have developed throughout your lifetime are being tested.

Many of the general questions just described provide all the data needed to answer the questions and ask you to use your reasoning ability to find the answers. Your best preparation for these tests, as well as for tests of facts and ideas, is to be at your physical and mental best. You, no doubt, have your own methods of getting into an exam-taking mood and keeping "in shape." The next section lists some ideas on this subject.

IV. KINDS OF QUESTIONS

Only rarely is the "essay" question, which you answer in narrative form, used in civil service tests. Civil service tests are usually of the short-answer type. Full instructions for answering these questions will be given to you at the examination. But in case this is your first experience with short-answer questions and separate answer sheets, here is what you need to know:

1) Multiple-choice Questions

Most popular of the short-answer questions is the "multiple choice" or "best answer" question. It can be used, for example, to test for factual knowledge, ability to solve problems or judgment in meeting situations found at work.

A multiple-choice question is normally one of three types—
- It can begin with an incomplete statement followed by several possible endings. You are to find the one ending which *best* completes the statement, although some of the others may not be entirely wrong.
- It can also be a complete statement in the form of a question which is answered by choosing one of the statements listed.

- It can be in the form of a problem – again you select the best answer.

Here is an example of a multiple-choice question with a discussion which should give you some clues as to the method for choosing the right answer:

When an employee has a complaint about his assignment, the action which will *best* help him overcome his difficulty is to
   A. discuss his difficulty with his coworkers
   B. take the problem to the head of the organization
   C. take the problem to the person who gave him the assignment
   D. say nothing to anyone about his complaint

In answering this question, you should study each of the choices to find which is best. Consider choice "A" – Certainly an employee may discuss his complaint with fellow employees, but no change or improvement can result, and the complaint remains unresolved. Choice "B" is a poor choice since the head of the organization probably does not know what assignment you have been given, and taking your problem to him is known as "going over the head" of the supervisor. The supervisor, or person who made the assignment, is the person who can clarify it or correct any injustice. Choice "C" is, therefore, correct. To say nothing, as in choice "D," is unwise. Supervisors have and interest in knowing the problems employees are facing, and the employee is seeking a solution to his problem.

2) True/False Questions

The "true/false" or "right/wrong" form of question is sometimes used. Here a complete statement is given. Your job is to decide whether the statement is right or wrong.

SAMPLE: A roaming cell-phone call to a nearby city costs less than a non-roaming call to a distant city.

This statement is wrong, or false, since roaming calls are more expensive.

This is not a complete list of all possible question forms, although most of the others are variations of these common types. You will always get complete directions for answering questions. Be sure you understand *how* to mark your answers – ask questions until you do.

V. RECORDING YOUR ANSWERS

Computer terminals are used more and more today for many different kinds of exams.
For an examination with very few applicants, you may be told to record your answers in the test booklet itself. Separate answer sheets are much more common. If this separate answer sheet is to be scored by machine – and this is often the case – it is highly important that you mark your answers correctly in order to get credit.
An electronic scoring machine is often used in civil service offices because of the speed with which papers can be scored. Machine-scored answer sheets must be marked with a pencil, which will be given to you. This pencil has a high graphite content which responds to the electronic scoring machine. As a matter of fact, stray dots may register as answers, so do not let your pencil rest on the answer sheet while you are pondering the correct answer. Also, if your pencil lead breaks or is otherwise defective, ask for another.

Since the answer sheet will be dropped in a slot in the scoring machine, be careful not to bend the corners or get the paper crumpled.

The answer sheet normally has five vertical columns of numbers, with 30 numbers to a column. These numbers correspond to the question numbers in your test booklet. After each number, going across the page are four or five pairs of dotted lines. These short dotted lines have small letters or numbers above them. The first two pairs may also have a "T" or "F" above the letters. This indicates that the first two pairs only are to be used if the questions are of the true-false type. If the questions are multiple choice, disregard the "T" and "F" and pay attention only to the small letters or numbers.

Answer your questions in the manner of the sample that follows:

32. The largest city in the United States is
    A. Washington, D.C.
    B. New York City
    C. Chicago
    D. Detroit
    E. San Francisco

1) Choose the answer you think is best. (New York City is the largest, so "B" is correct.)
2) Find the row of dotted lines numbered the same as the question you are answering. (Find row number 32)
3) Find the pair of dotted lines corresponding to the answer. (Find the pair of lines under the mark "B.")
4) Make a solid black mark between the dotted lines.

VI. BEFORE THE TEST

Common sense will help you find procedures to follow to get ready for an examination. Too many of us, however, overlook these sensible measures. Indeed, nervousness and fatigue have been found to be the most serious reasons why applicants fail to do their best on civil service tests. Here is a list of reminders:

- Begin your preparation early – Don't wait until the last minute to go scurrying around for books and materials or to find out what the position is all about.
- Prepare continuously – An hour a night for a week is better than an all-night cram session. This has been definitely established. What is more, a night a week for a month will return better dividends than crowding your study into a shorter period of time.
- Locate the place of the exam – You have been sent a notice telling you when and where to report for the examination. If the location is in a different town or otherwise unfamiliar to you, it would be well to inquire the best route and learn something about the building.
- Relax the night before the test – Allow your mind to rest. Do not study at all that night. Plan some mild recreation or diversion; then go to bed early and get a good night's sleep.
- Get up early enough to make a leisurely trip to the place for the test – This way unforeseen events, traffic snarls, unfamiliar buildings, etc. will not upset you.
- Dress comfortably – A written test is not a fashion show. You will be known by number and not by name, so wear something comfortable.

- Leave excess paraphernalia at home – Shopping bags and odd bundles will get in your way. You need bring only the items mentioned in the official notice you received; usually everything you need is provided. Do not bring reference books to the exam. They will only confuse those last minutes and be taken away from you when in the test room.
- Arrive somewhat ahead of time – If because of transportation schedules you must get there very early, bring a newspaper or magazine to take your mind off yourself while waiting.
- Locate the examination room – When you have found the proper room, you will be directed to the seat or part of the room where you will sit. Sometimes you are given a sheet of instructions to read while you are waiting. Do not fill out any forms until you are told to do so; just read them and be prepared.
- Relax and prepare to listen to the instructions
- If you have any physical problem that may keep you from doing your best, be sure to tell the test administrator. If you are sick or in poor health, you really cannot do your best on the exam. You can come back and take the test some other time.

VII. AT THE TEST

The day of the test is here and you have the test booklet in your hand. The temptation to get going is very strong. Caution! There is more to success than knowing the right answers. You must know how to identify your papers and understand variations in the type of short-answer question used in this particular examination. Follow these suggestions for maximum results from your efforts:

1) Cooperate with the monitor

The test administrator has a duty to create a situation in which you can be as much at ease as possible. He will give instructions, tell you when to begin, check to see that you are marking your answer sheet correctly, and so on. He is not there to guard you, although he will see that your competitors do not take unfair advantage. He wants to help you do your best.

2) Listen to all instructions

Don't jump the gun! Wait until you understand all directions. In most civil service tests you get more time than you need to answer the questions. So don't be in a hurry. Read each word of instructions until you clearly understand the meaning. Study the examples, listen to all announcements and follow directions. Ask questions if you do not understand what to do.

3) Identify your papers

Civil service exams are usually identified by number only. You will be assigned a number; you must not put your name on your test papers. Be sure to copy your number correctly. Since more than one exam may be given, copy your exact examination title.

4) Plan your time

Unless you are told that a test is a "speed" or "rate of work" test, speed itself is usually not important. Time enough to answer all the questions will be provided, but this does not mean that you have all day. An overall time limit has been set. Divide the total time (in minutes) by the number of questions to determine the approximate time you have for each question.

5) Do not linger over difficult questions

If you come across a difficult question, mark it with a paper clip (useful to have along) and come back to it when you have been through the booklet. One caution if you do this – be sure to skip a number on your answer sheet as well. Check often to be sure that you have not lost your place and that you are marking in the row numbered the same as the question you are answering.

6) Read the questions

Be sure you know what the question asks! Many capable people are unsuccessful because they failed to *read* the questions correctly.

7) Answer all questions

Unless you have been instructed that a penalty will be deducted for incorrect answers, it is better to guess than to omit a question.

8) Speed tests

It is often better NOT to guess on speed tests. It has been found that on timed tests people are tempted to spend the last few seconds before time is called in marking answers at random – without even reading them – in the hope of picking up a few extra points. To discourage this practice, the instructions may warn you that your score will be "corrected" for guessing. That is, a penalty will be applied. The incorrect answers will be deducted from the correct ones, or some other penalty formula will be used.

9) Review your answers

If you finish before time is called, go back to the questions you guessed or omitted to give them further thought. Review other answers if you have time.

10) Return your test materials

If you are ready to leave before others have finished or time is called, take ALL your materials to the monitor and leave quietly. Never take any test material with you. The monitor can discover whose papers are not complete, and taking a test booklet may be grounds for disqualification.

VIII. EXAMINATION TECHNIQUES

1) Read the general instructions carefully. These are usually printed on the first page of the exam booklet. As a rule, these instructions refer to the timing of the examination; the fact that you should not start work until the signal and must stop work at a signal, etc. If there are any *special* instructions, such as a choice of questions to be answered, make sure that you note this instruction carefully.

2) When you are ready to start work on the examination, that is as soon as the signal has been given, read the instructions to each question booklet, underline any key words or phrases, such as *least, best, outline, describe* and the like. In this way you will tend to answer as requested rather than discover on reviewing your paper that you *listed without describing*, that you selected the *worst* choice rather than the *best* choice, etc.

3) If the examination is of the objective or multiple-choice type – that is, each question will also give a series of possible answers: A, B, C or D, and you are called upon to select the best answer and write the letter next to that answer on your answer paper – it is advisable to start answering each question in turn. There may be anywhere from 50 to 100 such questions in the three or four hours allotted and you can see how much time would be taken if you read through all the questions before beginning to answer any. Furthermore, if you come across a question or group of questions which you know would be difficult to answer, it would undoubtedly affect your handling of all the other questions.

4) If the examination is of the essay type and contains but a few questions, it is a moot point as to whether you should read all the questions before starting to answer any one. Of course, if you are given a choice – say five out of seven and the like – then it is essential to read all the questions so you can eliminate the two that are most difficult. If, however, you are asked to answer all the questions, there may be danger in trying to answer the easiest one first because you may find that you will spend too much time on it. The best technique is to answer the first question, then proceed to the second, etc.

5) Time your answers. Before the exam begins, write down the time it started, then add the time allowed for the examination and write down the time it must be completed, then divide the time available somewhat as follows:
    - If 3-1/2 hours are allowed, that would be 210 minutes. If you have 80 objective-type questions, that would be an average of 2-1/2 minutes per question. Allow yourself no more than 2 minutes per question, or a total of 160 minutes, which will permit about 50 minutes to review.
    - If for the time allotment of 210 minutes there are 7 essay questions to answer, that would average about 30 minutes a question. Give yourself only 25 minutes per question so that you have about 35 minutes to review.

6) The most important instruction is to *read each question* and make sure you know what is wanted. The second most important instruction is to *time yourself properly* so that you answer every question. The third most important instruction is to *answer every question*. Guess if you have to but include something for each question. Remember that you will receive no credit for a blank and will probably receive some credit if you write something in answer to an essay question. If you guess a letter – say "B" for a multiple-choice question – you may have guessed right. If you leave a blank as an answer to a multiple-choice question, the examiners may respect your feelings but it will not add a point to your score. Some exams may penalize you for wrong answers, so in such cases *only*, you may not want to guess unless you have some basis for your answer.

7) Suggestions
    a. Objective-type questions
        1. Examine the question booklet for proper sequence of pages and questions
        2. Read all instructions carefully
        3. Skip any question which seems too difficult; return to it after all other questions have been answered
        4. Apportion your time properly; do not spend too much time on any single question or group of questions

5. Note and underline key words – *all, most, fewest, least, best, worst, same, opposite*, etc.
6. Pay particular attention to negatives
7. Note unusual option, e.g., unduly long, short, complex, different or similar in content to the body of the question
8. Observe the use of "hedging" words – *probably, may, most likely*, etc.
9. Make sure that your answer is put next to the same number as the question
10. Do not second-guess unless you have good reason to believe the second answer is definitely more correct
11. Cross out original answer if you decide another answer is more accurate; do not erase until you are ready to hand your paper in
12. Answer all questions; guess unless instructed otherwise
13. Leave time for review

  b. Essay questions
    1. Read each question carefully
    2. Determine exactly what is wanted. Underline key words or phrases.
    3. Decide on outline or paragraph answer
    4. Include many different points and elements unless asked to develop any one or two points or elements
    5. Show impartiality by giving pros and cons unless directed to select one side only
    6. Make and write down any assumptions you find necessary to answer the questions
    7. Watch your English, grammar, punctuation and choice of words
    8. Time your answers; don't crowd material

8) Answering the essay question

Most essay questions can be answered by framing the specific response around several key words or ideas. Here are a few such key words or ideas:

M's: manpower, materials, methods, money, management
P's: purpose, program, policy, plan, procedure, practice, problems, pitfalls, personnel, public relations

  a. Six basic steps in handling problems:
    1. Preliminary plan and background development
    2. Collect information, data and facts
    3. Analyze and interpret information, data and facts
    4. Analyze and develop solutions as well as make recommendations
    5. Prepare report and sell recommendations
    6. Install recommendations and follow up effectiveness

  b. Pitfalls to avoid
    1. *Taking things for granted* – A statement of the situation does not necessarily imply that each of the elements is necessarily true; for example, a complaint may be invalid and biased so that all that can be taken for granted is that a complaint has been registered

2. *Considering only one side of a situation* – Wherever possible, indicate several alternatives and then point out the reasons you selected the best one
3. *Failing to indicate follow up* – Whenever your answer indicates action on your part, make certain that you will take proper follow-up action to see how successful your recommendations, procedures or actions turn out to be
4. *Taking too long in answering any single question* – Remember to time your answers properly

IX. AFTER THE TEST

Scoring procedures differ in detail among civil service jurisdictions although the general principles are the same. Whether the papers are hand-scored or graded by machine we have described, they are nearly always graded by number. That is, the person who marks the paper knows only the number – never the name – of the applicant. Not until all the papers have been graded will they be matched with names. If other tests, such as training and experience or oral interview ratings have been given, scores will be combined. Different parts of the examination usually have different weights. For example, the written test might count 60 percent of the final grade, and a rating of training and experience 40 percent. In many jurisdictions, veterans will have a certain number of points added to their grades.

After the final grade has been determined, the names are placed in grade order and an eligible list is established. There are various methods for resolving ties between those who get the same final grade – probably the most common is to place first the name of the person whose application was received first. Job offers are made from the eligible list in the order the names appear on it. You will be notified of your grade and your rank as soon as all these computations have been made. This will be done as rapidly as possible.

People who are found to meet the requirements in the announcement are called "eligibles." Their names are put on a list of eligible candidates. An eligible's chances of getting a job depend on how high he stands on this list and how fast agencies are filling jobs from the list.

When a job is to be filled from a list of eligibles, the agency asks for the names of people on the list of eligibles for that job. When the civil service commission receives this request, it sends to the agency the names of the three people highest on this list. Or, if the job to be filled has specialized requirements, the office sends the agency the names of the top three persons who meet these requirements from the general list.

The appointing officer makes a choice from among the three people whose names were sent to him. If the selected person accepts the appointment, the names of the others are put back on the list to be considered for future openings.

That is the rule in hiring from all kinds of eligible lists, whether they are for typist, carpenter, chemist, or something else. For every vacancy, the appointing officer has his choice of any one of the top three eligibles on the list. This explains why the person whose name is on top of the list sometimes does not get an appointment when some of the persons lower on the list do. If the appointing officer chooses the second or third eligible, the No. 1 eligible does not get a job at once, but stays on the list until he is appointed or the list is terminated.

X. HOW TO PASS THE INTERVIEW TEST

The examination for which you applied requires an oral interview test. You have already taken the written test and you are now being called for the interview test – the final part of the formal examination.

You may think that it is not possible to prepare for an interview test and that there are no procedures to follow during an interview. Our purpose is to point out some things you can do in advance that will help you and some good rules to follow and pitfalls to avoid while you are being interviewed.

What is an interview supposed to test?

The written examination is designed to test the technical knowledge and competence of the candidate; the oral is designed to evaluate intangible qualities, not readily measured otherwise, and to establish a list showing the relative fitness of each candidate – as measured against his competitors – for the position sought. Scoring is not on the basis of "right" and "wrong," but on a sliding scale of values ranging from "not passable" to "outstanding." As a matter of fact, it is possible to achieve a relatively low score without a single "incorrect" answer because of evident weakness in the qualities being measured.

Occasionally, an examination may consist entirely of an oral test – either an individual or a group oral. In such cases, information is sought concerning the technical knowledges and abilities of the candidate, since there has been no written examination for this purpose. More commonly, however, an oral test is used to supplement a written examination.

Who conducts interviews?

The composition of oral boards varies among different jurisdictions. In nearly all, a representative of the personnel department serves as chairman. One of the members of the board may be a representative of the department in which the candidate would work. In some cases, "outside experts" are used, and, frequently, a businessman or some other representative of the general public is asked to serve. Labor and management or other special groups may be represented. The aim is to secure the services of experts in the appropriate field.

However the board is composed, it is a good idea (and not at all improper or unethical) to ascertain in advance of the interview who the members are and what groups they represent. When you are introduced to them, you will have some idea of their backgrounds and interests, and at least you will not stutter and stammer over their names.

What should be done before the interview?

While knowledge about the board members is useful and takes some of the surprise element out of the interview, there is other preparation which is more substantive. It *is* possible to prepare for an oral interview – in several ways:

1) Keep a copy of your application and review it carefully before the interview

This may be the only document before the oral board, and the starting point of the interview. Know what education and experience you have listed there, and the sequence and dates of all of it. Sometimes the board will ask you to review the highlights of your experience for them; you should not have to hem and haw doing it.

2) Study the class specification and the examination announcement

Usually, the oral board has one or both of these to guide them. The qualities, characteristics or knowledges required by the position sought are stated in these documents. They offer valuable clues as to the nature of the oral interview. For example, if the job involves supervisory responsibilities, the announcement will usually indicate that knowledge of modern supervisory methods and the qualifications of the candidate as a supervisor will be tested. If so, you can expect such questions, frequently in the form of a hypothetical situation which you are expected to solve. NEVER go into an oral without knowledge of the duties and responsibilities of the job you seek.

3) Think through each qualification required

Try to visualize the kind of questions you would ask if you were a board member. How well could you answer them? Try especially to appraise your own knowledge and background in each area, *measured against the job sought*, and identify any areas in which you are weak. Be critical and realistic – do not flatter yourself.

4) Do some general reading in areas in which you feel you may be weak

For example, if the job involves supervision and your past experience has NOT, some general reading in supervisory methods and practices, particularly in the field of human relations, might be useful. Do NOT study agency procedures or detailed manuals. The oral board will be testing your understanding and capacity, not your memory.

5) Get a good night's sleep and watch your general health and mental attitude

You will want a clear head at the interview. Take care of a cold or any other minor ailment, and of course, no hangovers.

What should be done on the day of the interview?

Now comes the day of the interview itself. Give yourself plenty of time to get there. Plan to arrive somewhat ahead of the scheduled time, particularly if your appointment is in the fore part of the day. If a previous candidate fails to appear, the board might be ready for you a bit early. By early afternoon an oral board is almost invariably behind schedule if there are many candidates, and you may have to wait. Take along a book or magazine to read, or your application to review, but leave any extraneous material in the waiting room when you go in for your interview. In any event, relax and compose yourself.

The matter of dress is important. The board is forming impressions about you – from your experience, your manners, your attitude, and your appearance. Give your personal appearance careful attention. Dress your best, but not your flashiest. Choose conservative, appropriate clothing, and be sure it is immaculate. This is a business interview, and your appearance should indicate that you regard it as such. Besides, being well groomed and properly dressed will help boost your confidence.

Sooner or later, someone will call your name and escort you into the interview room. *This is it.* From here on you are on your own. It is too late for any more preparation. But remember, you asked for this opportunity to prove your fitness, and you are here because your request was granted.

What happens when you go in?

The usual sequence of events will be as follows: The clerk (who is often the board stenographer) will introduce you to the chairman of the oral board, who will introduce you to the other members of the board. Acknowledge the introductions before you sit down. Do not be surprised if you find a microphone facing you or a stenotypist sitting by. Oral interviews are usually recorded in the event of an appeal or other review.

Usually the chairman of the board will open the interview by reviewing the highlights of your education and work experience from your application – primarily for the benefit of the other members of the board, as well as to get the material into the record. Do not interrupt or comment unless there is an error or significant misinterpretation; if that is the case, do not hesitate. But do not quibble about insignificant matters. Also, he will usually ask you some question about your education, experience or your present job – partly to get you to start talking and to establish the interviewing "rapport." He may start the actual questioning, or turn it over to one of the other members. Frequently, each member undertakes the questioning on a particular area, one in which he is perhaps most competent, so you can expect each member to participate in the examination. Because time is limited, you may also expect some rather abrupt switches in the direction the questioning takes, so do not be upset by it. Normally, a board member will not pursue a single line of questioning unless he discovers a particular strength or weakness.

After each member has participated, the chairman will usually ask whether any member has any further questions, then will ask you if you have anything you wish to add. Unless you are expecting this question, it may floor you. Worse, it may start you off on an extended, extemporaneous speech. The board is not usually seeking more information. The question is principally to offer you a last opportunity to present further qualifications or to indicate that you have nothing to add. So, if you feel that a significant qualification or characteristic has been overlooked, it is proper to point it out in a sentence or so. Do not compliment the board on the thoroughness of their examination – they have been sketchy, and you know it. If you wish, merely say, "No thank you, I have nothing further to add." This is a point where you can "talk yourself out" of a good impression or fail to present an important bit of information. Remember, *you close the interview yourself.*

The chairman will then say, "That is all, Mr. _____, thank you." Do not be startled; the interview is over, and quicker than you think. Thank him, gather your belongings and take your leave. Save your sigh of relief for the other side of the door.

How to put your best foot forward

Throughout this entire process, you may feel that the board individually and collectively is trying to pierce your defenses, seek out your hidden weaknesses and embarrass and confuse you. Actually, this is not true. They are obliged to make an appraisal of your qualifications for the job you are seeking, and they want to see you in your best light. Remember, they must interview all candidates and a non-cooperative candidate may become a failure in spite of their best efforts to bring out his qualifications. Here are 15 suggestions that will help you:

1) Be natural – Keep your attitude confident, not cocky

If you are not confident that you can do the job, do not expect the board to be. Do not apologize for your weaknesses, try to bring out your strong points. The board is interested in a positive, not negative, presentation. Cockiness will antagonize any board member and make him wonder if you are covering up a weakness by a false show of strength.

2) Get comfortable, but don't lounge or sprawl

Sit erectly but not stiffly. A careless posture may lead the board to conclude that you are careless in other things, or at least that you are not impressed by the importance of the occasion. Either conclusion is natural, even if incorrect. Do not fuss with your clothing, a pencil or an ashtray. Your hands may occasionally be useful to emphasize a point; do not let them become a point of distraction.

3) Do not wisecrack or make small talk

This is a serious situation, and your attitude should show that you consider it as such. Further, the time of the board is limited – they do not want to waste it, and neither should you.

4) Do not exaggerate your experience or abilities

In the first place, from information in the application or other interviews and sources, the board may know more about you than you think. Secondly, you probably will not get away with it. An experienced board is rather adept at spotting such a situation, so do not take the chance.

5) If you know a board member, do not make a point of it, yet do not hide it

Certainly you are not fooling him, and probably not the other members of the board. Do not try to take advantage of your acquaintanceship – it will probably do you little good.

6) Do not dominate the interview

Let the board do that. They will give you the clues – do not assume that you have to do all the talking. Realize that the board has a number of questions to ask you, and do not try to take up all the interview time by showing off your extensive knowledge of the answer to the first one.

7) Be attentive

You only have 20 minutes or so, and you should keep your attention at its sharpest throughout. When a member is addressing a problem or question to you, give him your undivided attention. Address your reply principally to him, but do not exclude the other board members.

8) Do not interrupt

A board member may be stating a problem for you to analyze. He will ask you a question when the time comes. Let him state the problem, and wait for the question.

9) Make sure you understand the question

Do not try to answer until you are sure what the question is. If it is not clear, restate it in your own words or ask the board member to clarify it for you. However, do not haggle about minor elements.

10) Reply promptly but not hastily

A common entry on oral board rating sheets is "candidate responded readily," or "candidate hesitated in replies." Respond as promptly and quickly as you can, but do not jump to a hasty, ill-considered answer.

11) Do not be peremptory in your answers

A brief answer is proper – but do not fire your answer back. That is a losing game from your point of view. The board member can probably ask questions much faster than you can answer them.

12) Do not try to create the answer you think the board member wants

He is interested in what kind of mind you have and how it works – not in playing games. Furthermore, he can usually spot this practice and will actually grade you down on it.

13) Do not switch sides in your reply merely to agree with a board member

Frequently, a member will take a contrary position merely to draw you out and to see if you are willing and able to defend your point of view. Do not start a debate, yet do not surrender a good position. If a position is worth taking, it is worth defending.

14) Do not be afraid to admit an error in judgment if you are shown to be wrong

The board knows that you are forced to reply without any opportunity for careful consideration. Your answer may be demonstrably wrong. If so, admit it and get on with the interview.

15) Do not dwell at length on your present job

The opening question may relate to your present assignment. Answer the question but do not go into an extended discussion. You are being examined for a *new* job, not your present one. As a matter of fact, try to phrase ALL your answers in terms of the job for which you are being examined.

Basis of Rating

Probably you will forget most of these "do's" and "don'ts" when you walk into the oral interview room. Even remembering them all will not ensure you a passing grade. Perhaps you did not have the qualifications in the first place. But remembering them will help you to put your best foot forward, without treading on the toes of the board members.

Rumor and popular opinion to the contrary notwithstanding, an oral board wants you to make the best appearance possible. They know you are under pressure – but they also want to see how you respond to it as a guide to what your reaction would be under the pressures of the job you seek. They will be influenced by the degree of poise you display, the personal traits you show and the manner in which you respond.

ABOUT THIS BOOK

This book contains tests divided into Examination Sections. Go through each test, answering every question in the margin. We have also attached a sample answer sheet at the back of the book that can be removed and used. At the end of each test look at the answer key and check your answers. On the ones you got wrong, look at the right answer choice and learn. Do not fill in the answers first. Do not memorize the questions and answers, but understand the answer and principles involved. On your test, the questions will likely be different from the samples. Questions are changed and new ones added. If you understand these past questions you should have success with any changes that arise. Tests may consist of several types of questions. We have additional books on each subject should more study be advisable or necessary for you. Finally, the more you study, the better prepared you will be. This book is intended to be the last thing you study before you walk into the examination room. Prior study of relevant texts is also recommended. NLC publishes some of these in our Fundamental Series. Knowledge and good sense are important factors in passing your exam. Good luck also helps. So now study this Passbook, absorb the material contained within and take that knowledge into the examination. Then do your best to pass that exam.

EXAMINATION SECTION

EXAMINATION SECTION
TEST 1

DIRECTIONS: Each question or incomplete statement is followed by several suggested answers or completions. Select the one that BEST answers the question or completes the statement. *PRINT THE LETTER OF THE CORRECT ANSWER IN THE SPACE AT THE RIGHT.*

1. A long-term liability of a corporation is represented by

   A. stock certificates issued
   B. stock subscriptions received
   C. the balance of a sinking fund
   D. bonds issued

2. Which is an advantage of incorporating?

   A. Establishing good will
   B. Acquiring treasury stock
   C. Limiting the liability of the owners
   D. Avoiding governmental control

3. Undistributed profits of a corporation are shown in the _____ account.

   A. earned surplus   B. treasury stock
   C. capital stock   D. bonds payable

4. The TOTAL amount of equity, or ownership, in a corporation is found by adding

   A. treasury stock and surplus
   B. capital stock and subscriptions
   C. capital stock and surplus
   D. capital stock and good will

5. On January 1, 2018, the earned surplus account of the Kalfur Corporation had a credit balance of $42,300. The net income for 2018 (after taxes) was $12,500. The dividends declared for 2018 amounted to $8,400.
   The balance of the earned surplus account on December 31, 2018 after the books were closed was

   A. $4,100   B. $33,900   C. $38,200   D. $46,400

6. The State Disability Benefits Insurance law provides benefits for an employee or his family when the employee

   A. dies
   B. retires
   C. is temporarily unable to work because of an off-the-job accident
   D. is temporarily unable to work because of an on-the-job accident

7. Which account does NOT belong in the current liability section of a balance sheet? _____ payable.

   A. Interest   B. Notes   C. Accounts   D. Mortgage

8. If the merchandise inventory on hand at the end of 2018 was overstated, what would be the effect?

   A. Understatement of income for 2018
   B. Overstatement of income for 2018
   C. Understatement of assets at the end of 2018
   D. No effect on income or assets

9. The face value of a 45-day, 6% promissory note is $740. The maturity value of the note will be

   A. $734.45   B. $740.00   C. $745.55   D. $747.40

10. When cash is received as a result of sales, the PROPER business procedure is to

    A. put the cash in the petty cash box
    B. deposit the cash in a checking account at the end of the day
    C. deposit the cash in a savings account at the end of the day
    D. use the cash to pay current bills

11. Which item can be determined from information on the Income Statement (Profit and Loss Statement)?

    A. Working capital
    B. Rate of merchandise turnover
    C. Total liabilities
    D. Owner's worth

12. Which item belongs on the Income Statement for the year?

    A. B. Rand, Drawing
    B. Accrued Salaries, Payable
    C. Purchases Discount
    D. Allowance for Depreciation of Furniture and Fixtures

13. _____ tax is affected by the number of exemptions claimed.

    A. FICA
    B. State unemployment insurance
    C. State income tax
    D. Federal unemployment insurance

14. The source of an entry in the Cash Payments Journal is a

    A. sales invoice   B. checkbook stub
    C. petty cash voucher   D. general ledger

15. If a partnership agreement does not indicate how profits and losses are to be divided, then they will be distributed

    A. equally
    B. in proportion to investment
    C. according to duties and responsibilities
    D. by a court

16. The two parties on a promissory note are known as the _____ and _____.

    A. drawee; maker
    B. drawee; drawer
    C. payee; drawee
    D. payee; maker

17. In order to find the correct available cash balance when reconciling the checkbook balance with the bank balance, outstanding checks should be _____ balance.

    A. added to the checkbook
    B. subtracted from the checkbook
    C. added to the bank
    D. subtracted from the bank

18. A check drawn by a bank on funds that it has on deposit in another bank is known as a

    A. bank draft
    B. certified check
    C. cashier's check
    D. money order

19. _____ tax is contributed by the employee and matched by the employer.

    A. State unemployment insurance
    B. State income tax
    C. FICA
    D. Federal unemployment insurance

20. Which general ledger account would appear in a post-closing trial balance?

    A. Interest Income
    B. Notes Receivable
    C. Sales Discount
    D. Bad Debts Expense

21. A time draft frequently used in connection with a purchase of merchandise is a

    A. trade acceptance
    B. check
    C. cashier's check
    D. bank draft

22. A list of accounts and their balances prepared from a subsidiary ledger is called a

    A. statement of account
    B. trial balance
    C. balance sheet
    D. schedule

23. A time draft which states on its face that it resulted from the sale or purchase of merchandise is called a

    A. promissory note
    B. purchase order
    C. bank draft
    D. trade acceptance

24. A truck is purchased for $14,800. It is estimated that the truck will be used for four years. At the end of the four years, it is estimated that the truck will have a scrap value of $10,900.
    The amount of annual depreciation is

    A. $3,900
    B. $1,425
    C. $1,200
    D. $975

25. The current ratio is found by

    A. *dividing* current assets by current liabilities
    B. *subtracting* current liabilities from current assets
    C. *subtracting* total liabilities from total assets
    D. *dividing* current assets by net income

KEY (CORRECT ANSWERS)

1. D
2. C
3. A
4. C
5. D

6. C
7. D
8. B
9. C
10. B

11. B
12. C
13. C
14. B
15. A

16. D
17. D
18. A
19. C
20. B

21. A
22. D
23. D
24. D
25. A

TEST 2

DIRECTIONS: Each question or incomplete statement is followed by several suggested answers or completions. Select the one that BEST answers the question or completes the statement. *PRINT THE LETTER OF THE CORRECT ANSWER IN THE SPACE AT THE RIGHT.*

1. The Federal individual income tax return must be filed by   1.____

   A. December 31   B. March 15
   C. April 15   D. June 30

2. When a firm discounts its own note at a bank, the account to be credited is   2.____

   A. Cash
   B. Notes Payable
   C. Notes Receivable Discounted
   D. Accounts Payable

3. Brooks and Carton are partners with an investment of $50,000 and $25,000, respectively.   3.____
   How much should be credited to Brooks as his share of a $60,000 profit if their agreement provides that the partners are to share profits and losses in proportion to their investments?

   A. $20,000   B. $30,000   C. $40,000   D. $50,000

4. At the end of the month, the total of the Schedule of Accounts Payable should equal the   4.____

   A. total of the Purchases column in the Purchases Journal
   B. total of the Accounts Payable column in the Cash Payments Journal
   C. balance of the Accounts Payable account in the General Ledger
   D. balance of the Purchases account in the General Ledger

5. When depreciation on a fixed asset is recorded, the effect of the entry on the fundamental bookkeeping equation is that the   5.____

   A. assets and capital remain unchanged
   B. assets increase; capital decreases
   C. assets decrease; capital decreases
   D. assets decrease; capital increases

6. The ORIGINAL source of an entry in the Purchases Journal is a   6.____

   A. purchase invoice   B. stock inventory card
   C. purchase order   D. creditor's account

7. The business form which is sent to each customer at the end of the month summarizing the transactions with him is called a   7.____

   A. schedule   B. statement of account
   C. sales invoice   D. voucher

8. When we receive a bank draft from a customer, our bookkeeper should debit   8.____

   A. Notes Payable   B. Notes Receivable
   C. Accounts Receivable D. Cash

9. The gross sales of a business are $170,000 and Sales Returns and Allowances $450. It is estimated that an additional allowance of 1% of net sales will be required. The amount listed for Bad Debts Expense on the Income Statement should be

   A. $1,250   B. $1,695.50   C. $1,700   D. $1,704.50

9.____

10. Which group of accounts will appear on a post-closing trial balance?

    A. Assets, liabilities, and expenses
    B. Income and expenses
    C. Liabilities, capital, and income
    D. Assets, liabilities, and capital

10.____

Questions 11-16.

DIRECTIONS: Questions 11 through 16 are to be answered SOLELY on the basis of the last part of the bank statement below, mailed to Arthur Greene for the month of June.

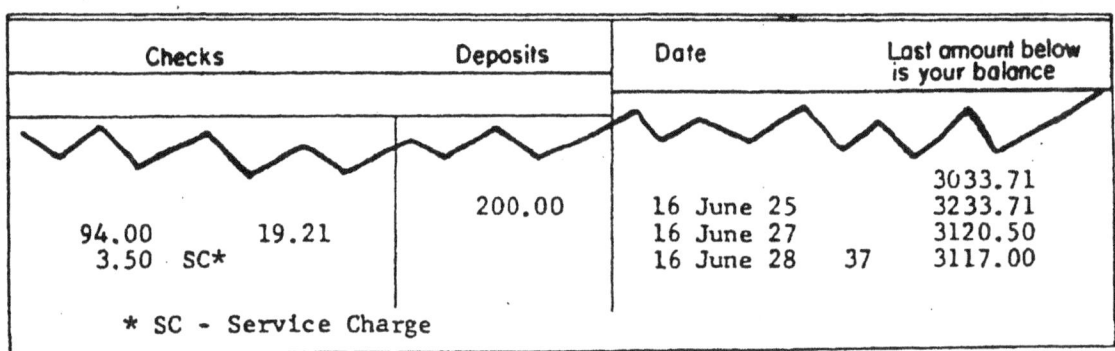

All the checks written have been paid except four. The last check written in June is No. 316. The stubs for the four outstanding checks are:

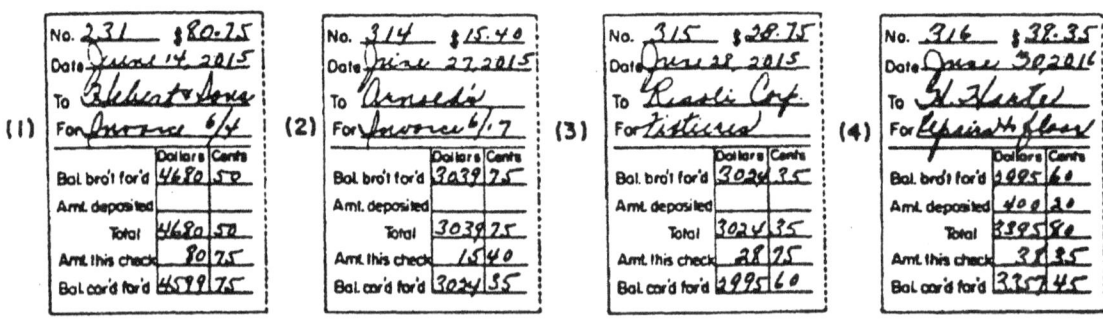

11. From the information available, what was Greene's corrected checkbook balance on June 30?

    A. $3,357.45   B. $3,117.00
    C. $3,353.95   D. $3,120.50

11.____

12. Which is the BEST reason that the deposit of $400.20, shown on Stub No. 316, does not appear on the bank statement?   12._____

    A. The bank has made an error.
    B. The bank has not credited his account.
    C. The withdrawals equal the deposits.
    D. The checks included in the deposit have not cleared the banks on which they were written.

13. When he examined the checks returned by his bank, Greene discovered that a check he had written for $44 had been incorrectly entered on the stub as $24.   13._____
    He should correct this error by

    A. adding $20 to his checkbook balance
    B. notifying his bank to add $20 to his account
    C. subtracting $20 from his checkbook balance
    D. subtracting $24 from his checkbook balance

14. On May 25, Greene wrote and had his bank certify a check for $150, which he mailed to Garcia, the payee. Garcia received the check on May 27 and deposited it in his bank on June 1. It was presented to Greene's bank and cleared for payment on June 2.   14._____
    On which date did Greene's bank deduct the $150 from his account?

    A. May 25   B. May 27   C. June 1   D. June 2

15. The journal entry to record the bank service charge shown on the bank statement should be made in the   15._____

    A. Petty Cashbook   B. General Journal
    C. Cash Receipts Journal   D. Cash Payments Journal

16. Greene's bookkeeper should prepare a bank reconciliation for June MAINLY to determine   16._____

    A. possible errors by comparing Greene's checkbook balance with the bank balance
    B. the total amount of checks written during the month
    C. which checks are still outstanding
    D. the total amount of cash deposited during the month

17. Which statement concerning a check is MOST accurate?   17._____

    A. A canceled check may be used to prove payment.
    B. Two signatures are required on each check drawn on a joint checking account.
    C. The corporation's name should be signed on the signature line of a check.
    D. Checks mailed for deposit should be endorsed by means of a blank endorsement.

18. If a check which has been certified is not used, which is the RECOMMENDED business practice?   18._____

    A. Mark the check *Void* and add the amount to the checkbook balance.
    B. Send a *stop payment* order to the bank.
    C. Deposit the check.
    D. Destroy the check.

19. Ames' bank returned a check which he had deposited, marked N.S.F. This notation indicates that the

    A. check has been improperly endorsed
    B. drawer has overdrawn his bank account
    C. drawer has stopped payment on the check
    D. signature on the check has been forged

20. In order to determine the correct available bank balance, the amount of a deposit made, but not yet recorded in an account, should be _____ balance.

    A. *added* to the checkbook
    B. *added* to the bank balance
    C. *subtracted* from the checkbook
    D. *subtracted* from the bank

Questions 21-25.

DIRECTIONS: Questions 21 through 25 are to be answered on the basis of the following depreciation record.

DEPRECIATION RECORD

Delivery Truck	Tractson	04387A	July 1, 2015
Asset	Make	Number	Acquired
$4,000	5 years	$500	straight-line
Cost	Estimated Life	Salvage Value	Meth. of Depr.

Year	1st quarter	2nd quarter	3rd quarter	4th quarter
1			$175	$175
2	...	...	$175	$175
3	$175	$175		
4	$175			
5				
6				

21. According to the record, the LAST adjusting entry had been made on or about

    A. June 1, 2015   B. June 1, 2016
    C. December 31, 2016   D. March 31, 2017

22. The book value on the date of the latest entry is

    A. $500   B. $2,275   C. $2,775   D. $3,500

23. The TOTAL amount of depreciation which would be recorded during the lifetime of the truck is

    A. $4,500   B. $4,000   C. $3,500   D. $500

24. What is the annual rate of depreciation for the truck?

    A. 17.5%   B. 2%   C. 20%   D. 5%

25. If a business uses the straight-line method of depreciation, which is CORRECT? 25.____
    A. All assets are depreciated at the same rate.
    B. The older the asset, the greater the amount of depreciation recorded each year.
    C. The rate of depreciation is the same each year for a particular asset.
    D. The salvage value will be the same for all fixed assets.

KEY (CORRECT ANSWERS)

1.	C	11.	C
2.	B	12.	B
3.	C	13.	C
4.	C	14.	A
5.	C	15.	D
6.	A	16.	A
7.	B	17.	A
8.	D	18.	C
9.	B	19.	B
10.	D	20.	B

21. D
22. C
23. C
24. A
25. C

TEST 3

DIRECTIONS: Each question or incomplete statement is followed by several suggested answers or completions. Select the one that BEST answers the question or completes the statement. *PRINT THE LETTER OF THE CORRECT ANSWER IN THE SPACE AT THE RIGHT.*

1. Entries in the Cash Payments Journal are USUALLY recorded from 1.____

   A. purchase invoices B. check stubs
   C. cancelled checks D. expense sheets

2. A bank draft received from a customer is recorded in the 2.____

   A. General Journal B. Note Register
   C. Sales Journal D. Cash Receipts Journal

3. When sales taxes are collected from cash customers, the account credited is 3.____

   A. Sales Tax Payable B. Sales Tax
   C. Cash D. Accounts Payable

4. One advantage of the corporate form of business is 4.____

   A. limited life
   B. limited capital
   C. limited liability
   D. dissolution on death of an officer

5. Current assets minus current liabilities equals 5.____

   A. current turnover B. current ratio
   C. asset ratio D. working capital

6. What is the LATEST date that an invoice dated October 15 with terms net 10 E.O.M. should be paid? 6.____

   A. October 25 B. October 31
   C. November 10 D. November 30

7. The deduction allowed to a customer for an early payment of his account is known as a 7.____

   A. cash discount B. mark down
   C. credit memorandum D. trade discount

8. In a C.O.D. freight shipment, the business form that the seller attaches to the bill of lading is a 8.____

   A. sight draft B. promissory note
   C. check D. time draft

9. The form prepared to test the equality of debits and credits in the General Ledger is called 9.____

   A. statement of account B. balance sheet
   C. trial balance D. income statement

10. If the depreciation of a truck is calculated by the straight-line method, which statement is CORRECT?

    A. As the truck becomes older, the rate of depreciation increases.
    B. The rate of depreciation is the same each year.
    C. The amount of annual depreciation is based on the truck's mileage.
    D. On a statement of profit and loss, the depreciation appears as a deferred expense.

11. A computer program used to create spreadsheets, graphs and charts, and maintain financial records is

    A. Quickbooks
    B. Adobe Reader
    C. Microsoft Powerpoint
    D. Microsoft Excel

12. An inventory of merchandise prepared from an actual count of stock items on hand is described as a(n) _____ inventory.

    A. perpetual   B. physical   C. estimated   D. fixed

13. Which is NOT classified as a current asset on the balance sheet?

    A. Petty Cash
    B. Notes Receivable
    C. Land
    D. Accounts Receivable

14. Which error will cause a trial balance to be out of balance?

    A. Failure to post the debit part of a journal entry
    B. Failure to record an entire journal entry
    C. Error in totaling the sales journal
    D. Posting a debit in the debit side of the wrong account

15. If a customer's check which you had deposited is returned to you by the bank labeled *dishonored*, what entry would be made?
    Debit

    A. Cash and credit customer's account
    B. Miscellaneous Expense and credit Cash
    C. customer's account and credit Capital
    D. customer's account and credit Cash

16. The total of the Purchases Journal for the month of May was incorrectly computed as $6,500. The correct amount was $5,500. The $6,500 was used to record and post the summary entry for the month.
    To correct the error, the bookkeeper should debit

    A. Merchandise Purchases and credit Accounts Payable $5,500
    B. Merchandise Purchases and credit Accounts Payable $1,000
    C. Accounts Payable and credit Merchandise Purchases $1,000
    D. Accounts Payable and credit Merchandise Purchases $6,500

17. Entries in the Purchases Journal are USUALLY recorded from

    A. purchase requisitions
    B. purchase invoices
    C. check stubs
    D. credit memorandums

18. Merchandise was sold on April 10, 2018 for $400 less a trade discount of 25%, terms 2/10, n/30.
    The amount required to settle the invoice on April 20 is

    A. $294   B. $300   C. $392   D. $400

    18._____

19. When the books were closed at the end of the business fiscal year, there was a failure to record depreciation on Office Equipment for the year.
    This error had the effect of

    A. *understating* the book value of the asset Office Equipment
    B. *overstating* the book value of the asset Office Equipment
    C. *understating* the net income of the asset Office Equipment
    D. *overstating* operating expenses

    19._____

Questions 20-25.

DIRECTIONS: Questions 20 through 25 are to be answered SOLELY on the basis of the following bank reconciliation statement.

CONDON, INC. Bank Reconciliation March 31.			
Checkbook balance	$3,148.70	Bank Balance	$3,830.65
Less: Service Charge	4.15	Add: Deposit in Transit	310.00
		Total	4,140.65
		Less: Outstanding Checks	
		No. 815 $470.20	
		817 525.90	996.10
		(No. 813 certified 920.00)	
Adjusted checkbook balance	$3,144.55	Available bank balance	$3,144.55

20. Which entry will be made on the books of Condon, Inc. to record the bank service charge?
    Debit

    A. Cash, credit Bank Charges
    B. Bank Charges, credit Accounts Payable
    C. Bank Charges, credit Cash
    D. Bank Account, credit Bank Charges

    20._____

21. The deposit in transit of $310 will be listed on the

    A. bank statement for the month of March
    B. bank statement for the month of April
    C. bank statement for the month of February
    D. check stub record *only*

    21._____

22. The bookkeeper determined which checks were outstanding by   22._____

    A. counting the cancelled checks
    B. examining the bank statement
    C. comparing the cancelled checks with the bank statement
    D. comparing the cancelled checks with the check stubs

23. The certified check of $920 was NOT deducted with the other outstanding checks   23._____
    because it

    A. was deducted from our bank balance at the time it was certified
    B. was not deducted from our checkbook balance when it was written
    C. will not be cashed by our bank
    D. will not be deducted from our bank balance until it clears our bank

24. The MAIN reason for preparing the bank reconciliation statement is to determine the   24._____

    A. total amount of cancelled checks
    B. total amount of outstanding checks
    C. total deposits with withdrawals for the month
    D. errors that might have been made

25. A trial balance is prepared to   25._____

    A. see if the totals agree with the subsidiary ledgers
    B. see if the total debit balances in the General Ledger agree with the total credit balances in the General Ledger
    C. show the worth of the business
    D. make up statements of customers' accounts

KEY (CORRECT ANSWERS)

1.	B	11.	D
2.	D	12.	B
3.	A	13.	C
4.	C	14.	A
5.	D	15.	D
6.	C	16.	C
7.	A	17.	B
8.	A	18.	A
9.	C	19.	B
10.	B	20.	C

21. B
22. D
23. A
24. D
25. B

TEST 4

DIRECTIONS: Each question or incomplete statement is followed by several suggested answers or completions. Select the one that BEST answers the question or completes the statement. *PRINT THE LETTER OF THE CORRECT ANSWER IN THE SPACE AT THE RIGHT.*

1. The due date of a 60-day promissory note dated June 15 is August   1.____

    A. 13   B. 14   C. 15   D. 16

2. Using the information that can be found in the Income Statement, one can find the   2.____

    A. current ratio
    B. merchandise turnover
    C. working capital
    D. rate of return on capital

3. Which of the following is NOT a computer program commonly used for accounting and finance purposes?   3.____

    A. QuarkXPress   B. Peachtree
    C. Quicken   D. Quickbooks

4. The ABC Corporation has 100,000 shares of stock outstanding. The Corporation decides to distribute to the stockholders a $200,000 profit.
If a stockholder owns 100 shares of stock, he will receive a TOTAL dividend of   4.____

    A. $50.00   B. $2.00   C. $200.00   D. $.50

5. A transaction that will cause a DECREASE in capital is a   5.____

    A. purchase of office equipment on credit
    B. payment of a creditor's account less a cash discount
    C. payment of an interest-bearing note
    D. prepayment of freight for a customer, to be charged to the customer's account

6. Mr. Davis is married and has three children who go to school. His oldest son, age 17, earned $900 during the year working parttime.
On his joint Federal income tax return, Mr. Davis may claim a MAXIMUM of _____ exemptions.   6.____

    A. five   B. two   C. three   D. four

7. If the total of the Schedule of Accounts Receivable does not agree with the balance in the Accounts Receivable Controlling account, the difference may have been caused by   7.____

    A. adding the Sales Journal incorrectly
    B. failing to enter a sale in the Sales Journal
    C. posting a sale to the wrong customer's account
    D. failing to record a check received from a customer

8. An entry in the general journal is USUALLY made from the   8.____

    A. sales invoice   B. purchase invoice
    C. credit memorandum   D. incoming check

9. An example of a tax collected by the Federal government is the 9.____

   A. sales tax
   B. real estate tax
   C. automobile registration fee
   D. social security tax

10. The adjusting entry at the end of the year to record the estimated depreciation for the year results in a(n) 10.____

    A. *increase* in liabilities and a decrease in capital
    B. *decrease* in assets and an increase in assets
    C. *decrease* in assets and a decrease in capital
    D. *decrease* in assets and an increase in capital

11. On December 28, the total in the Salaries Expense Account was $59,500. On December 31, the bookkeeper recorded accrued salaries of $600. 11.____
    The entry to close the Salaries Expense Account on December 31 should be debit the _____ and credit the _____ .

    A. Income and Expense Summary Account for $59,500;
       Salaries Expense Account for $59,500
    B. Income and Expense Summary Account for $60,100;
       Salaries Expense Account for $60,100
    C. Income and Expense Summary Account for $58,900;
       Salaries Expense Account for $58,900
    D. Salaries Expense Account for $59,500; Income and
       Expense Summary Account for $59,500

12. The tax paid by the employee to provide benefits upon his retirement is the 12.____

    A. FICA tax
    B. State Disability Benefits
    C. Federal withholding tax
    D. workmen's compensation insurance

13. The Federal income tax form that is given to the employee to show his total salary for the year and the amount of withholding tax for the year is called Form 13.____

    A. 941   B. W-4   C. 1099   D. W-2

14. An error that would cause the trial balance to be out of balance would be INCORRECTLY adding 14.____

    A. the Purchase Journal
    B. the cash column in the Cash Receipts Journal
    C. the Schedule of Accounts Receivable
    D. extensions on an invoice

15. An account that would be shown in a post-closing trial balance is 15.____

    A. Notes Receivable   B. Sales Income
    C. Discount on Purchases   D. Freight Out

16. You have just posted an entry from the Sales Journal to the customer's account. The correct amount in the Sales Journal is $125, but you posted $12.50. To correct the error, you should

    A. draw a single line through the $12.50 in the account and write $125 above it
    B. debit in the General Journal the customer's account for $112.50 and credit the Sales Income Account for $112.50
    C. credit in the General Journal the customer's account for $12.50 and debit the Sales Income Account for $12.50
    D. debit in the Sales Journal the customer's account for $112.50 and credit the Sales Income Account for $112.50

17. When the bookkeeper added the trial balance, she found that it did not balance. To find the reason, a logical FIRST step would be to

    A. check the pencil footings in ledger accounts
    B. add the trial balance a second time
    C. check whether figures were copied correctly from the ledger to the trial balance
    D. check postings from the journals

18. A column or group of columns containing data of a specific nature on a punched card is called a

    A. zone   B. field   C. row   D. file

19. *Allowance for Doubtful Accounts* is BEST described as a(n) _____ account.

    A. contingent liability
    B. capital
    C. expense
    D. asset valuation

20. A sales invoice to Judy Burns for $50 was entered in the Sales Journal as $150. Which would occur as a result of this error? The

    A. trial balance will not balance at the end of the month
    B. balance of the monthly statement to Judy Burns will be overstated
    C. check received from Judy Burns in payment of her account will be larger than the correct amount
    D. Accounts Receivable controlling account will not agree with the Schedule of Accounts Receivable at the end of the month

21. Sales taxes which are collected from customers and which will subsequently be remitted to the State Tax Bureau are recorded by the retailer as a(n)

    A. operating expense in the Income Statement
    B. addition to sales in the Income Statement
    C. current asset in the Balance Sheet
    D. current liability in the Balance Sheet

22. When the payee of a check writes as an endorsement *Pay to the order of (name of the firm)* before his signature, he has used a _____ endorsement.

    A. blank
    B. qualified
    C. restrictive
    D. full

23. Entries in the Purchases Journal are USUALLY made from which source document? 23.____

    A. Purchase order
    B. Purchase requisition
    C. Incoming invoice
    D. Outgoing invoice

24. Which is shown on the bank statement sent by the bank each month? 24.____

    A. Outstanding checks
    B. Deposits in transit
    C. Checks paid by the bank during the month
    D. The amount of interest earned during the month

25. The authorization by the State of New York which permits a group of persons to do business as a corporation is called the 25.____

    A. charter
    B. by-laws
    C. trade acceptance
    D. articles of copartnership

KEY (CORRECT ANSWERS)

1. B
2. B
3. A
4. C
5. C

6. A
7. A
8. C
9. D
10. C

11. B
12. A
13. D
14. B
15. A

16. A
17. B
18. B
19. D
20. B

21. D
22. D
23. C
24. C
25. A

EXAMINATION SECTION
TEST 1

DIRECTIONS: Each question or incomplete statement is followed by several suggested answers or completions. Select the one that BEST answers the question or completes the statement. *PRINT THE LETTER OF THE CORRECT ANSWER IN THE SPACE AT THE RIGHT.*

Questions 1-5.

DIRECTIONS: Questions 1 through 5 are to be answered on the basis of the following information.

The balance on our bank statement is $6,842.50. The bank had made a service charge of $4.50. Our check stubs reveal a final balance of $5,747.50. A comparison of the check stubs with the bank statement indicated that a deposit we had mailed on the 29th for $585 had not been recorded by the monthly closing. Four checks which we had made out ($1,001, $645, $38.50, and a certified check for $1,200) had not been cleared by the monthly closing.

1. The effect of the deposit in transit is to _____ balance.

    A. *increase* the final check stub
    B. *decrease* the final check stub
    C. *increase* the bank
    D. *decrease* the bank

2. The effect of the bank service charge is to _____ balance.

    A. *increase* the final check stub
    B. *decrease* the final check stub
    C. *increase* the bank
    D. *decrease* the bank

3. The CORRECTED check stub balance after reconciliation is

    A. $5,743   B. $5,752   C. $6,337   D. $6,843

4. The TOTAL of the outstanding checks to be subtracted from the bank balance is

    A. $484.50   B. $1,684.50   C. $2,269.50   D. $2,885.50

5. The CORRECTED bank balance after reconciliation is

    A. $5,743   B. $5,789   C. $6,843   D. $7,428

Questions 6-8.

DIRECTIONS: Questions 6 through 8 are to be answered on the basis of the worksheet below, which is for the first quarter of the Argo Taxi Company.

2 (#1)

[Worksheet image: ARGC TAXI CO., INC WORKSHEET FOR QUARTER ENDED 3/31/—]

Account	Trial Balance Dr	Trial Balance Cr	Adjustments Dr	Adjustments Cr	Income Statement Dr	Income Statement Cr	Balance Sheet Dr	Balance Sheet Cr
Cash	1700						1700	
Oil Products Inventory	5000			3600			1400	
Prepaid Insurance	1000			680			320	
Automobiles	105000						105000	
Allow. for Depreciation of Autos		23000		8750				31750
Maintenance Equipment	20000						20000	
Allow. for Dep. of Maintenance Equip.		7000		500				7500
Accounts Payable		1200						1200
Dividends Payable		200						200
Capital Stock		55000						55000
Retained Earnings		13200						13200
Fares Income		80000				80000		
Miscellaneous Expenses	4500				4500			
Rent Expense	1500				1500			
Repair Expense	5200				5200			
Salary Expense	24000				24000			
	192200	192200						
Oil Products Expense			3600		3600			
Insurance Expense			680		680			
Depreciation of Automobiles Exp.			8750		8750			
Dep. of Maintenance Equip.			500		500			
			13530	13530	48730	80000	152720	124750
Federal Income Taxes					7817.50			7817.50
Net Profit after Income Taxes					23452.50			23452.50
					80000	80000	152720	152720

6. The balance of the Automobiles account after the June adjustment is 6.____

   A. $8,750   B. $23,000   C. $31,750   D. $105,000

7. The book value of the asset Maintenance Equipment, after adjusting entries, is 7.____

   A. $7,500   B. $12,500   C. $13,000   D. $20,000

8. Assuming that the entire net profit after taxes was transferred to Retained Earnings, the balance of the Retained Earnings account would be 8.____

   A. $10,252.50
   C. $23,452.50
   B. $13,200
   D. $36,652.50

9. The TOTAL operating expenses for the quarter were 9.____

   A. $13,530   B. $48,730   C. $121,450   D. $192,200

10. Closing entries are prepared from _____ columns. 10.____

    A. Trial Balance
    C. Income Statement
    B. Adjustment
    D. Balance Sheet

11. When sales taxes are collected from cash customers, the account credited is 11.____

    A. Sales Taxes Payable
    C. Cash
    B. Sales Taxes
    D. Accounts Payable

12. What type of data processing equipment would arrange punched cards alphabetically? 12.____

    A. Card punch
    C. Sorter
    B. Card verifier
    D. Tabulator

13. _____ tax is affected by the number of exemptions claimed by the employee. 13.____

    A. State Unemployment Insurance
    C. FICA
    B. Federal Unemployment Insurance
    D. Federal income

20

14. The merchandise turnover is found by dividing _____ merchandise inventory.　　　14.____

    A. net sales by ending
    B. net sales by average
    C. cost of goods sold by average
    D. cost of goods sold by ending

15. The process of summarizing the income and expense accounts and transferring the net　　15.____
    result to the Retained Earnings account is known as

    A. adjusting the accounts
    B. reversing the accounts
    C. closing the ledger
    D. preparing a post-closing trial balance

16. An example of a fixed asset is　　　16.____

    A. equipment   B. merchandise inventory
    C. cash   D. prepaid insurance

17. Determining that the amount of cash on hand agrees with the balance of the cash　　17.____
    account is known as

    A. recording
    B. proving cash
    C. reconciling the bank statement
    D. establishing the petty cash fund

18. The balance in the Accounts Receivable controlling account on December 31 is $20,500.　　18.____
    The balance in the Allowance for Bad Debts account is $750 after adjustments.
    The amount believed to be collectible from customers is

    A. $750   B. $19,750   C. $20,500   D. $21,250

19. The FIRST record of any transaction of a business is made in the　　19.____

    A. ledger   B. account
    C. journal   D. balance sheet

20. A decrease in owner's capital that results from a business transaction is called　　20.____

    A. income   B. expense   C. asset   D. liability

21. The difference between the sales and the cost of goods sold is called　　21.____

    A. net sales   B. sales returns
    C. gross profit on sales   D. sales discount

22. A customer sent a check for $50 in partial payment of her account.　　22.____
    What would be the effect of erroneously posting the check as a debit to the customer's
    account?

    A. *Overstatement* of the total of the Schedule of Accounts Receivable
    B. *Understatement* of the Accounts Receivable controlling account
    C. *Overstatement* of the Accounts Receivable controlling account
    D. *Understatement* of the total of the Schedule of Accounts Receivable

23. In the absence of any statement in the partnership agreement as to the manner of sharing profits and losses, such profits and losses will be shared

    A. equally
    B. according to investments
    C. according to work performed
    D. according to sales

24. At the end of the year, which account should be closed into the Income and Expense Summary account?

    A. Petty Cash
    B. Depreciation of Furniture and Fixtures
    C. Allowance for Bad Debts
    D. Notes Payable

25. On an Income Statement, losses from bad debts will appear as a(n)

    A. operating expense
    B. deduction from Accounts Receivable
    C. addition to the cost of goods sold
    D. deduction from the cost of goods sold

KEY (CORRECT ANSWERS)

1.	C	11.	A
2.	B	12.	C
3.	A	13.	D
4.	B	14.	C
5.	A	15.	C
6.	D	16.	A
7.	B	17.	B
8.	D	18.	B
9.	B	19.	C
10.	C	20.	B

21.	C
22.	A
23.	A
24.	B
25.	A

TEST 2

DIRECTIONS: Each question or incomplete statement is followed by several suggested answers or completions. Select the one that BEST answers the question or completes the statement. *PRINT THE LETTER OF THE CORRECT ANSWER IN THE SPACE AT THE RIGHT.*

1. A bookkeeping worksheet is prepared

    A. to be used as a source document
    B. to distribute to the stockholders at the end of the year
    C. as an aid in the preparation of financial statements
    D. to be used as a financial statement

2. When a set of books for a partnership is opened, the CORRECT procedure is to set up

    A. a capital account for each partner
    B. a capital account for each partner except *silent* partners
    C. one capital account that would show the combined investment of the partners
    D. an account showing stock already subscribed

3. At the end of the fiscal period, it is determined that the interest owed and not paid on the mortgage amounts to $420. This amount will be debited to

    A. Interest Expense
    B. Mortgage Payable
    C. Interest Receivable
    D. Interest Income

4. Income that has been earned but not yet received is referred to as _____ income.

    A. deferred   B. accrued   C. unearned   D. prepaid

5. The account Mortgage Payable is a(n)

    A. current liability
    B. prepaid expense
    C. accrued expense
    D. fixed liability

6. Under the cash basis of keeping books, all items of income are recorded when

    A. paid   B. billed   C. received   D. ordered

7. A financial statement prepared by a data processing system is an example of

    A. a source document
    B. output
    C. a flowchart
    D. input

8. On an income statement, net sales minus cost of goods sold is the

    A. gross profit
    B. merchandise available for sale
    C. net operating profit
    D. net profit before taxes

9. Allowance for Depreciation of Delivery Equipment is a(n) _____ account.

    A. liability   B. expense   C. accrual   D. valuation

10. When the totals of the two columns of a Trial Balance are equal, it proves that

    A. all debits and credits have been posted to the proper accounts
    B. there have been no offsetting errors
    C. no entries have been omitted
    D. equal amounts of debits and credits have been posted

11. The TOTAL of the Sales Journal is posted as a debit to

    A. Accounts Receivable   B. Accounts Payable
    C. Sales   D. Cash

12. Unexpired insurance is recorded as a debit to

    A. Insurance Receivable   B. Prepaid Insurance
    C. Insurance Payable   D. Insurance Expense

13. The cost price of a fixed asset minus the Allowance for Depreciation is known as its _____ value.

    A. cash   B. par   C. market   D. book

14. The payment in cash by The Lake Corporation on April 1, 2008 of a dividend declared and recorded on March 10, 2008 results in

    A. a decrease in assets and a decrease in capital
    B. both an increase and a decrease in assets
    C. a decrease in assets and a decrease in liabilities
    D. a decrease in liabilities and an increase in capital

15. Current assets minus current liabilities equals

    A. current ratio   B. current turnover
    C. merchandise turnover   D. working capital

16. The proprietor withdrew cash for his personal use. The effect on the fundamental bookkeeping equation is to

    A. *increase* assets and decrease owner's worth
    B. *increase* assets and increase owner's worth
    C. *decrease* assets and decrease liabilities
    D. *decrease* assets and decrease owner's worth

17. A payment for gasoline and oil was incorrectly debited to the Delivery Equipment account instead of to the Delivery Expense account.
    This error, if not corrected, would result in

    A. understatement of the total assets
    B. no effect on the net profit
    C. an understatement of the net profit
    D. an overstatement of the net profit

18. A bookkeeper made an entry debiting the Bad Debts Expense account and crediting the Allowance for Bad Debts account. The credit represents a(n)

    A. *increase* in the liabilities
    B. *increase* in the net worth

C. *decrease* in the value of the assets
D. *decrease* in the liabilities

19. Adjusting entries are NORMALLY made

    A. before the Trial Balance is taken
    B. whenever price changes occur in inventory costs
    C. at the beginning of each fiscal period
    D. at the end of the current fiscal period

19.____

20. The declaration of a cash dividend by the Yule Corporation will result in a(n)

    A. *increase* in assets and an increase in liabilities
    B. *increase* in liabilities and a decrease in capital
    C. *decrease* in assets and a decrease in liabilities
    D. *decrease* in assets and a decrease in capital

20.____

21.

Accounts Payable

May	31		CP6	178	00	May	31		P3	320	00
June	31		J4	80	00						
	2		J5	75	00						

The above account was taken from the General Ledger of Clarke & Scott. The above account is classified as a

A. fixed liability   B. contingent asset
C. deferred asset   D. current liability

21.____

22. When a corporation declares a dividend on its stock, the account debited is

    A. Dividends Payable   B. Retained Earnings
    C. Capital Stock   D. Stock Subscriptions

22.____

23. The payroll tax for the State unemployment insurance is paid by

    A. the employee *only*
    B. both the employee and the employer
    C. the employer *only*
    D. the insurance company

23.____

24. Which computer application would MOST likely be used for accounting purposes?

    A. Microsoft Powerpoint   B. Adobe Reader
    C. Internet Explorer   D. Microsoft Excel

24.____

25. A diagram of a bookkeeping operation through a computerized system is called a

    A. floor plan   B. worksheet
    C. flowchart   D. CPU

25.____

KEY (CORRECT ANSWERS)

1.	C	11.	A
2.	A	12.	B
3.	A	13.	D
4.	B	14.	C
5.	D	15.	D
6.	C	16.	D
7.	B	17.	D
8.	A	18.	C
9.	D	19.	D
10.	D	20.	B

21. D
22. B
23. C
24. D
25. C

TEST 3

DIRECTIONS: Each question or incomplete statement is followed by several suggested answers or completions. Select the one that BEST answers the question or completes the statement. *PRINT THE LETTER OF THE CORRECT ANSWER IN THE SPACE AT THE RIGHT.*

1. The process of transferring information from the journal to the ledger is called 1.____

   A. journalizing B. posting
   C. closing D. balancing

2. Which is NOT an asset account? 2.____

   A. Supplies on Hand B. Prepaid Insurance
   C. Office Equipment D. Sales

3. Which journal entries are used at the end of each accounting period to clear the balances from the temporary accounts so that these accounts may be used in accumulating data for preparing the next period's statement. _____ entries. 3.____

   A. Correcting B. Closing
   C. Adjusting D. Opening

4. The verification of the equality of debits and credits in the General Ledger is called a 4.____

   A. trial balance B. schedule
   C. statement D. worksheet

5. Which account would NOT be listed on the Balance Sheet as a current liability? 5.____

   A. Accounts Payable
   B. Sales Taxes Payable
   C. Mortgage Payable
   D. FICA Taxes Payable

6. Debts owed by a business enterprise are referred to as 6.____

   A. capital B. income C. assets D. liabilities

7. If insurance premiums were recorded as an asset when paid, the adjusting entry needed to record the expired insurance would require a debit to which account? 7.____

   A. Miscellaneous Expense B. Prepaid Insurance
   C. Insurance Expense D. John Green, Capital

8. A diagram showing the sequence of steps involved in an automated data processing procedure is called a 8.____

   A. flowchart B. source document
   C. coding sheet D. spreadsheet

9. If a business enterprise paid $3,000 to its creditors on account, what was the effect of the transaction on the accounting equation? A(n)

   A. *increase* in an asset, an increase in a liability
   B. *decrease* in an asset, a decrease in a liability
   C. *increase* in an asset, an increase in capital
   D. *increase* in one asset, a decrease in another asset

10. Which three steps of an automated data processing system are listed in the PROPER order?

    A. Input, storage, process
    B. Process, data origination, output
    C. Output, input, storage
    D. Input, process, output

11. The Merchandise Inventory account is GENERALLY adjusted

    A. when inventory is purchased
    B. when inventory is sold
    C. at the end of the accounting period
    D. at the beginning of each month

12. Which transaction is recorded in the Sales Journal? The sale of

    A. merchandise for cash
    B. merchandise on account
    C. vacant land (plant asset) for cash
    D. vacant land (plant asset) on account

13. Which is an example of a transposition error? Recording $450 as

    A. $540   B. $4,500.00   C. $455   D. $4.50

14. The accounting equation is CORRECTLY stated as

    A. Owner's Equity = Assets + Liabilities
    B. Owner's Equity - Assets = Liabilities
    C. Owner's Equity = Liabilities - Assets
    D. Assets = Liabilities + Owner's Equity

15. The Wage and Tax statement, Form W-2, is a form which shows

    A. a listing of deductions taken from an employee's salary
    B. an end-of-year listing of total wages and income tax and FICA withholdings
    C. the bonds purchased for an employee by an employer
    D. the marital status of an employee and the number of allowances claimed

16. A set of instructions which guides the processing of data by an electronic computer is called a

    A. file   B. diagram   C. program   D. record

17. An invoice is dated June 3. Terms of the sale are n/45. What is the LAST date for payment?   17.____

    A. June 30   B. July 17   C. July 18   D. July 19

18. The accounting equation is summarized in the   18.____

    A. Balance Sheet
    B. Trial Balance
    C. Income Statement
    D. Schedule of Accounts Payable

19. The Accounts Payable Subsidiary Ledger contains the amounts   19.____

    A. owed to the business by charge customers
    B. owed by the business to creditors
    C. of all cash purchases of merchandise
    D. of all sales discounts

20. Which procedure is followed in a journalless accounting system for handling accounts receivable?   20.____

    A. A trial balance must be prepared daily.
    B. Debits do not equal credits at the end of the accounting period when all postings have been made.
    C. Individual sales are recorded in a multicolumn Sales Journal instead of in a one-column Sales Journal.
    D. Posting to customers' accounts is made directly from the sales invoices.

21. _____ is a voluntary payroll deduction.   21.____

    A. FICA tax   B. Credit union savings
    C. Federal withholding tax   D. State income tax

22. On a worksheet, if the Trial Balance debit column is larger than the Trial Balance credit column, it indicates a(n)   22.____

    A. net income   B. net loss
    C. error   D. decrease in capital

23. In the General Ledger, the controlling account that summarizes the activities in the Customer's Ledger is called   23.____

    A. Accounts Receivable   B. Accounts Payable
    C. Purchases   D. Sales

24. The balance of the Insurance Expense account in the Income Statement debit column on the worksheet represents the   24.____

    A. insurance expired during the fiscal period
    B. face value of all insurance policies
    C. value of the prepaid insurance at the end of the fiscal period
    D. cash value of all insurance policies

25. A fee paid to the bank when securing a cashier's check should be recorded by a debit to 25._____
_____ and a credit to _____.
- A. Petty Cash; Cash
- B. Miscellaneous Expense; Bank Charges
- C. Accounts Receivable; Cash
- D. Miscellaneous Expense; Cash

KEY (CORRECT ANSWERS)

1.	B	11.	C
2.	D	12.	B
3.	B	13.	A
4.	A	14.	D
5.	C	15.	B
6.	D	16.	C
7.	C	17.	C
8.	A	18.	A
9.	B	19.	B
10.	D	20.	D

21.	B
22.	C
23.	A
24.	A
25.	D

TEST 4

DIRECTIONS: Each question or incomplete statement is followed by several suggested answers or completions. Select the one that BEST answers the question or completes the statement. *PRINT THE LETTER OF THE CORRECT ANSWER IN THE SPACE AT THE RIGHT.*

1. A 60-day promissory note dated April 12 will be due on June

   A. 11   B. 12   C. 13   D. 14

2. Failure to set up an allowance for doubtful accounts at the end of 2012 will result in an _____ 2012.

   A. *understatement* of net profit for
   B. *overstatement* of net profit for
   C. *understatement* of assets at the end of
   D. *overstatement* of liabilities at the end of

3. Which error will cause the trial balance to be out of balance?

   A. Forgetting to post from the Sales Journal to the H. Allen account in the Accounts Receivable Ledger
   B. Failing to record the purchase of a desk
   C. Incorrectly totaling the Purchase Journal
   D. Posting the $1,250 total of the accounts receivable column in the Cash Receipts Journal as $1,520

4. The checkbook balance on May 2, at the start of the day, was $1,500. During the day, a deposit of $75 was made, and checks for $100 and $50 were written.
   What was the checkbook balance at the end of the day?

   A. $1,275   B. $1,425   C. $1,575   D. $1,725

5. Data about Accounts Receivable to be fed into an automatic data processing system is often recorded in the form of

   A. statements of account
   B. punched cards
   C. schedule of accounts receivable
   D. sales journals

6. A purchase of merchandise on credit results in a(n) _____ in assets and a(n) _____ in liabilities.

   A. increase; increase   B. increase; decrease
   C. decrease; decrease   D. decrease; increase

7. During her vacation, Harriet Miller, age 45, was injured while driving her own car. For part of the 5 weeks she was unable to work, cash benefits MOST likely would be paid to her under

   A. Workers' Compensation
   B. the Social Security Administration

C. State Disability Benefits Insurance
D. Unemployment Insurance

8. The book value of a share of stock of a corporation may be found by

   A. dividing the net worth of the corporation by the number of shares of stock
   B. dividing the total amount of stock of the corporation by the number of shares of stock
   C. looking at the amount shown on the stock certificate
   D. looking at the price of the stock on the stock exchange page of the daily newspaper

8._____

9. In a business, which are MOST likely to be prepared by automatic data processing?

   A. Sales invoices
   B. Inspection reports by the night watchman
   C. Business correspondence (letters)
   D. Applications for employment

9._____

10. The entry recording the estimated depreciation for the year results in a(n) _____ in capital.

    A. increase in liabilities and a decrease
    B. decrease in liabilities and an increase
    C. increase in assets and an increase
    D. decrease in assets and a decrease

10._____

11. The balance of the Accounts Receivable controlling account would be different from the total of the Accounts Receivable Schedule if the bookkeeper

    A. made an error in totaling the Sales Journal and posted the incorrect total
    B. failed to record a sale made to S. Charles
    C. recorded the receipt of a check from a customer but neglected to record the cash discount
    D. added an invoice incorrectly and entered the incorrect total in the Sales Journal

11._____

12. Credits in the Notes Payable account USUALLY originate in the _____ Journal.

    A. Purchase   B. Cash Receipts
    C. Cash Payments   D. General

12._____

13. On the books of the seller, the deduction granted to a customer for early payment of the invoice is called a _____ discount.

    A. retail   B. purchase   C. trade   D. sales

13._____

14. A firm started the year with $25 worth of office supplies. During the year, the firm purchased $65 worth of office supplies. A count of the office supplies at the end of the year showed that $20 worth was still on hand.
    What was the TOTAL cost of the office supplies which the firm must have used during the year?

    A. $45   B. $60   C. $70   D. $110

14._____

15. A payroll check prepared by a computer is an example of _____ data processing _____.

    A. electronic; input
    B. electronic; output
    C. manual; output
    D. manual; input

16. A sale of $250 was made subject to a 7% sales tax.
    To record the sale CORRECTLY, the credits should be Sales Income

    A. $250, Sales Taxes $17.50
    B. $250, Sales Taxes Payable $17.50
    C. $267.50, Sales Taxes $17.50
    D. $267.50, Sales Taxes Payable $17.50

17. In order to determine which checks are outstanding, the bookkeeper should compare the

    A. cancelled checks with the stubs in the checkbook
    B. cancelled checks with the checks listed in the bank statement
    C. check stubs with entries made in the Cash Payments Journal
    D. checkbook deposits with entries made in the Cash Receipts Journal

18. In a sale on credit to B. Benson, the bookkeeper, by mistake, posted to the B. Boyers account.
    The error will PROBABLY be discovered when

    A. the schedule of the subsidiary ledger does not agree with the controlling account
    B. the trial balance does not balance
    C. B. Boyers receives his monthly statement
    D. the bookkeeper receives monthly statements from creditors

19. Which does a person receive as evidence of part ownership in a corporation? A

    A. certificate of incorporation
    B. stock certificate
    C. bond
    D. charter

20. The count of merchandise inventory on hand at the end of the year was overstated. This error will result in an _____ the year.

    A. *overstatement* of profit for
    B. *understatement* of profit for
    C. *overstatement* of liabilities at the end of
    D. *understatement* of assets at the end of

21. The Accounts Receivable account is an example of a _____ account.

    A. subsidiary
    B. controlling
    C. fixed asset
    D. valuation

22. The _____ check provides space for stating the purpose for which the check is written.

    A. cashier's   B. certified   C. preferred   D. voucher

23. If the assets of a firm at the end of the year were greater than the assets at the beginning of the year, then which statement would be CORRECT?   23._____

    A. The firm made a profit for the year.
    B. The firm was well managed for the year.
    C. The capital of the firm was greater at the end of the year.
    D. More information is needed before arriving at a conclusion.

24. Which is a legal characteristic of a general partnership? _____ liability.   24._____

    A. Long-term   B. Unlimited
    C. Contingent   D. Deferred

25. The term *double entry bookkeeping* means that, for each transaction, an entry is made   25._____

    A. in the journal and also in the ledger
    B. in the general ledger and also in a subsidiary ledger
    C. on the debit side of one account and on the credit side of another account
    D. on a business paper and also in the books

KEY (CORRECT ANSWERS)

1. A   11. A
2. B   12. D
3. D   13. D
4. B   14. C
5. B   15. B

6. A   16. B
7. C   17. A
8. A   18. C
9. A   19. B
10. D   20. A

21. B
22. D
23. D
24. B
25. C

EXAMINATION SECTION
TEST 1

DIRECTIONS: Each question or incomplete statement is followed by several suggested answers or completions. Select the one that BEST answers the question or completes the statement. *PRINT THE LETTER OF THE CORRECT ANSWER IN THE SPACE AT THE RIGHT.*

1. In the preparation of a balance sheet, failure to consider the inventory of office supplies will result in _____ assets and _____.

    A. overstating; overstating liabilities
    B. understating; overstating capital
    C. understating; understating capital
    D. overstating; understating liabilities

2. The annual federal unemployment tax is paid by the

    A. employer *only*
    B. employee *only*
    C. employer and the employee equally
    D. employee, up to a maximum of 30 cents per week, and the balance is paid by the employer

3. Which are NORMALLY considered as current assets?

    A. Bank overdrafts
    B. Prepaid expenses
    C. Accrued expenses
    D. Payroll taxes

4. What type of ledger account is a summary of a number of accounts in another ledger? The _____ account.

    A. controlling
    B. subsidiary
    C. asset
    D. proprietorship

5. The PRIMARY purpose of a petty cash fund is to

    A. provide a fund for paying all miscellaneous expenses
    B. take the place of the cash account
    C. provide a common drawing fund for the owners of the business
    D. avoid entering a number of small amounts in the Cash Payments Journal

6. In the absence of a written agreement, profits in a partnership would be divided

    A. in proportion to the investment of the partners
    B. on an equitable basis depending on the time and effort spent by the partners
    C. equally
    D. on a ratio of investment basis, giving the senior partner preference

7. Which account represents a subtraction or decrease to an income account?

    A. Purchase Returns & Allowances
    B. Sales Returns & Allowances
    C. Freight In
    D. Prepaid Rent

8. If the Interest Expense account showed a debit balance of $210 as of December 31, and $40 of this amount was prepaid on Notes Payable, which statement is CORRECT as of December 31?

   A. Prepaid Interest of $170 should be shown as a deferred expense in the balance sheet.
   B. Interest Expense should be shown in the Income Statement as $210.
   C. Prepaid Interest of $40 should be listed as a deferred credit to income in the balance sheet.
   D. Interest Expense should be shown in the Income Statement as $170.

9. When prices are rising, which inventory-valuation method results in the LOWEST inventory value?

   A. FIFO
   B. LIFO
   C. Average cost
   D. Declining balance

10. Which of the following is a CORRECT procedure in preparing a bank reconciliation?

    A. Deposits in transit should be added to the cash balance on the books, and outstanding checks should be deducted from the cash balance on the bank statement.
    B. The cash balance on the bank statement and the cash balance on the books should be equal if there are deposits in transit and outstanding checks.
    C. Outstanding checks should be deducted from the cash balance on the books.
    D. Any service charge should be deducted from the check stub balance.

11. Which ratio indicates that there may NOT be enough on hand to meet current obligations?

    A. $\dfrac{\text{fixed assets}}{\text{fixed liabilities}} = \dfrac{2}{3}$
    B. $\dfrac{\text{total assets}}{\text{total obligations}} = \dfrac{3}{5}$
    C. $\dfrac{\text{current assets}}{\text{current liabilities}} = \dfrac{1}{3}$
    D. $\dfrac{\text{current assets}}{\text{fixed liabilities}} = \dfrac{1}{2}$

12. Which asset is NOT subject to depreciation?

    A. Factory equipment
    B. Land
    C. Buildings
    D. Machinery

13. Which form is prepared to verify that the total of the account balances in the Customers Ledger agrees with the balance in the controlling account in the General Ledger?

    A. Worksheet
    B. Schedule of accounts payable
    C. Schedule of accounts receivable
    D. Trial balance

14. If the merchandise inventory on hand at the end of the year was overstated, what will be the result of this error?   14.____

    A. *Understatement* of income for the year
    B. *Overstatement* of income for the year
    C. *Understatement* of assets at the end of the year
    D. No effect on income or assets

15. Working capital is found by subtracting the total current liabilities from the total   15.____

    A. fixed liabilities
    B. fixed assets
    C. current income
    D. current assets

16. Which is the CORRECT procedure for calculating the rate of merchandise turnover?   16.____

    A. Gross Sales divided by Net Sales
    B. Cost of Sales divided by Average Inventory
    C. Net Purchases divided by Average Inventory
    D. Gross Purchases divided by Net Purchases

17. The books of the Atlas Cement Corporation show a net profit of $142,000. To close the Profit and Loss account of the corporation at the end of the year, the account CREDITED should be   17.____

    A. Earned Surplus
    B. Capital Stock
    C. C. Atlas, Capital
    D. C. Atlas, Personal

18. The bank statement at the end of the month indicated a bank charge for printing a new checkbook.
    How is this information recorded?
    Debit   18.____

    A. Cash and credit Office Supplies
    B. Office Supplies and credit the Bank Charges
    C. the Bank Charges and credit Office Supplies
    D. Miscellaneous Expense and credit Cash

19. The Allowance for Doubtful Accounts appears on the balance sheet as a deduction from   19.____

    A. Accounts Receivable
    B. Notes Receivable
    C. Accounts Payable
    D. Notes Payable

20. The Tucker Equipment Corporation had a $45,000 profit for the year ended December 31.
    Which would be the PROPER entry to close the Income and Expense account at the end of the year?
    Debit Income and Expense Summary; credit   20.____

    A. Tucker, Capital
    B. Tucker, Drawing
    C. Retained Earnings
    D. Capital Stock

21. A failure to record a purchases invoice would be discovered when the   21._____

    A. monthly statement of account is sent to the customer
    B. check is received from the customer
    C. check is sent to the creditor
    D. statement of account is received from the creditor

22. Which General Ledger account would appear in a post-closing trial balance?   22._____

    A. Notes Receivable   B. Bad Debts Expense
    C. Sales Discount   D. Fee Income

23. Which deduction is affected by the number of exemptions claimed?   23._____

    A. State Disability   B. State income tax
    C. FICA tax   D. Workers' Compensation

24. The face value of a 60-day, 12% promissory note is $900.   24._____
    The maturity value of this note will be

    A. $909   B. $900   C. $918   D. $1,008

25. An invoice dated March 10, terms 2/10, n/30, should be paid no later than   25._____

    A. March 20   B. March 31   C. April 9   D. April 10

KEY (CORRECT ANSWERS)

1. C
2. A
3. B
4. A
5. D

6. C
7. B
8. D
9. B
10. D

11. C
12. B
13. C
14. B
15. D

16. B
17. A
18. D
19. A
20. C

21. D
22. A
23. B
24. C
25. C

TEST 2

DIRECTIONS: Each question or incomplete statement is followed by several suggested answers or completions. Select the one that BEST answers the question or completes the statement. *PRINT THE LETTER OF THE CORRECT ANSWER IN THE SPACE AT THE RIGHT.*

1. Which is NOT an essential element of a computer system?

    A. Input
    C. Verifier
    B. Central processing unit
    D. Output

2. The general ledger account that would NOT appear in a post-closing trial balance would be

    A. Cash
    C. Furniture and Fixtures
    B. Accounts Payable
    D. Sales Income

3. Ralph Hanley, age 45, supports his wife and three children. Mr. Hanley is the only member of the family required to file an income tax return. What is the MAXIMUM number of exemptions he can claim?

    A. One   B. Five   C. Three   D. Four

4. The cost of a fixed asset minus the allowance for depreciation (accumulated depreciation) is the _____ value.

    A. market   B. cost   C. liquidation   D. book

5. The form used by a bookkeeper in summarizing adjustments and information which will be used in preparing statements is called a

    A. journal
    C. ledger
    B. balance sheet
    D. worksheet

6. When a large number of transactions of a particular kind are to be entered in bookkeeping records, it is USUALLY advisable to use

    A. cash records
    C. special journals
    B. controlling accounts
    D. special ledgers

7. The petty cash book shows a petty cash balance of $9.80 on May 31. The petty cash box contains only $9.10. What account will be debited to record the $.70 difference?

    A. Cash
    C. Cash Short and Over
    B. Petty Cash
    D. Petty Cash Expense

8. The ONLY difference between the books of a partnership and those of a sole proprietorship appears in the _____ accounts.

    A. proprietorship
    C. asset
    B. liability
    D. expense

9. The earnings of a corporation are FIRST recorded as a credit to an account called

    A. Dividends Payable
    C. Retained Earnings
    B. Capital Stock Authorized
    D. Profit and Loss Summary

10. A firm purchased a new delivery truck for $2,900 and sold it four years later for $500. The Allowance for Depreciation of Delivery Equipment account was credited for $580 at the end of each of the four years.
    When the machine was sold, there was a

    A. loss of $80
    B. loss of $1,820
    C. loss of $2,400
    D. gain of $80

    10._____

11. FICA taxes are paid by

    A. employees *only*
    B. employers *only*
    C. both employees and employers
    D. neither employees nor employers

    11._____

12. Which phase of the data processing cycle is the SAME as calculating net pay in a manual system?

    A. Input   B. Processing   C. Storing   D. Output

    12._____

13. Which error will cause the trial balance to be out of balance?

    A. A sales invoice for $60 was entered in the Sales Journal for $600.
    B. A credit to office furniture in the journal was posted as a credit to office machines in the ledger.
    C. A debit to advertising expense in the journal was posted as a debit to miscellaneous expense in the ledger.
    D. A debit to office equipment in the journal was posted as a credit to office equipment in the ledger.

    13._____

14. The collection of a bad debt previously written off will result in a(n)

    A. *decrease* in assets
    B. *decrease* in capital
    C. *increase* in assets
    D. *increase* in liabilities

    14._____

15. Which account does NOT belong in the group?

    A. Notes Receivable
    B. Building
    C. Office Equipment
    D. Delivery Truck

    15._____

16. The adjusting entry to record the estimated bad debts is debit _____ and credit _____.

    A. Allowance for Bad Debts; Bad Debts Expense
    B. Bad Debts Expense; Allowance for Bad Debts
    C. Allowance for Bad Debts; Accounts Receivable
    D. Bad Debts Expense; Accounts Receivable

    16._____

17. At the end of the year, which account should be closed into the income and expense summary?

    A. Freight In
    B. Allowance for Doubtful Accounts
    C. Notes Receivable
    D. Petty Cash

    17._____

18. Which form is prepared to aid in verifying that the customer's account balances in the customer's ledger agree with the balance in the Accounts Receivable account in the general ledger?

A. Worksheet
B. Schedule of Accounts Payable
C. Schedule of Accounts Receivable
D. Trial Balance

19. In the preparation of an income statement, failure to consider accrued wages will result in

A. *overstating* operating expense and understating net profit
B. *overstating* net profit *only*
C. *understating* operating expense and overstating net profit
D. *understating* operating expense *only*

20. The CORRECT formula for determining the rate of merchandise turnover is

A. cost of goods sold divided by average inventory
B. net sales divided by net purchases
C. gross sales divided by ending inventory
D. average inventory divided by cost of goods sold

21. A legal characteristic of a corporation is _____ liability.

A. contingent
B. limited
C. unlimited
D. deferred

22. A customer's check you had deposited is returned to you by the bank labeled *Dishonored*.
What entries would be made as a result of this action? Debit _____ and credit _____.

A. cash; customer's account
B. miscellaneous expense; cash
C. customer's account; capital
D. customer's account; cash

23. The TOTAL capital of a corporation may be found by adding

A. assets and liabilities
B. assets and capital stock
C. liabilities and capital stock
D. earned surplus and capital stock

24. The source of an entry made in the Petty Cash book is the

A. general ledger
B. voucher
C. register
D. general journal

25. Which account is debited to record interest earned but not yet due?

A. Deferred Interest
B. Interest Receivable
C. Interest Income
D. Income and Expense Summary

KEY (CORRECT ANSWERS)

1. C
2. D
3. B
4. D
5. D

6. C
7. C
8. A
9. C
10. A

11. C
12. B
13. D
14. C
15. A

16. B
17. A
18. C
19. C
20. A

21. B
22. D
23. D
24. B
25. B

TEST 3

DIRECTIONS: Each question or incomplete statement is followed by several suggested answers or completions. Select the one that BEST answers the question or completes the statement. *PRINT THE LETTER OF THE CORRECT ANSWER IN THE SPACE AT THE RIGHT.*

1. Which reason should NOT generally be used by an employer when making a hiring decision?
   An applicant('s)

   A. resume reveals a lack of job-related skills
   B. attendance record on a previous job is poor
   C. has improperly prepared the job application
   D. is married

   1.____

2. Graves, Owens, and Smith formed a partnership and invested $15,000 each. If the firm made a profit of $18,000 last year and profits and losses were shared equally, what was Owens' share of the net profit?

   A. $1,000   B. $5,000   C. $6,000   D. $9,000

   2.____

3. The bank statement balance of the Bedford Co. on May 31 was $3,263.28. The checkbook balance was $3,119.06. A reconciliation showed that the outstanding checks totaled $147.22 and that there was a bank service charge of $3.00. The CORRECT checkbook balance should be

   A. $3,260.28   B. $3,122.06   C. $3,116.06   D. $3,266.28

   3.____

4. Which account is shown in a post-closing trial balance?

   A. Prepaid Insurance   B. Fees Income
   C. Purchases   D. Freight In

   4.____

5. A check endorsed *For deposit only (signed) Samuel Jones* is an example of a _____ endorsement.

   A. full   B. blank   C. complete   D. restrictive

   5.____

6. The selling price of a share of stock as published in a daily newspaper is called the _____ value.

   A. book   B. face   C. par   D. market

   6.____

7. Which is obtained by dividing the cost of goods sold by the average inventory?

   A. Current ratio
   B. Merchandise inventory turnover
   C. Average rate of mark-up
   D. Acid-test ratio

   7.____

8. A Suzuki truck costing $39,000 is expected to have a useful life of six years and a salvage value of $3,000.
   If $6,000 is debited to the depreciation expense account each year for six years, what method of depreciation is used?

   A. Units of production   B. Straight line
   C. Declining balance   D. Sum of the years digits

   8.____

9. Which form is prepared to aid in verifying that the customer's account balances in the customer's ledger agree with the balance in the Accounts Receivable account in the General Ledger?

   A. Worksheet
   B. Schedule of Accounts Payable
   C. Schedule of Accounts Receivable
   D. Trial Balance

10. In the preparation of a balance sheet, failure to consider commissions owed to salespersons will result in _____ liabilities and _____ capital.

    A. understating; overstating
    B. understating; understating
    C. overstating; overstating
    D. overstating; understating

11. A financial statement generated by a computer is an example of a(n)

    A. audit trail
    B. output
    C. input
    D. program

12. Merchandise was sold for $150 cash plus a 3% sales tax. The CORRECT credit(s) should be

    A. Sales Income $150, Sales Taxes Payable $4.50
    B. Sales Income $154.50
    C. Merchandise $150, Sales Taxes Payable $4.50
    D. Sales Income $150

13. The bookkeeper should prepare a bank reconciliation MAINLY to determine

    A. which checks are outstanding
    B. whether the checkbook balance and the bank statement balance are in agreement
    C. the total amount of checks written during the month
    D. the total amount of cash deposited during the month

14. Which is the CORRECT procedure for calculating the rate of merchandise turnover?

    A. Gross Sales divided by Net Sales
    B. Cost of Goods Sold divided by Average Inventory
    C. Net Purchases divided by Average Inventory
    D. Gross Purchases divided by Net Purchases

15. Which previous job should be listed FIRST on a job application form? The

    A. least recent job
    B. most recent job
    C. job you liked best
    D. job which paid the most

16. Failure to record cash sales will result in

    A. *overstatement* of profit
    B. *understatement* of profit
    C. *understatement* of liabilities
    D. *overstatement* of capital

17. When a fixed asset is repaired, the cost of the repairs should be _____ account.   17.____

    A. *debited* to the asset
    B. *debited* to the expense
    C. *credited* to the proprietor's capital
    D. *credited* to the asset

18. The form used by a bookkeeper to summarize information which will be used in preparing financial statements is called a   18.____

    A. journal   B. balance sheet
    C. ledger   D. worksheet

19. Which type of ledger account is a summary of a number of accounts in another ledger? _____ account.   19.____

    A. Controlling   B. Subsidiary
    C. Asset   D. Proprietorship

20. What is the summary entry on the Purchases Journal?   20.____
    Debit _____ and credit _____.

    A. Accounts Payable; Merchandise Purchases
    B. Accounts Receivable; Merchandise Purchases
    C. Merchandise Purchases; Accounts Receivable
    D. Merchandise Purchases; Accounts Payable

21. The source document for entries made in the Sales Journal is a(n)   21.____

    A. credit memo   B. statement of accounts
    C. invoice   D. bill of lading

22. A Trial Balance which is in balance would NOT reveal the   22.____

    A. omission of the credit part of an entry
    B. posting of the same debit twice
    C. omission of an entire transaction
    D. omission of an account with a balance

23. A financial statement prepared by a computerized accounting system is an example of   23.____

    A. input   B. output
    C. flowcharting   D. programming

24. The form which the payroll clerk gives to each employee to show gross earnings and taxes withheld for the year is a   24.____

    A. W-2   B. W-3   C. W-4   D. 1040

25. Who would be the LEAST appropriate reference on an application for a job? A   25.____

    A. relative
    B. guidance counselor
    C. former employer
    D. prominent member of the community

KEY (CORRECT ANSWERS)

1. D
2. C
3. C
4. A
5. D

6. D
7. B
8. B
9. C
10. A

11. B
12. A
13. B
14. B
15. B

16. B
17. B
18. D
19. A
20. D

21. C
22. C
23. B
24. A
25. A

EXAMINATION SECTION
TEST 1

DIRECTIONS: Each question or incomplete statement is followed by several suggested answers or completions. Select the one that BEST answers the question or completes the statement. *PRINT THE LETTER OF THE CORRECT ANSWER IN THE SPACE AT THE RIGHT.*

1. A line of a Federal Income Tax Rate Schedule reads:
   over   but not over   your tax is:
   $6,000 $8,000 $1,130 plus 25% of excess over $6,000.
   The income tax due on taxable income of $7,200 is

   A. $1,130   B. $1,430   C. $1,630   D. $1,800

   1._____

2. We discounted at our bank a customer's promissory note for $3,000. The proceeds were $2,985.
   The CORRECT credit part of the entry to record this transaction is

   A. Notes Payable, $3,000
   B. Notes Receivable Discounted, $3,000
   C. Notes Payable, $2,985
   D. Notes Receivable Discounted, $2,985

   2._____

3. A payment for gasoline and oil was incorrectly debited to the Delivery Equipment account instead of to the Delivery Expense account.
   This error, if not corrected, would result in

   A. an overstatement of the net profit
   B. an understatement of the net profit
   C. no change in the net profit
   D. no change in the total assets

   3._____

4. A federal depository receipt is issued when a firm

   A. reports to an employee the amount of federal taxes withheld from his wages during the year
   B. purchases United States government bonds
   C. deposits its surplus cash in a bank
   D. deposits in a bank FICA taxes and federal withholding taxes

   4._____

5. As evidence of part ownership in a corporation, a person receives a

   A. certificate of incorporation
   B. stock certificate
   C. bond
   D. charter

   5._____

6. One advantage resulting from the use of controlling accounts in the general ledger is that fewer

   A. bookkeepers are needed to do the work
   B. pages are needed in each journal

   6._____

C. accounts are needed in the subsidiary ledgers
D. postings are required in the general ledger

7. The proprietor took home an office desk from the business for his personal use. The effect on the fundamental bookkeeping equation is to

   A. *increase* assets, decrease owner's worth
   B. *increase* assets, increase liabilities
   C. *increase* assets, increase owner's worth
   D. *decrease* owner's worth, decrease assets

   7.____

8. Which can be determined from information found on the Balance Sheet?

   A. Current ratio
   B. Ratio of net profit to sales
   C. Total operating expenses
   D. Total income

   8.____

9. In recording the amount of State sales tax collected on cash sales, the amount to be credited is

   A. Sales
   B. Sales Taxes Payable
   C. Sales Taxes Receivable
   D. Sales Taxes Expense

   9.____

10. The rate of return on capital investment is found by dividing the amount of investment into

    A. total sales
    B. proprietor's drawings
    C. net income
    D. total current assets

    10.____

Questions 11-15.

DIRECTIONS: Questions 11 through 15 are to be answered on the basis of the following account.

Name   Grey-Jackson, Inc.   Terms: 2/10, N/30
Address   75 E. 43, New York, N.Y.   10017

DATE	EXPLANATION	POST. REF.	DEBIT	CREDIT	BALANCE
May 3		J 21	630 00		630 00
7		Ja 11		25 00	605 00
10		CR 34		605 00	
June 13		S 32	230 00		230 00
15		Ja 27		15 00	245 00

11. This account will be found in

    A. Accounts Receivable Subsidiary
    B. Accounts Payable Subsidiary
    C. General
    D. Sales

    11.____

12. From which business paper did the entry on May 3 originate? 12.____
    A

    A. purchases invoice   B. shipping memo
    C. sales invoice   D. statement of account

13. The MOST probable reason for the entry on May 7 is that 13.____

    A. a partial payment was made
    B. merchandise was returned
    C. a cash discount on the transaction of May 3 was allowed
    D. shipping charges were prepaid

14. In order to obtain more information regarding the entry of May 7, the bookkeeper should refer to 14.____

    A. invoice number 11
    B. page 11 of the Grey-Jackson, Inc. file
    C. the 11th entry in the General Journal
    D. page 11 of the General Journal

15. If the debit on June 15 represents a freight charge, how much should be paid on June 22? 15.____

    A. $245.00   B. $240.40   C. $240.10   D. $230.00

16. Which error will cause the Trial Balance to be out of balance? 16.____
    The

    A. bookkeeper charged an item to Miscellaneous Expense instead of to Advertising Expense
    B. bookkeeper failed to post an entire entry from the General Journal
    C. bookkeeper incorrectly entered the amount of a purchase into the Purchases Journal
    D. Petty Cash account was omitted from the Trial Balance

17. On October 14, the bookkeeper received in the mail a customer's check for $500. The identical amount, $500, is also due to a creditor on October 14. 17.____
    Which is the recommended bookkeeping procedure?

    A. Endorse the check to the creditor, and mail it to him.
    B. Request your firm's bank to certify the customer's cheek, and mail it to your creditor.
    C. Deposit the customer's check, and mail a separate check to the creditor.
    D. Return the customer's check to him, and request him to mail it to the creditor.

18. A sale is made on June 16, terms 2/10, EOM. 18.____
    In order for the discount to be allowed, payment must be made no later than

    A. June 26   B. June 30   C. July 2   D. July 10

19. When a petty cash fund is established, the effect on the fundamental accounting equation is that total assets 19.____

    A. and total liabilities remain unchanged
    B. decrease; total liabilities increase

49

C. decrease; proprietorship decreases
D. increase; proprietorship increases

20. One of the reasons for preparing a Schedule of Accounts Receivable is to

    A. make up statements of customers accounts
    B. determine if the subsidiary ledger agrees with the controlling account
    C. determine the worth of the business
    D. determine the total sales for the fiscal period

21. The current price of a share of stock traded on the stock exchange is called the _____ value.

    A. market   B. par   C. book   D. face

22. In a certain industry, firm A had a current ratio of 4:1; while firm B had a current ratio of 1:1.
    A logical conclusion would be that firm A

    A. had a higher merchandise turnover than firm B
    B. had more cash than firm B
    C. had more assets than firm B
    D. was better able to pay its current debts than firm B

23. When a bank certifies a $100 check for the person who wrote the check, it

    A. pays $100 to the person who wrote the check
    B. tells the depositor that he should remember this check so as to avoid overdrawing his account
    C. immediately deducts the $100 from the balance of the account
    D. asks the depositor for $100 to cover the check

24. A 90-day, 6% interest-bearing note for $340 was paid on the due date.
    The amount of the check was

    A. $345.10   B. $343.40   C. $340.00   D. $334.90

25. The declaration by a corporation of dividend to be paid at a future date results in a decrease in

    A. assets and a decrease in net worth
    B. assets and an increase in liabilities
    C. liabilities and a decrease in net worth
    D. net worth and an increase in liabilities

KEY (CORRECT ANSWERS)

1.	B	11.	A
2.	B	12.	D
3.	A	13.	B
4.	D	14.	D
5.	B	15.	B
6.	D	16.	D
7.	D	17.	B
8.	A	18.	D
9.	B	19.	A
10.	C	20.	B

21. A
22. D
23. C
24. A
25. D

TEST 2

DIRECTIONS: Each question or incomplete statement is followed by several suggested answers or completions. Select the one that BEST answers the question or completes the statement. *PRINT THE LETTER OF THE CORRECT ANSWER IN THE SPACE AT THE RIGHT.*

1. Which can be determined from information found on the Balance Sheet?

    A. Current ratio
    B. Rate of net profit based on sales
    C. Merchandise turnover
    D. Total operating expenses

2. Which statement BEST describes the function of a source document in an automatic data processing system?

    A. Input is recorded on it.
    B. Output is recorded on it.
    C. Raw data is obtained from it.
    D. It manipulates the central processing unit.

3. Postings to the debit side of Accounts Payable in the General Ledger USUALLY come from the _____ Journal.

    A. Cash Payments   B. Sales
    C. Purchases   D. Cash Receipts

4. The PRIMARY purpose of a trial balance is to

    A. check the accuracy of control accounts
    B. locate errors in posting
    C. assure the accuracy of financial reports
    D. determine if the general ledger is in balance

5. An outstanding check is a check that has

    A. been voided   B. been deposited
    C. not been written   D. not been paid

6. If the total of the credit column on the Income Statement of the worksheet is larger than the total of the debit column, the difference is called net

    A. income   B. loss   C. worth   D. value

7. Which is NOT an input device in an electronic data processing system? A(n)

    A. optical scanner   B. magnetic tape unit
    C. printer   D. console keyboard

8. After all closing entries are recorded and posted, the _____ account would still have a balance.

    A. Income and Expense Summary   B. Purchases
    C. Owner's Drawing   D. Owner's Capital

9. Failure to replenish Petty Cash at the end of the fiscal period will result in

    A. *understatement* of Net Income
    B. *overstatement* of Net Income
    C. *understatement* of Petty Cash
    D. *overstatement* of Expenses

10. Which item should NOT appear on a job application form?

    A. Current address
    B. Social security number
    C. Religion
    D. Education

11. If a person holds a civil service job, he or she is employed by

    A. the government
    B. a private accounting firm
    C. a large engineering firm
    D. a nonprofit charitable organization

12. Which is NOT given by an employer to an employee as a fringe benefit?

    A. Paid vacation days
    B. Paid sick leave
    C. Group life insurance coverage
    D. Payment of federal income taxes

13. A source of current job openings is(are)

    A. DICTIONARY OF OCCUPATIONAL TITLES
    B. CAREER INFORMATION HANDBOOK
    C. classified advertisements in a newspaper
    D. OCCUPATIONAL OUTLOOK HANDBOOK

14. Which reason should NOT generally be used by an employer when making a hiring decision?
    An applicant('s)

    A. resume reveals a lack of job-related skills
    B. attendance record on a previous job is poor
    C. has improperly prepared the job application
    D. is married

15. When listing previous jobs on an employment application, the prospective employer should list his/her _____ job first.

    A. least recent
    B. most recent
    C. favorite
    D. highest salaried

16. The LEAST appropriate reference on an application for a job would be a

    A. relative
    B. guidance counselor
    C. former employer
    D. prominent member of the community

17. Receipt of a $300 check from a customer in payment of his $300 account results in   17._____

    A. an increase in total value of assets
    B. a decrease in total value of assets
    C. no change in total value of assets
    D. an increase in net worth

18. The monthly report sent to each customer to remind him of the amount he owes is called a(n)   18._____

    A. invoice
    B. statement of account
    C. bank statement
    D. credit memorandum

19. Entries in the Cash Payments Journal are USUALLY made from   19._____

    A. Sales Invoices
    B. Petty Cash Vouchers
    C. Checkbook stubs
    D. Purchase orders

20. The Petty Cash book shows a petty cash balance of $10 on June 30. An actual count of the petty cash on hand on June 30 shows $9.00 in the petty cash box.   20._____
    The account to be debited to record the difference between the book balance and the petty cash on hand would be

    A. Petty Cash
    B. Cash
    C. Cash Short and Over
    D. Petty Cash Expense

KEY (CORRECT ANSWERS)

1. A
2. C
3. A
4. D
5. D

6. A
7. C
8. D
9. B
10. C

11. A
12. D
13. C
14. D
15. B

16. A
17. C
18. B
19. C
20. C

TEST 3

DIRECTIONS: Each question or incomplete statement is followed by several suggested answers or completions. Select the one that BEST answers the question or completes the statement. *PRINT THE LETTER OF THE CORRECT ANSWER IN THE SPACE AT THE RIGHT.*

1. Information prepared in machine-readable form for processing by automatic data processing equipment is commonly referred to as

    A. output
    B. business data
    C. input
    D. financial data

2. Mr. H. Brown, the owner of a small business, withdrew money for his own use. The bookkeeper debited the H. Brown Capital account and credited the Cash account. To correct this error, the bookkeeper should debit the _____ account and credit the _____ account.

    A. H. Brown Personal; H. Brown Capital
    B. H. Brown Personal; Cash
    C. Cash; H. Brown Personal
    D. H. Brown Capital; H. Brown Personal

3. The Dale Corporation earned a net profit of $50,000 for the year. Before closing the books, the Capital Stock account showed a balance of $300,000, and the Retained Earnings account had a balance of $40,000.
The net worth of the firm on December 31 was

    A. $340,000   B. $350,000   C. $390,000   D. $310,000

4. Of the following examples of computer programs, the one most commonly associated with standard bookkeeping procedures is

    A. Microsoft Word
    B. Adobe Acrobat Pro
    C. Microsoft PowerPoint
    D. Microsoft Excel

5. The receipt of a check in settlement of an interest-bearing note will result in an increase in assets(,)

    A. and a decrease in assets
    B. a decrease in assets, and an increase in capital
    C. a decrease in assets, and a decrease in capital
    D. a decrease in liabilities, and an increase in capital

6. A sale on credit to George Rogers for $200 was incorrectly posted to his account as $20. This error would mean that the

    A. Schedule of Accounts Receivable would be understated
    B. Accounts Receivable controlling account would be overstated
    C. Schedule of Accounts Receivable would be overstated
    D. trial balance would not balance

7. A cash sale of $250 worth of merchandise subject to a 6% sales tax should be recorded as a debit to the Cash account for

   A. $250 and a credit to the Sales Income account for $250
   B. $265 and a credit to the Sales Income account for $265
   C. $250, a debit to the Sales Tax Expense account for $15, and a credit to the Sales Income account for $265
   D. a credit to the Sales Income account for $250, and a credit to the Sales Taxes Payable account for $15

8. To determine which checks are outstanding at the end of each month, the bookkeeper should

   A. ask the bank to send a list of these outstanding checks
   B. find the necessary information in the bank statement
   C. compare the cancelled checks with the bank statement
   D. compare the cancelled checks with the checkbook stubs

9. An error was made in writing the amount of a check. The BEST business procedure to be followed is to

   A. cross off the incorrect amount on the check and neatly write the correct amount above the incorrect figure
   B. erase the incorrect amount on the check and neatly fill in the correct amount
   C. write *void* across the check and the stub and write a new check
   D. tear up the check and write a new check

10. When a posting machine is used, Accounts Receivable and Accounts Payable are USUALLY kept in a

    A. bound ledger with money columns for debit and credit
    B. looseleaf ledger with money columns for debit and credit
    C. card ledger with money columns for debit, credit, and balance
    D. bound ledger with money columns for debit, credit, and balance

11. The federal individual income tax return MUST be filed by

    A. December 31   B. March 15
    C. April 15   D. June 30

12. When cash is received as a result of sales, the PROPER business procedure is to

    A. put the cash in the petty cash box
    B. deposit the cash in a checking account at the end of the day
    C. deposit the cash in a savings account at the end of the day
    D. use the cash to pay current bills

13. Which of the following is computer software used for bookkeeping purposes?

    A. Adobe InDesign   B. Microsoft Outlook
    C. Adobe Dreamweaver   D. Sage 50

14. The bookkeeper failed to record depreciation for the year. As a result, the

    A. assets will be understated
    B. profit will be understated
    C. profit will be overstated
    D. liabilities will be overstated

15. The TOTAL of the Schedule of Accounts Receivable should agree with the

    A. total of the Accounts Receivable column in the cash receipts journal
    B. total of the Accounts Receivable column in the general journal
    C. balance of the Accounts Receivable controlling account
    D. balance in the Sales account

16. Which error would cause the trial balance to be out of balance?

    A. Incorrectly totaling the Sales Journal
    B. Failing to post to a customer's account from the Sales Journal
    C. Incorrectly debiting the Office Expense account instead of the Furniture and Fixtures account
    D. Incorrectly adding the debits in the Notes Payable account

17. The business paper which is used as a source for an entry in the Petty Cash book is a

    A. voucher
    B. purchase order
    C. check stub
    D. credit memorandum

18. On December 31, the Capital Stock account of the Rogers Corporation showed a balance of $75,000, and the Retained Earnings account showed a balance of $15,000. If 1,000 shares of stock were in the hands of stockholders, the book value of each share of stock was

    A. $90   B. $75   C. $60   D. 15

19. A 60-day promissory note dated July 7 will be due on

    A. August 6
    B. September 5
    C. September 6
    D. September 7

20. A bank reconciliation showed a deposit in transit, a bank charge, outstanding checks, and a certified outstanding check.
    On the basis of this information, the bookkeeper should make an entry to record the

    A. deposit in transit
    B. bank charge
    C. outstanding checks
    D. certified outstanding check

21. Merchandise was sold on February 8 for $175 less a trade discount of 20%, terms 2/10, n/30.
    The amount of the check received on March 9 should be

    A. $137.20   B. $140.00   C. $171.50   D. $175.00

22. The monthly report sent by a bank to a depositor showing his balance in the bank, deposits made during the month, and checks paid during the month is called a

    A. bank reconciliation
    B. monthly report
    C. bank statement
    D. balance sheet

23. A $200 check received from John Howard, a customer, in payment of his $200 promissory note was entered incorrectly by debiting the Cash account and crediting the John Howard account.
The CORRECTING entry should debit the _____ account and credit the _____ account.

   A. Cash; Notes Receivable
   B. Notes Receivable; John Howard
   C. John Howard; Notes Receivable
   D. Cash; John Howard

23._____

24. Bond holders of a corporation are _____ of the corporation.

   A. owners   B. creditors   C. customers   D. directors

24._____

25. Which error will cause the trial balance to be out of balance?

   A. Posting to the wrong side of a customer's account in the Accounts Receivable Ledger
   B. Failure to record a sale in the Sales Journal
   C. Totaling the Purchase Journal incorrectly
   D. Posting a $1,450 debit to the Accounts Payable controlling account as $1,540

25._____

KEY (CORRECT ANSWERS)

1. C		11. C	
2. A		12. B	
3. C		13. D	
4. D		14. C	
5. B		15. C	
6. A		16. D	
7. D		17. A	
8. D		18. A	
9. C		19. B	
10. C		20. B	

21. B
22. C
23. C
24. B
25. D

BOOKKEEPING PROBLEMS
EXAMINATION SECTION
TEST 1

DIRECTIONS: Each question or incomplete statement is followed by several suggested answers or completions. Select the one that BEST answers the question or completes the statement. *PRINT THE LETTER OF THE CORRECT ANSWER IN THE SPACE AT THE RIGHT.*

1. The accounts in a general ledger are BEST arranged

    A. in numerical order
    B. according to the frequency with which each account is used
    C. according to the order in which the headings of the columns in the cash journals are arranged
    D. according to the order in which they are used in preparing financial statements

1._____

2. A physical inventory is an inventory obtained by

    A. an actual count of the items on hand
    B. adding the totals of the stock record cards
    C. deducting the cost of goods sold from the purchases for the period
    D. deducting the purchases from the sales for the period

2._____

3. Modern accounting practice favors the valuation of the inventories of a going concern at

    A. current market prices, if higher than cost
    B. cost or market, whichever is lower
    C. estimated selling price
    D. probable value at forced sale

3._____

4. A subsidiary ledger contains accounts which show

    A. details of contingent liabilities of undetermined amount
    B. totals of all asset accounts in the general ledger
    C. totals of all liability accounts in the general ledger
    D. details of an account in the general ledger

4._____

5. A statement of the assets, liabilities, and net worth of a business is called a

    A. trial balance
    B. budget
    C. profit and loss statement
    D. balance sheet

5._____

6. The one of the following which is NEVER properly considered a negotiable instrument is a(n)

    A. invoice
    B. bond
    C. promissory note
    D. endorsed check

6._____

7. The term *current assets* USUALLY includes such things as

    A. notes payable
    B. machinery and equipment
    C. furniture and fixtures
    D. accounts receivable

7._____

8. An accounting system which records revenues as soon as they are earned and records liabilities as soon as they are incurred regardless of the date of payment is said to operate on a(n) _____ basis.

   A. accrual   B. budgetary   C. encumbrance   D. cash

9. A *trial balance* is a list of

   A. the credit balances in all accounts in a general ledger
   B. all general ledger accounts and their balances
   C. the asset accounts in a general ledger and their balances
   D. the liability accounts in a general ledger and their balances

10. A controlling account contains the totals of

    A. the accounts used in preparing the balance sheet at the end of the fiscal period
    B. the individual amounts entered in the accounts of a subsidiary ledger during the fiscal period
    C. all entries in the general journal during the fiscal period
    D. the accounts used in preparing the profit and loss statement for the fiscal period

11. The ESSENTIAL nature of an asset is that it(s)

    A. must be tangible
    B. must be easily converted into cash
    C. must have value
    D. cost must be included in the profit and loss statement

12. When an asset is depreciated on the straight-line basis, the amount charged off for depreciation

    A. is greater in the earlier years of the asset's life
    B. is greater in the later years of the asset's life
    C. varies each year according to the extent to which the asset is used during the year
    D. is equal each full year of the asset's life

Questions 13-27.

DIRECTIONS: Questions 13 to 27 consist of a list of some of the accounts in a general ledger. Indicate whether each account listed generally contains a debit or a credit balance by putting the letter D (for debit balance) or the letter C (for credit balance) in the correspondingly numbered space on the right for each account listed. For example, for the account Cash, which generally contains a debit balance, you would give the letter D as your answer.

13. Sales Taxes Collected

14. Social Security Taxes Paid by Employer

15. Deposits from Customers

16. Freight Inward

17. Sales Discount

18. Withholding Taxes Payable   18.____
19. L. Norton, Drawings   19.____
20. Office Salaries   20.____
21. Merchandise Inventory   21.____
22. L. Norton, Capital   22.____
23. Purchases Returns   23.____
24. Unearned Rent Income   24.____
25. Reserve for Bad Debts   25.____
26. Depreciation of Machinery   26.____
27. Insurance Prepaid   27.____

Questions 28-42.

DIRECTIONS: Questions 28 to 42 consist of a list of some of the accounts in a general ledger. For the purpose of preparing financial statements, each of these accounts is to be classified into one of the following five major classifications, lettered A to E, as follows:
A. Assets   B. Liabilities   C. Proprietorship
D. Income   E. Expense

You are to indicate the classification to which each account belongs by printing the correct letter, A, B, C, D, or E, in the correspondingly numbered space on the right. For example, for the account Furniture and Fixtures, which is an asset account, you would print the letter A.

28. Notes Receivable   28.____
29. Sales   29.____
30. Wages Payable   30.____
31. Office Salaries   31.____
32. Capital Stock Authorized   32.____
33. Goodwill   33.____
34. Capital Surplus   34.____
35. Office Supplies Used   35.____
36. Interest Payable   36.____
37. Prepaid Rent   37.____
38. Interest Cost   38.____
39. Accounts Payable   39.____

40. Prepaid Insurance 40.____

41. Merchandise Inventory 41.____

42. Interest Earned 42.____

43. A trial balance will NOT indicate that an error has been made in 43.____

    A. computing the balance of an account
    B. entering an amount in the wrong account
    C. carrying forward the balance of an account
    D. entering an amount on the wrong side of an account

44. Many business firms maintain a book of original entry in which all bills to be paid are recorded. 44.____
    This book is known as a

    A. purchase returns journal   B. subsidiary ledger
    C. voucher register   D. notes payable register

45. Many business firms provide a petty cash fund from which to pay for small items in order to avoid the issuing of many small checks. 45.____
    If this fund is replenished periodically to restore it to its original amount, the fund is called a(n) _____ fund.

    A. imprest   B. debenture
    C. adjustment   D. expense reserve

46. A firm which voluntarily terminates business, selling its assets and paying its liabilities, is said to be in 46.____

    A. receivership   B. liquidation
    C. depletion   D. amortization

47. The phrase *3%-10 days* on an invoice ORDINARILY means that 47.____

    A. 3% of the amount must be paid each 10 days
    B. the purchaser is entitled to only ten days credit
    C. a discount of 3% will be allowed for payment in 10 days
    D. the entire amount must be paid in 10 days or a penalty of 3% of the amount due will be added

48. The CHIEF disadvantage of *single-entry* bookkeeping is that it 48.____

    A. is too difficult to operate
    B. is illegal for income tax purposes
    C. provides no possibility of determining net profits
    D. furnishes an incomplete picture of the business

49. Sales *minus* cost of goods sold *equals* 49.____

    A. net profit   B. gross sales
    C. gross profit   D. net sales

50. The amounts of the transactions recorded in a journal are transferred to the general ledger accounts by a process known as   50.____

    A. auditing   B. balancing   C. posting   D. verifying

51. A merchant purchased a stock of goods and priced these goods so as to gain 40% on the cost to him.   51.____
    If the merchant sold these goods for $840, the COST of these goods to him was

    A. $556   B. $600   C. $348   D. $925

52. In the interest at 6% for one full year on a principal sum amounts to $12, the *principal sum* is   52.____

    A. $150   B. $96   C. $196   D. $200

53. On October 17, a business man discounted a customer's 90-day non-interest bearing note at his bank. The face of the note was $960, and it was dated September 28. The discount rate was 5%.   53.____
    Using a 360-day year, the amount in cash that the business man received from the bank was MOST NEARLY

    A. $899.33   B. $950.67   C. $967.50   D. $989.75

54. A certain correctly totaled cash receipts journal contained the following columns: Net Cash Debit, Accounts Receivable, Sales Discounts, and General.   54.____
    At the end of April, the totals of the columns were as follows: Net Cash Debit - $18,925.15, Accounts Receivable (not given), Sales Discounts - $379.65, General - $5,639.25.
    The TOTAL of the Accounts Receivable column was

    A. $11,194.50   B. $21,344.32   C. $7,621.19   D. $13,665.55

55. In its first year of operation, a retail store had cash sales of $49,000 and installment sales of $41,000.   55.____
    If 12% of the amount of these installment sales were collected in that year, the TOTAL amount of cash received from sales was

    A. $22,176   B. $34,987   C. $53,920   D. $55,650

56. I. Conklin and J. Ulster formed a partnership and agreed to share profits in proportion to their initial capital investments. I. Conklin invested $15,000 and J. Ulster invested $12,500.   56.____
    If the profits for the year were $16,500, J. Ulster's share of the profits was

    A. $6,750   B. $7,500   C. $8,100   D. $8,300

57. In a certain city, the tax rate on real estate one year was $48.75 per thousand dollars of assessed valuation. If an apartment house in that city was assessed for $185,000, the real estate tax payable by the owner of that house was MOST NEARLY   57.____

    A. $9,018.75   B. $9,009.75   C. $8,900.00   D. $8,905.25

58. A correctly totaled cash payments journal contained the following columns: Net Cash, Accounts Payable, Purchase Discounts, General.
At the end of April, the totals of the columns were as follows: Net Cash - $18,375.60, Accounts Payable - $16,981.19, Purchase Discounts (not given), General - $1,875.37.
The TOTAL of the Purchase Discounts column was

   A. $120.36 B. $239.87 C. $480.96 D. $670.51

58._____

59. On January 1, the credit balance of the Accounts Payable account in a general ledger was $9,139.87. For the month of January, the Purchase Journal total amounted to $3,467.81; the Accounts Payable column in the Cash Disbursements Journal amounted to $2,935.55; the total of the Returned Purchases Journal for January amounted to $173.15; and the Miscellaneous column in the Cash Disbursements Journal showed that $750 had been paid in January on notes given to creditors and entered in previous months.
The BALANCE in the Accounts Payable account at the end of January was

   A. $8,437.89 B. $9,498.98 C. $9,998.98 D. $10,132.68

59._____

60. The bank statement received from his bank by a business man showed a certain balance for the month of June. This bank statement showed a service charge of $5.19 for the month. He discovered that a check drawn by him in the amount of $83.75 and returned by the bank had been entered on the stub of his checkbook as $38.75. He also found that two checks which he had issued, #29 for $37.18 and #33 for $18.69, were not listed on the statement and had not been returned by the bank. The balance in his checkbook before he reconciled it with the balance shown on the bank statement was $8,917.91.
The BALANCE on the bank statement was

   A. $8,903.97 B. $8,923.59 C. $8,997.65 D. $9,303.95

60._____

KEY (CORRECT ANSWERS)

1.	D	16.	D	31.	E	46.	B
2.	A	17.	D	32.	C	47.	C
3.	B	18.	C	33.	A	48.	D
4.	D	19.	D	34.	C	49.	C
5.	D	20.	D	35.	E	50.	C
6.	A	21.	D	36.	B	51.	B
7.	D	22.	C	37.	A	52.	D
8.	A	23.	C	38.	E	53.	B
9.	B	24.	C	39.	B	54.	D
10.	B	25.	C	40.	A	55.	C
11.	C	26.	D	41.	A	56.	B
12.	D	27.	D	42.	D	57.	A
13.	C	28.	A	43.	B	58.	C
14.	D	29.	D	44.	C	59.	B
15.	C	30.	B	45.	A	60.	B

TEST 2

Questions 1-25.

DIRECTIONS:
1. Below you will find the general ledger balances on February 28 in the books of C. Dutton.
2. On the following pages, you will find all the entries on the books of C. Dutton for the month of March.
3. In the appropriate spaces on the right, you are to supply the new balances for the accounts called for at the end of March.

The correct balances in the general ledger of C. Dutton on February 28 were as follows: (NOTE: The accounts below have not been arranged in the customary trial balance form.)

Cash	$4,336
Accounts Receivable	8,165
Notes Receivable	2,200
Furniture and Fixtures	9,000
Merchandise Inventory 1/1	4,175
Accounts Payable	5,560
Notes Payable	1,500
Reserve for Depreciation of Furniture and Fixtures	1,800
C. Dutton, Capital	14,162
C. Dutton, Drawing	900
Purchases	42,600
Freight In	36
Rent	1,750
Light	126
Telephone	63
Salaries	4,076
Shipping Expenses	368
Sales	53,200
Sales Biscount	637
Purchase Biscount	596
City Sales Tax Collected	804
Social Security Taxes Payable	96
Withholding Taxes Payable	714

CASH RECEIPTS

Date	Name	Net Cash	Accounts Receivable	Sales Disc.	Miscellaneous Acct.	Amount
3/1	T. Blint	6,027.00	6,150.00	123.00		
	K. Crowe	1,015.00			Notes Rec.	1,000.00
					Int. Income	15.00
3/10	N. Tandy	3,969.00	4,050.00	81.00		
3/17	Rebuilt Desk Co.	45.00			Furn. & Fixt.	45.00
3/24	J. Walter	2,910.00	3,000.00	90.00		
3/31	National Federal Bank	3,000.00			Notes Payable	3,000.00
		16,966.00	13,200.00	294.00		4,060.00

CASH DISBURSEMENTS

Date		Net Cash	Accts. Pay.	Purch. Disc.	Soc. Sec. Tax	With-hold Tax	Miscellaneous Acct.	Amount
3/1	Bliss Realty Co.	875.00					Rent	875.00
3/4	Con. Edison	54.00					Light	54.00
3/10	D. LaRue	2,891.00	2,950.00	59.00				
3/15	Payroll	747.00			26.00	175.	Sal.	948.00
3/19	Rebuilt Desk Co.	115.00					Furn/Fixt	115.00
3/26	Jiggs & Co.	3,686.00	3,800.00	114.00				
3/30	Nat'l Fed Bank	1,218.00					Notes Pay.	1200.00
							Int. Cost	18.00
3/31	Payroll	733.00			22.00	171.	Salary	926.00
3/31	C. Dutton	600.00					Draw	600.00
		10,919.00	6,750.00	173.00	48.00	346.00		4736.00

SALES BOOK

Date	Name	Accts. Rec.	Sales	City Sales Tax
3/3	K. Crowe	6,850.00	6,665.00	185.00
3/10	J. Walters	5,730.00	5,730.00	
3/16	N. Tandy	3,100.00	3,007.00	93.00
3/25	Willis & Co.	7,278.00	7,069.00	209.00
3/30	V. Clyburne	2,190.00	2,190.00	
		25,148.00	24,661.00	487.00

PURCHASE BOOK

Date		Accts. Pay.	Purchases	Freight In	Miscellaneous Acct.	Amount
3/4	Jiggs & Co.	5,212.00	5,070.00	142.00		
3/11	Barton & Co.	320.00			Ins. Prepd.	320.00
3/16	A. Field	6,368.00	6,179.00	189.00		
3/19	Smith Delivery	22.00			Ship. Exp.	22.00
3/23	N.Y. Telephone	29.00			Telephone	29.00
3/26	D. LaRue	3,000.00	3,000.00			
3/29	App & App	7,531.00	7,168.00	363.00		
		22,482.00	21,417.00	694.00		371.00

Supply the balances of the following accounts on March 31 after all posting has been done for March. Put answers in the appropriate spaces on the right. Give amounts only.

1. Cash   1._____

2. Accounts Receivable   2._____

3. Notes Receivable   3._____

4. Insurance Prepaid   4._____

5. Furniture and Fixtures   5._____

6. Accounts Payable   6._____

7. Notes Payable   7._____

8. Reserve for Depreciation of Furniture and Fixtures   8.____

9. C. Dutton, Capital   9.____

10. C. Dutton, Drawing   10.____

11. Purchases   11.____

12. Freight In   12.____

13. Rent   13.____

14. Light   14.____

15. Telephone   15.____

16. Salaries   16.____

17. Shipping Expenses   17.____

18. Sales   18.____

19. Sales Discount   19.____

20. Purchase Discount   20.____

21. City Sales Tax Collected   21.____

22. Social Security Taxes Payable   22.____

23. Withholding Taxes Payable   23.____

24. Interest Income   24.____

25. Interest Cost   25.____

Questions 26-35.

DIRECTIONS: Mr. Adams has a complete set of books - Cash Journals, Purchase and Sales Journals, and a General Journal. Below you will find the General Journal used by Mr. Adams. Under the heading of each money column, you will find a letter of the alphabet. Following the General Journal, there is a series of transactions. You are to determine the correct entry for each transaction and then show on the right in the appropriate space the columns to be used. For example, if a certain transaction results in an entry of $100 in the Notes Receiving Column (on the left side) and an entry of $100 in the General Ledger Column (on the right side), in the appropriate space on the right, you should write A, D. If the record of the transaction requires the use of more than two columns, your answer should contain more than two letters. DO NOT PUT THE AMOUNTS IN YOUR ANSWER SPACE. The LETTERS of the columns to be used are sufficient. If a transaction requires no entry in the General Journal, write *None* in the appropriate space in your answer space, even though a record would be made in some other journal.

GENERAL JOURNAL

Notes Receivable	Accounts Payable	General Ledger	L. F.		General Ledger	Accounts Receivable	Notes Payable
A	B	C			D	E	F

26. We sent Tripp & Co. a 30-day trade acceptance for $500 for merchandise sold him today. They accepted it. 26.____

27. The proprietor, Mr. Adams, returned $100 in cash to be deposited, representing Traveling Expenses he had not used. 27.____

28. An entry in the purchase journal last month for a purchase invoice from V. Valides for $647 was erroneously entered in the purchase journal as $746 and posted as such. 28.____

29. A check for $200 received from Mr. Breen was erroneously credited to account of P. Ungar. 29.____

30. In posting the totals of the cash receipts journal last month, an item of bank discount of $30 on our note for $1500 discounted for 60 days was included in the total posted to the sales discount account. 30.____

31. M. Hogan paid his note of $600 and interest of $12 and his account was credited for $612. 31.____

32. Mr. Blow informed us he could not pay his invoice of $2000 due today. Instead, he sent us his 30-day note for $2000 for 30 days bearing interest at 6% per annum. 32.____

33. The proprietor, Mr. Adams, drew $75 to buy his daughter a U.S. Bond. 33.____

34. Mr. O'Brien wrote to us that we overcharged him on an invoice last week. 34.____

35. Returned $120 worth of merchandise to Pecora & Co. and received their credit memorandum. 35.____

Questions 36-50.

DIRECTIONS: In Questions 36 to 50, you will find a list of accounts with a number before each.

1. Cash
2. Accounts Receivable
3. Notes Receivable
4. Notes Receivable Discounted
5. Furniture and Fixtures
6. Delivery Equipment
7. Insurance Prepaid
8. Depreciation on Delivery Equipment
9. Bad Debts
10. Purchases
11. Discount on Purchases
12. Sales
13. Discount on Sales
14. Accounts Payable
15. Notes Payable
16. Interest Cost
17. Reserve for Depreciation on Delivery Equipment
18. Reserve for Bad Debts
19. Sales Taxes Collected
20. Ben Miller, Capital
21. Ben Miller, Drawing
22. Interest Income
23. Purchase Returns

Using the number in front of each account title (using no accounts not listed), make journal entries for the transactions given below. Do not write the names of the accounts in your answer space. Simply indicate in the proper space on the right the numbers of the accounts to be debited or credited. Always give the number or numbers of the accounts to be debited first, then give the number or numbers of accounts to be credited. For example, if furniture and fixtures and delivery equipment are to be debited, and cash and notes payable are to be credited in a certain transaction, then write in your answer space 5, 6 - 1, 15 (use a dash to separate the debits from the credits).

36. F. Pierce, a customer, went into bankruptcy owing us $600. We received a check for $200. 36.____

37. Later in the month, we are informed that there is no possibility of collecting the balance from F. Pierce. There is a sufficient balance in the Reserve for Bad Debts to take care of the above. 37.____

38. Set up the Depreciation on the Delivery Equipment for the year amounting to $240. 38.____

39. Discounted M. Colby's note for $500 today and received $490 in proceeds. 39.____

40. Mr. Miller, the proprietor, invested $2000 in the business. 40.____

41. Paid our note due to Dillon & Co. today for $800 with interest of $16. 41.____

42. Accepted Finnegan's trade acceptance for $1500 for merchandise bought today. 42.____

43. Create a Reserve for Bad Debts of $2000 at the end of the year. 43.____

44. Returned to Dillon & Co. $30 worth of damaged merchandise for credit. They allowed it. 44.____

45. G. Garry claimed a discount of $12 which we had failed to allow him. He had already paid his bill. Sent him check for $12. 45.____

46. On one sale during the month, we had failed to collect the Sales Tax of $15. Wrote to the customer and he sent us a check for $15. 46.____

47. M. Colby paid his note due today which we had discounted two months ago. 47.____

48. Bought a new safe for $875 from Cramer & Co., terms 2/10, n/60 days. Agreed to pay them in 60 days. 48.____

49. Bought merchandise during the month amounting to $17,500 - all on account. 49.____

50. On December 31, paid for a Fire Insurance policy to run for three years from that date - premium was $480. 50.____

51. The following information was taken from the ledger of Peter Dolan on Dec. 31 after adjusting entries had been posted to the ledger. 51.____

Sales Income	$60,000
Sales Returns	3,500
Mdse. Purchases	42,000
Inventory of 1/1	9,400
Sales Taxes Payable	360
Freight Inward	225
Inventory 12/31	7,640
Insurance Unexpired	163

Find the gross profit on Sales for the year.

52. On March 31, your bank sent you a statement of account. You compared the canceled checks with the stubs in your checkbook and found the following:
    Check #34 - $56.00 had not been paid by the bank
    #44 - $38.00 had been paid by the bank as $38.89 because the amount on the check did not agree with your stub in the checkbook
    #52 - $76.50 had not been returned by the bank, though the check had been certified
    #57 - $127.42 had not been paid by the bank
    What total amount would you deduct from the balance on the bank's statement as checks outstanding?

53. On April 30, Mr. Jolley received his statement of account from the bank. A comparison of the bank statement and your checkbook revealed the following: Checkbook balance $5,640; this included a deposit of $325 on the last day of April which had not been entered on the bank statement.
    You also find the following:
    Check #69 - $89.00 had not been paid by the bank
    #70 - Paid by the bank as $47.55, had been entered in your checkbook as $45.57
    #76 - $114.30 had not been paid by the bank
    The bank statement included a debit memo of $4.00 for excessive activity during the month.
    What was the balance on the bank statement?

54. An invoice dated January 15 for merchandise you bought added up to $876.00. The terms were 3/10, n/60, F.O.B. DESTINATION. When the goods arrived, you paid freight amounting to $8.50. On January 20, you returned goods billed at $26 and received credit therefor. You paid the bill on January 24.
    What was the amount of your check?

55. Income taxes paid by residents of a certain state are based on the balance of taxable income at the following
    rates: 2% on first $1000 or less
            3% on 2nd and 3rd $1000
            4% on 4th and 5th $1000
            5% on 6th and 7th $1000
            6% on 8th and 9th $1000
            7% on all over $9000
    What would be the NORMAL income tax to be paid by a resident of that state whose taxable balance of income was $6,750?

56. A salesman's gross earnings for the year came to $8,820. His rate of Commission was 5% of his sales to customers after deducting returns by customers. During the year, his customers returned 10% of the goods they purchased. What were his total sales during the year before deducting returns?

57. On December 31, the insurance account contained a debit for $144 for a three-year fire insurance policy dated August 1. What amount should be listed on the balance sheet of December 31 of that year?

58. A partnership began business on January 1 with partners' investments of $26,000. During the year, the partners drew $18,500 for personal use. On December 31, the assets of the firm were $46,300, and the liabilities were $15,600. What was the firm's net profit for the year? (Write P or L before your answer.)

58.____

59. The rent income account of a real estate firm showed a total balance of $75,640 at the end of 1986. Of this amount, $3,545 represented prepaid 1987 rents. The account also included entries for 1986 rents due from tenants but not yet collected, amounting to $2,400.
What amount should be listed on the profit and loss statement as rent income for 1986?

59.____

60. You discounted a customer's note for $7,200 at your bank at the rate of 6% and received net proceeds of $7,182.
How many days did the note have to run from date of discount to date of maturity? (Use 360 days to the year.)

60.____

Questions 61-90.

DIRECTIONS: In Questions 61 to 90, you will find a list of ledger accounts. Indicate whether an account is generally listed in the Trial Balance as a DEBIT or as a CREDIT by putting the letter *D* or the letter *C* in the correct space on the right for each account listed.

61. Sales   61.____
62. Land   62.____
63. Notes Payable   63.____
64. Traveling Expenses   64.____
65. Purchases   65.____
66. Buildings   66.____
67. Merchandise Inventory   67.____
68. Machinery and Equipment   68.____
69. Notes Receivable   69.____
70. Bonds Payable   70.____
71. Advertising   71.____
72. Delivery Expense   72.____
73. Cash   73.____

74. Accounts Payable — 74. ____
75. Interest on Bonds — 75. ____
76. Real Estate Taxes — 76. ____
77. Accounts Receivable — 77. ____
78. Don Burch, Proprietor — 78. ____
79. Sales Discount — 79. ____
80. Withholding Taxes — 80. ____
81. Depreciation — 81. ____
82. Prepaid Insurance — 82. ____
83. Reserve for Dep. on Buildings — 83. ____
84. Rent Income — 84. ____
85. Reserve for Bad Debts — 85. ____
86. Don Burch, Drawing Account — 86. ____
87. Sales Returns — 87. ____
88. Bad Debts — 88. ____
89. Purchase Discount — 89. ____
90. Reserve for Dep. on Machinery & Equipment — 90. ____

KEY (CORRECT ANSWERS)

1.	$ 10,383	31.	C,D,D	61.	C
2.	$ 20,113	32.	A,E	62.	D
3.	$ 1,200	33.	None	63.	C
4.	$ 320	34.	C,E	64.	D
5.	$ 9,070	35.	B,D	65.	D
6.	$ 21,292	36.	1-2	66.	D
7.	$ 3,300	37.	18-2	67.	D
8.	$ 1,800	38.	8-17	68.	D
9.	$ 14,162	39.	1,16-4	69.	D
10.	$ 1,500	40.	1-20	70.	C
11.	$ 64,017	41.	15,16-1	71.	D
12.	$ 730	42.	14-15	72.	D
13.	$ 2,625	43.	9-18	73.	D
14.	$ 180	44.	14-23	74.	C
15.	$ 92	45.	13-1	75.	D
16.	$ 5,950	46.	1-19	76.	D
17.	$ 390	47.	4-3	77.	D
18.	$ 77,861	48.	5-14	78.	C
19.	$ 931	49.	10-14	79.	D
20.	$ 769	50.	7-1	80.	C
21.	$ 1,291	51.	$12,515	81.	D
22.	$ 144	52.	$ 183.42	82.	D
23.	$ 1,060	53.	$ 5,512.32	83.	C
24.	$ 15	54.	$ 816	84.	C
25.	$ 18	55.	$ 247.50	85.	C
26.	A-E	56.	$196,000	86.	D
27.	None	57.	$ 124	87.	D
28.	B-D	58.	P $23,200	88.	D
29.	C,E	59.	$72,095	89.	C
30.	C,D	60.	15	90.	C

TEST 3

DIRECTIONS: Each question or incomplete statement is followed by several suggested answers or completions. Select the one that BEST answers the question or completes the statement. *PRINT THE LETTER OF THE CORRECT ANSWER IN THE SPACE AT THE RIGHT.*

1. Of the following taxes, the one which is levied MOST NEARLY in accordance with ability to pay is a(n) _____ tax.

    A. excise
    B. income
    C. general property
    D. sales

   1._____

2. When a check has been lost, the bank on which it is drawn should ORDINARILY be notified and instructed to

    A. stop payment on the check
    B. issue a duplicate of the check
    C. charge the account of the drawer for the amount of the check
    D. certify the check

   2._____

3. The profit and loss statement prepared for a retail store does NOT ordinarily show

    A. the cost of goods sold
    B. depreciation of fixtures and equipment
    C. expenditures for salaries of employees
    D. the net worth of the proprietor

   3._____

4. When two business corporations join their assets and liabilities to form a new corporation, the procedures is called a(n)

    A. merger
    B. liquidation
    C. receivership
    D. exchange

   4._____

5. The method of depreciation which deducts an equal amount each full year of an asset's life is called _____ depreciation.

    A. sum-of-years digits
    B. declining balance
    C. straight-line
    D. service-hours

   5._____

6. A fixed asset is an asset that

    A. is held primarily for sale to customers
    B. is used in the conduct of the business until worn out or replaced
    C. is readily convertible into cash
    D. has no definite value

   6._____

7. The gross profit on sales for a period is determined by

    A. subtracting the cost of goods sold from the sales
    B. subtracting the sales returns and the discounts on sales from the gross sales
    C. subtracting the sales from the purchases for the period
    D. finding the difference between the inventory of merchandise at the beginning of the period and the inventory of merchandise at the end of the period

   7._____

8. The term *auditing* refers to the

   A. entering of amounts from the journals into the general ledger
   B. reconciliation of the accounts in a subsidiary ledger with the controlling account in the general ledger
   C. preparation of a trial balance of the accounts in the general ledger
   D. examination of the general ledger and other records of a concern to determine its true financial condition

9. A voucher register is a

   A. type of electric cash register
   B. list of customers whose accounts are past due
   C. list of the assets of a business
   D. book in which bills to be paid are recorded

10. The account DISCOUNT ON PURCHASES is *properly* closed directly to the _____ account.

    A. Accounts Payable
    B. Sales
    C. Purchases
    D. Fixtures

11. The account UNEARNED RENTAL INCOME is *usually* considered a(n) _____ account.

    A. asset
    B. nominal
    C. capital
    D. liability

12. A controlling account is an account which contains

    A. the totals of *all* the expense accounts in the general ledger
    B. the total of the amounts entered in the accounts in a subsidiary ledger
    C. the total of the depreciation on fixtures claimed in *all* preceding years
    D. *all* totals of the income and expense accounts before closing to the Profit and Loss account

13. The purpose of the DRAWING account in the general ledger of an individual enterprise is to show the

    A. salaries paid to the employees
    B. amounts paid to independent contractors for services rendered
    C. amounts taken by the proprietor for his personal use
    D. total of payments made for general expenses of the business

14. The phrase *2%/10 net 30 days* on an invoice ORDINARILY means that

    A. 2% of the amount must be paid within 30 days
    B. the purchaser must add 2% to the amount of the invoice if he fails to pay within 30 days
    C. the entire amount must be paid within 30 days
    D. the purchaser may deduct 2% from the amount if he pays within 30 days

15. The ESSENTIAL characteristic of a C.O.D. sale of merchandise is that the

    A. purchaser pays for the merchandise upon its receipt by him
    B. seller guarantees the merchandise to be as specified by him
    C. merchandise is delivered by a common carrier
    D. purchaser is permitted to pay for the merchandise in convenient installments

16. If the drawer of a check makes an error in writing the amount of the check, he should

    A. erase the error and insert the correct amount
    B. cross out the error and insert the correct amount
    C. destroy the check and prepare another one
    D. write the correct amount directly above the incorrect one

17. States do NOT levy a(n) _____ tax.

    A. unemployment insurance   B. income
    C. corporation franchise   D. export

18. The cost of goods sold by a retail store is PROPERLY determined by

    A. *adding* the closing inventory to the total of the opening inventory and the purchases for the year
    B. *deducting* the closing inventory from the total of the opening inventory and the purchases for the year
    C. *deducting* the total of the opening and closing inventories from the purchases for the year
    D. *adding* the total of the opening and closing inventories

19. The PRIMARY purpose of a trial balance is to determine

    A. that all transactions have been entered in the journals
    B. the accuracy of the totals in the general ledger
    C. the correctness of the amounts entered in the journals
    D. that amounts have been posted to the proper accounts in the general ledger

20. The SURPLUS account of a corporation is *ordinarily* used to record

    A. the actual amount subscribed by stockholders
    B. the amount of profits earned by the corporation
    C. any excess of current assets over current liabilities
    D. the total of the fixed assets of the corporation

Questions 21-30.

DIRECTIONS: Each of Questions 21 to 30 consists of a typical transaction of Our Business followed by the debit and credit (amounts omitted) of the journal entry for that transaction. For each of these questions, the debit and credit given may be appropriately classified under one of the following categories:

    A. The debit of the journal entry is CORRECT but the credit is INCORRECT.
    B. The debit of the journal entry is INCORRECT but the credit is CORRECT.
    C. BOTH the debit and the credit of the journal entry are correct.
    D. BOTH the debit and the credit of the journal entry are incorrect.

Examine each question carefully. Then, in the correspondingly numbered space on the right, mark as your answer the letter preceding the category which is the BEST of the four suggested above.

SAMPLE QUESTION: We purchased a desk for cash.
                  Debit: Office Equipment
                  Credit: Accounts Payable

In this example, the debit is correct but the credit is incorrect. Therefore, you should mark A as your answer.

21. We sent a check for $500 to R. Thomas in payment for an invoice for that amount. 21._____
    Debit: Cash   Credit: Accounts Receivable

22. We took merchandise, amounting to $35, for our own use. 22._____
    Debit: Proprietor, Personal   Credit: Purchases

23. Arthur Townsend's 90-day note for $350, which was discounted by us at our bank last month, was paid by him today. 23._____
    Debit: Notes Receivable Discounted
    Credit: Accounts Receivable

24. We sold merchandise to T. Wilson on account of $275. 24._____
    Debit: Accounts Payable   Credit: Sales

25. We returned damaged merchandise to B. Lowell and received a credit memorandum from him for $28. 25._____
    Debit: Accounts Payable
    Credit: Sales Returns and Allowances

26. We paid our 30-day note given to Mr. Kane for $650 without interest. 26._____
    Debit: Notes Receivable   Credit: Cash

27. We sent Chet Carr a check for $10.50 for a discount he had forgotten to take when he paid us for merchandise this week. 27._____
    Debit: Sales Discounts   Credit: Cash

28. The bank loaned us $1000, and we invested it in the business. 28._____
    Debit: Cash   Credit: Loan Receivable

29. We recorded depreciation for the year on our office equipment. 29._____
    Debit: Reserve for Depreciation of Office Equipment
    Credit: Depreciation of Office Equipment

30. One of our customers, Allen Koren, was declared bankrupt and his debt of $25 to us was canceled. 30._____
    Debit: Reserve for Bad Debts Credit: Accounts Receivable

Questions 31-45.

DIRECTIONS: Questions 31 to 45 consist of a list of some of the accounts in the general ledger of a corporation which operates a retail store. Indicate whether each account listed contains generally a debit or credit balance by marking the letter D (for debit balance) or the letter C (for credit balance) in the correspondingly numbered space on the right.
For example, for the account Cash, which generally contains a debit balance, you would mark the letter D as your answer.

5 (#3)

31. Rent Expense   31.____
32. Allowance for Depreciation of Fixtures   32.____
33. Sales Returns and Allowances   33.____
34. Security Deposit for Electricity   34.____
35. Accrued Salaries Payable   35.____
36. Dividends Payable   36.____
37. Petty Cash Fund   37.____
38. Notes Receivable Discounted   38.____
39. Surplus   39.____
40. Capital Stock Authorized   40.____
41. Insurance Expense   41.____
42. Sales for Cash   42.____
43. Purchase Discounts   43.____
44. Automobile Delivery Equipment   44.____
45. Bad Debts Expense   45.____

Questions 46-60.

DIRECTIONS: Questions 46 to 60 consist of a list of some of the accounts in a general ledger. For the purpose of preparing financial statements, each of these accounts is to be classified into one of the following five major classifications, lettered A to E, as follows:
A. Assets   B. Liabilities   C. Income   D. Expense   E. Capital You are to indicate the classification to which each belongs by marking the appropriate letter, A, B, C, D or E. in the correspondingly numbered space on the right. For example, for the account MERCHANDISE INVENTORY, which is an asset account, you would mark the letter A as your answer.

46. Purchases   46.____
47. Prepaid Interest   47.____
48. Cash in Bank   48.____
49. Depreciation of Fixtures   49.____

50. Accounts Receivable 50._____
51. Mortgage Payable 51._____
52. Accrued Interest Receivable 52._____
53. Bad Debts 53._____
54. Insurance Expired 54._____
55. Treasury Stock 55._____
56. Investments 56._____
57. Loan to Partner 57._____
58. Unearned Rent Received 58._____
59. Petty Cash Fund 59._____
60. Loss on Sale of Equipment 60._____

KEY (CORRECT ANSWERS)

1.	B	16.	C	31.	D	46.	D
2.	A	17.	D	32.	C	47.	A
3.	D	18.	B	33.	D	48.	A
4.	A	19.	B	34.	D	49.	D
5.	C	20.	B	35.	C	50.	A
6.	B	21.	D	36.	C	51.	B
7.	A	22.	C	37.	D	52.	A
8.	D	23.	A	38.	C	53.	D
9.	D	24.	B	39.	C	54.	D
10.	C	25.	A	40.	C	55.	E
11.	D	26.	B	41.	D	56.	A
12.	B	27.	C	42.	C	57.	A
13.	C	28.	A	43.	C	58.	B
14.	C	29.	D	44.	D	59.	A
15.	A	30.	C	45.	D	60.	D

EXAMINATION SECTION

TEST 1

DIRECTIONS: Each question or incomplete statement is followed by several suggested answers or completions. Select the one that BEST answers the question or completes the statement. *PRINT THE LETTER OF THE CORRECT ANSWER IN THE SPACE AT THE RIGHT.*

Questions 1-25.

DIRECTIONS: Below you will find the Cash Receipts Journal of John Walker, a merchant. Under the heading of each money column of the Journals, there is a letter of the alphabet. Following the Journals there is a series of transactions. You are to determine the entry for each transaction and then show in the space at the right the columns to be used.

For example: If a certain transaction entered in the Cash Receipts Journal results in an entry of $100 in the General Ledger Column and $100 in the Net Cash Column, in the appropriate space at the right you should write: A,E. If the record of the transaction requires the use of more than two columns, your answer should contain more than two letters.

Do not put the amounts in your answer space. The letters of the columns in the Cash Journals to be used are sufficient.

If a transaction requires no entry in the Cash Journals, write "None" in the appropriate space at the right, even though a record would be made in some other journal.

CASH RECEIPTS JOURNAL

Date	Account Credited	Explanation	F	General Ledger	Accts. Rec.	Cash Sales	Disc. on Sales	Net Cash
				A	B	C	D	E

CASH PAYMENTS JOURNAL

Date	Acct. Debited	Explanation	F	General Ledger	Accts. Pay.	Soc. Sec. Taxes Pay.	With. Taxes Pay.	Disc. on Purch.	Net Cash
				F	G	H	I	J	K

1. Cash Sales amounted to $280.   1.____

2. Paid employees' salaries for the week. The check amounted to $346 after deducting $4.00 for Social Security Taxes and $30 for Income Taxes withheld.   2.____

3. A check received in the mail from R. Walters was in payment of a bill of $150, terms 2/10, n/30. The customer had taken the discount.   3.____

2 (#1)

4. The proprietor, Mr. Walker, took merchandise valued at $30 from the stockroom for his personal use.   4.____

5. Prepaid $15 freight on shipment of goods to H. Lane, a customer, and charged his account.   5.____

6. Sent a check for $250 to P. Packer to apply on account.   6.____

7. Drew a check for $75 to start a Petty Cash fund.   7.____

8. H. Wall sent us a check for $700 in payment of his 60-day note for $700. The note was interest bearing (6%), but he failed to pay us the interest. We deposited the $700 check and wrote to him requesting an additional check.   8.____

9. Paid rent for month $180.   9.____

10. Received a check for $70 from K. London to apply on account.   10.____

11. H. Wall sent us a check for the interest due on note (see Item 8).   11.____

12. Paid our 30-day note for $460 due today which we had given to G. Thompson.   12.____

13. Accepted a trade acceptance drawn by R. Sparks on us for invoice of $722.   13.____

14. Borrowed at our bank on our $1,500 note. Net proceeds, $1,485. (The bookkeeper used only one journal to make a complete and correct entry. You are to do likewise.)   14.____

15. Received a check for $60 from W. Saks, a creditor, refunding our overpayment to him on our account.   15.____

16. A check from H. Low, which was deposited by us last month, was returned to us marked "insufficient funds." The check amounted to $55 and had been sent to us to settle his account.   16.____

17. Drew a sight draft on R. Coe for overdue account of $120. Left draft at bank for collection.   17.____

18. Paid $26 freight on goods purchased from W. Lincoln of Chicago, terms f.o.b. Chicago.   18.____

19. Mailed a credit memorandum to E. Stern for return of defective merchandise sold him on account for $65.   19.____

20. The proprietor, John Walker, drew $90 cash for personal use.   20.____

21. Received a money order for $110 from B. Kiner for invoice of merchandise charged to him.   21.____

22. Mr. Walker, proprietor, drew $1,200 from his personal savings account and invested the entire sum in his business. 22.____

23. Issued check to Clark & Co. in payment of invoice amounting to $500. Discount of 3% was taken. 23.____

24. Received a 30-day non-interest bearing note for $610 from A. Allen for merchandise sold him today. 24.____

25. Sent a check for $51 to Collector of Internal Revenue for Social Security Taxes collected for the past three months. 25.____

Questions 26-35.

DIRECTIONS: Below you will find the General Journal used by D. Prince, wholesaler. Under the heading of each money column you will find a letter of the alphabet. Following the General Journal, there is a series of transactions. You are to determine the correct entry for each transaction and then show in the appropriate space at the right the columns to be used.

For example: If a certain transaction results in an entry of $100 in the Notes Receivable Column (on the left side) and an entry of $100 in the General Ledger Column (on the right side), in the appropriate space at the right you should write A, D.

If the record of the transaction requires the use of more than two columns, your answer should contain more than two letters.

Do not put the amounts on your answer space. The letters of the columns to be used are sufficient.

If a transaction requires no entry in the General Journal, write "None" in the appropriate space at the right, even though a record would be made in some other journal.

GENERAL JOURNAL

Notes Rec.	Accts. Pay.	General Ledger	L. F.		General Ledger	Accts. Rec.	Notes Payable
A	B	C			D	E	F

26. Issued a credit memorandum for $68 to J. Winston for goods returned to us. 26.____

27. P. Jones sent us his 60-day note for $750 in full settlement of his account. 27.____

28. Sent a 60-day note to J. O'Connor for invoice of $375 less 2%. 28.____

29. H. Owens sent us a credit memorandum for overcharge of $75 on invoice. 29.____

30. Mailed a 30-day draft to W. Kinder, a customer, for his acceptance amounting to $375 for invoice of goods sold him yesterday. 30.____

31. A. Hocker, a customer, went out of business owing us $170. The claim is considered worthless. 31._____

32. The proprietor requested the bookkeeper to provide a reserve of $500 for expected losses on customers' accounts. 32._____

33. P. Winston sent us a $350 bank draft in full settlement of his account. 33._____

34. Accepted a 30-day trade acceptance drawn by A. Hall for bill of goods amounting to $316 purchased by us last week. 34._____

35. Mr. D. Prince, the proprietor, takes his brother, L. Prince, into the business as an equal partner. Mr. L. Prince invests merchandise worth $3,500 in the business and becomes a partner. 35._____

Questions 36-50.

DIRECTIONS: Below you will find a list of accounts from the ledger of R. Lincoln. There is a letter of the alphabet before each account.
Using the letter in front of each account title (using no accounts not listed), make journal entries for the transactions given below.
Do not write the names of the accounts in your answer space. Simply indicate in the proper space at the right the letters of the accounts to be debited or credited.
Always give the letter or letters of accounts to be debited first, then give the letter or letters of accounts to be credited.
For example, if Office Supplies and Delivery Expenses are to be debited and Notes Payable and Cash are to be credited in a certain transaction, then write as your answer L, D; K, C.

- A. Accounts Payable
- B. Accounts Receivable
- C. Cash
- D. Delivery Expense
- E. Discount on Purchases
- F. Freight Inward
- G. Interest Cost
- H. Purchases
- I. Notes Receivable
- J. Notes Receivable Discounted
- K. Notes Payable
- L. Office Supplies
- M. R. Lincoln, Personal
- N. Petty Cash
- O. Purchase Returns
- P. Sales Discount
- R. Sales Returns
- S. Sales Income

36. Paid the Fox Transportation Co. $15 by check for express charges on goods delivered to us. 36._____

37. Accepted a 30-day trade acceptance for $850 drawn on us by Allen & Co. 37._____

38. Returned damaged goods to H. Parker and he sent us a credit memorandum for $47. 38._____

5 (#1)

39. John Smith's 30-day note for $800, which was discounted by us at our bank last month, was paid by him today. 39.____

40. Paid our 60-day note due today in favor of S. Paul for $600 with interest. The check amounted to $606. 40.____

41. The total of the Notes Payable column in the General Journal amounted to $450 at the end of last month. It was posted in error to the Notes Receivable Discounted account. Make the correction entry. 41.____

42. Issued a check to J. News in settlement of invoice $500 less 2%. 42.____

43. Paid Stern Stationers $5.00 by check for four reams of paper for office use. 43.____

44. Sent a check for $48 to Gregory's Garage for storage, gasoline, oil, and service on auto trucks. 44.____

45. Drew a check for $100 to establish a Petty Cash fund. 45.____

46. A. Black, a customer, settled his account of $400 by sending us a check for $100 and a 30-day note for the balance. 46.____

47. J. Walters failed to deduct a discount of $10 when he paid us last month. He called the matter to our attention and we sent him a check for $10. 47.____

48. Donated to the Salvation Army merchandise out of stock costing the proprietor $75. 48.____

49. At the end of the year, the Sales Returns account had a balance of $225. make the entry to close this account. 49.____

50. At the end of the year, the Freight Inward account had a balance of $450. Make the entry to close this account. 50.____

Questions 51-60.

DIRECTIONS: In answering Questions 51 through 60, print the CORRECT answer in the space at the right.

51. On December 31, a bookkeeper prepared a Profit and Loss Statement in which the following are some of the items listed: 51.____

    Sales $50,000
    Purchases   45,000
    Inventory (Jan. 1)   7,500
    Sales Returns   400
    Gross Profit   15,000
    Selling expense   3,200

Find the Inventory of Merchandise on December 31.

52. A. Landers invested $5,000 in cash in a new business. At the end of the year, he finds he has $2,500 in cash, $1,000 in furniture, $1,800 in merchandise on which he owes $750. During the year, Mr. Landers drew $2,400 for his own use. What was his profit or loss for the year? (Write P or L before the figure.)

52.____

53. Wm. Abbott purchased a machine for $2,800. The estimated life of the machine was five years. At the end of five years, the machine could be sold for scrap for $400. Find the depreciation charge at the end of the first six months of use.

53.____

54. On January 1, A. Menton's Capital was $2,400. His partner, P. King, had a Capital of $6,000. Their agreement provided for dividing profits in proportion to Capital. During the year the Net Profit was $12,480. What was A. Menton's share of the Net Profit?

54.____

55. On December 31, J. Klein's ledger, after all closing entries, contained the following balances:

Cash	$5,000
Merchandise Inventory	1,500
Accounts Receivable	8,000
Notes Receivable	2,000
Deferred Expense	300
Furniture and Fixtures	1,200
Accounts Payable	4,000
Reserve for Bad Debts	600
Notes Receivable Discounted	800
Reserve for Depreciation of Furniture and Fixtures	900

What was J. Klein's Capital on December 31?

55.____

56. An employer paid $160 in Social Security taxes at the rate of 1% on taxable wages. He expects to employ more persons next year and pay out 50% more in taxable wages than he did. What will be his Social Security costs at the new rate of 1½% next year?

56.____

57. On June 17, you discounted a customer's 60-day note at your bank. The face of the note was $840 and it was dated June 5, discount rate 6%. What was the amount of the net proceeds?

57.____

58. On June 18, you sold I. Cohen, of Chicago, merchandise. The invoice totaled $684, which included $38 freight which you had prepaid. Terms were 2, 10, n/30, f.o.b. New York. If Mr. Cohen pays you on June 27, what should be the CORRECT amount of the check?

58.____

59. A bankrupt firm agrees to pay its creditors 30 cents on the dollar. It pays Klein & Co. $12,600. What was Klein & Co.'s loss?

59.____

60. A salesman earned $15,600 in one year. His commissions were at the rate of 7½% of sales. What were his sales for the year?   60.____

Questions 61-80.

DIRECTIONS: Questions 61 through 80 are to be answered on the basis of the following:
The bookkeeper of Walters Co. began to make a trial balance of his General Ledger on December 31. Before he had completed his trial balance, you were permitted to examine his work.
If a balance is in the correct column, print "C" in the appropriate space at the right. If a balance is in the wrong column, print "W" in the appropriate space at the right.
Caution: Since the trial balance is not complete, do not attempt to strike a balance of the figures given in the question.

WALTER CO.
Trial Balance, December 31

#	Account	Debit	Credit	Answer
61.	Merchandise, Inventory, Jan. 1	16,000		61.____
62.	Freight Inward	150		62.____
63.	Petty Cash		75	63.____
64.	Interest Income	70		64.____
65.	Notes Receivable	4,000		65.____
66.	Sales		17,000	66.____
67.	Sales Discount		170	67.____
68.	Purchase Returns	250		68.____
69.	Auto Trucks	9,000		69.____
70.	Reserve for Depreciation of Furniture	770		70.____
71.	Bad Debts		160	71.____
72.	Sales Taxes Collected	225		72.____
73.	Sales Returns		485	73.____
74.	Reserve for Bad Debts		500	74.____
75.	Deposits with Landlord		150	75.____

76.	Accrued Interest on Notes Receivable	50	76._____
77.	Income from Commissions	900	77._____
78.	Purchase Discounts	110	78._____
79.	Depreciation of Furniture	225	79._____
80.	Notes and Acceptances from Customers	780	80._____

KEY (CORRECT ANSWERS)

#		#		#		#	
1.	C, E	21.	B, E	41.	J; K	61.	C
2.	F, H, I, K	22.	A, E	42.	A; C, E	62.	C
3.	B, D, E	23.	G, J, K	43.	L; C	63.	W
4.	None	24.	None	44.	D; C	64.	W
5.	F, K	25.	F, K	45.	N; C	65.	C
6.	G, K	26.	C, E	46.	I, C; B	66.	C
7.	F, K	27.	A, E	47.	P; C	67.	W
8.	A, E	28.	B, D, F	48.	M; H	68.	W
9.	F, K	29.	B, D	49.	H; F	69.	C
10.	B, E	30.	None	50.	H; F	70.	W
11.	A, E	31.	C, E	51.	17900	71.	W
12.	F, K	32.	C, D	52.	P1950	72.	W
13.	None	33.	None	53.	220	73.	W
14.	A, D, E	34.	B, F	54.	3565.71	74.	C
15.	A, E	35.	C, D	55.	11700	75.	W
16.	F, K	36.	F; C	56.	360	76.	W
17.	None	37.	A; K	57.	833.28	77.	C
18.	F, K	38.	A; O	58.	671.08	78.	C
19.	None	39.	J; K	59.	29400	79.	W
20.	F, K	40.	K, G; C	60.	208000	80.	W

TEST 2

DIRECTIONS: Each question or incomplete statement is followed by several suggested answers or completions. Select the one that BEST answers the question or completes the statement. *PRINT THE LETTER OF THE CORRECT ANSWER IN THE SPACE AT THE RIGHT.*

Questions 1-25.

DIRECTIONS: Below you will find:
1. General Ledger balances on January 31, appearing in books of A. New.
2. All entries on books of A. New for month of February
3. You are to supply balances of ledger accounts on February 29, in the appropriate spaces at the right, as indicated at the end of these questions.

The correct balances in A. New's General Ledger on January 31 were as follows: Cash $7,642; Notes Receivable $2,600; Accounts Receivable $3,100; Furniture and Fixtures $750; Delivery Equipment $1,200; Purchases $2,850; Telephone and Telegrams $110; Office Supplies $380; Salaries $300; Sales Discount $80; Purchase Discount $56; Insurance $160; Sales $3,150; Freight Inward $70; Accounts Payable $2,400; Freight Outward (debit) $40; Notes Payable $1,100; A. New Capital $12,200; A. New Personal (credit) $310; Sales Taxes Payable $35; Withholding Taxes Payable $28; and Social Security Taxes Payable $3.

CASH RECEIPTS

Date	Name	Net Cash	Sales Disc.	Accts. Rec.	Miscellaneous Account	Amount
2/2	S. Wilson	471.00	9.00	480.00		
2/5	First Nat'l Bank	500.00			Notes Pay.	500.00
2/16	M. Tower	350.00			Notes Rec.	340.00
					Int. Income	10.00
2/20	Paul Smith	245.00	5.00	250.00		
2/28	Sundry Customers	110.00			Sales	110.00
	TOTALS	$1675.00	$14.00	$730.00		$960.00

CASH DISBURSEMENTS

Date	Name	Net Cash	Purch. Disc.	Soc. Sec. Tax	With-hold. Taxes	Accts. Pay.	Miscellaneous Account	Amount
2/3	Sun Realty Co.	125					Rent	125
2/9	Bell Smith Co.	540	10			550		
2/10	First Nat'l Bank	808					Notes Pay.	800
							Int. Cost	8
2/14	James Roe Co.	1360	22			1382		
2/16	Roxy Desk Co.	125					Fur. & Fixt.	125
2/20	Baldwin Auto	1650					Del. & Equip.	1650
2/28	Payroll	360		4	36		Sal.	400
2/28	A. New	215					A. New Pers.	215
	TOTALS	$5183	32	4	36	1932		3323

2 (#2)

SALES BOOK

Date	Name	Accts. Rec.	Sales	Freight Out	Sales Tax
2/2	Booth &White	460.00	455.00	5.00	
2/10	Water & Co.	375.00	364.00	11.00	
2/14	Neville Bros.	204.00	200.00		4.00
2/16	A. Parker	918.00	900.00		18.00
	TOTALS	$1957.00	1919.00	16.00	22.00

PURCHASE BOOK

Date	Name	Accts. Payable	Purchases	Freight Inward	Miscellaneous Account	Amount
2/4	Walden Co.	800.00	800.00			
2/5	Power Telephone	17.00			Tel.	17.00
2/9	Mfgs. Ins. Co.	122.00			Insurance	122.00
2/12	Tower & Co.	756.00	748.00	8.00		
2/16	X-cel Express	13.00		13.00		
2/23	Braver & Co.	265.00	265.00			
2/28	Penn Stationers	65.00			Off. Suppl.	65.00
	TOTALS	$2038.00	1813.00	21.00		204.00

Supply the balances of the following accounts on February 29, after all posting has been done for February. Print the answers in the appropriate spaces at the right. (Give amounts only.)

1. Cash   1._____

2. Notes Receivable   2._____

3. Accounts Receivable   3._____

4. Furniture and Fixtures   4._____

5. Delivery Equipment   5._____

6. Purchases   6._____

7. Telephone   7._____

8. Office Supplies   8._____

9. Salaries   9._____

10. Sales Discount   10._____

11. Purchase Discount   11._____

12. Insurance   12._____

13. Freight Inward 13.____

14. Sales 14.____

15. Accounts Payable 15.____

16. Freight Outward 16.____

17. Notes Payable 17.____

18. A. New, Capital 18.____

19. A. New, Personal 19.____

20. Sales Taxes Payable 20.____

21. Withholding Taxes Payable 21.____

22. Social Security Taxes Payable 22.____

23. Interest Income 23.____

24. Rent 24.____

25. Interest Cost 25.____

Questions 26-50.

DIRECTIONS: Below is a list of some of the accounts containing balances in the ledger of the Ajax Company on December 31st after posting all entries for the year, except adjusting and closing entries.
If the account normally would have a debit balance, write "D" in the proper numbered space at the right. If the amount normally would have a credit balance, write "C" in the proper numbered space at the right.

26. Notes Receivable 26.____

27. Merchandise Inventory 27.____

28. Notes Payable 28.____

29. Interest on Notes Receivable 29.____

30. Freight Inward 30.____

31. Sales Discount 31.____

32. Samuel Ajax Proprietor 32.____

33. Purchase Returns and Allowances   33.____
34. Land and Buildings   34.____
35. Reserve for Depreciation of Furniture and Fixtures 35.____
36. Purchase Discount   36.____
37. Rent Collected from Sub-Tenants   37.____
38. Taxes Accrued   38.____
39. Notes Receivable Discounted   39.____
40. Accounts Payable   40.____
41. Interest on Notes Payable   41.____
42. Sales Returns and Allowances   42.____
43. Reserve for Bad Debts   43.____
44. Income from Commissions   44.____
45. Deposits from Customers on Containers   45.____
46. Sales   46.____
47. Accounts Receivable   47.____
48. United States Government Bonds   48.____
49. Sales Taxes Collected   49.____
50. Deposit with Gas Company   50.____

Questions 51-90.

DIRECTIONS: As an employee for Wallace and Pace, you have taken a trial balance of the General Ledger on December 31. After posting all adjusting entries but before closing the accounts, you find your adjusted trial balance is correct. You are now requested to prepare a classified balance sheet using only the following classifications:
- A. Current Assets
- B. Fixed Assets
- C. Deferred Charges
- D. Current Liabilities
- E. Fixed Liabilities
- F. Capital

5 (#2)

Indicate the balance sheet classification of the following items by putting the letter (A to F) in the corresponding spaces at the right. However, if any of the following items should *not* appear in our classified balance sheet, write the letter "P" in the corresponding space at the right.

51. Cash   51.____
52. Furniture and Fixtures   52.____
53. Notes Receivable   53.____
54. Reserve for Bad Debts   54.____
55. Merchandise Inventory 1/1   55.____
56. Freight In   56.____
57. A. Wallace, Capital   57.____
58. Sales Returns   58.____
59. Notes Payable   59.____
60. Purchase Discount   60.____
61. Reserve for Depreciation of Furniture and Fixtures   61.____
62. Insurance Unexpired   62.____
63. Interest Cost   63.____
64. Salaries   64.____
65. Shipping Supplies Inventory as of 12/31   65.____
66. Accounts Receivable   66.____
67. Bad Debts   67.____
68. Shipping Supplies   68.____
69. Mortgage Payable   69.____
70. Depreciation on Furniture and Fixtures   70.____
71. L. Pace, Personal (credit)   71.____
72. Land, Buildings   72.____

6 (#2)

73. Depreciation on Buildings   73._____

74. Interest Accrued on Notes Receivable   74._____

75. Petty Cash Fund   75._____

76. Taxes   76._____

77. Sales Discount   77._____

78. Merchandise Inventory 12/31   78._____

79. Sales   79._____

80. Interest Income   80._____

81. Purchases   81._____

82. Insurance   82._____

83. Accounts Payable   83._____

84. Salaries Accrued   84._____

85. Reserve for Depreciation of Buildings   85._____

86. Taxes Payable   86._____

87. Purchase Returns   87._____

88. Interest Accrued on Mortgage   88._____

89. A. Wallace, Personal (debit)   89._____

90. L. Pace, Capital   90._____

Questions 91-110.

DIRECTIONS: Below you will find a list of accounts with a number before each:

1. Accounts Payable
2. Accounts Receivable
3. Cash
4. Freight Inward
5. Freight Outward
6. Interest Cost
7. Interest Income
8. Notes Payable
9. Notes Receivable
10. Notes Receivable Discounted
11. Petty Cash Fund
12. Proprietor's Capital Account
13. Purchases
14. Purchase Discounts
15. Purchase Returns
16. Real Estate
17. Sales
18. Sales Discounts
19. Selling Expenses
20. Selling Expenses

7 (#2)

Using the number in front of each account, make journal entries for the transactions listed below.
    Do not write the names of the accounts in your answer space. Simply indicate in the proper space at the right the numbers of the accounts to be debited or credited. Always give the number of the account to be debited first, then give the number of the account to be credited.
    Example: If Cash is to be debited and Sales is to be credited, write as your answer 3-17.

91. Drew a check to establish a Petty Cash Fund. 91._____

92. A. Paul, a customer, sent us a 60-day interest-bearing note for an invoice previously entered on our books. 92._____

93. Sent a credit memorandum to a customer for goods returned to us. 93._____

94. Our bank notified us that a customer's check was returned marked "insufficient funds." 94._____

95. Accepted a 60-day draft drawn on us by a creditor for invoice previously entered on the books. 95._____

96. A customer sent us a check as a deposit on goods to be sent him. 96._____

97. Issued a certified check for the purchase of real estate. 97._____

98. Received notice from the bank that our account was charged for the payment of trade acceptance given to a creditor two months ago. 98._____

99. Returned merchandise to a creditor and received a credit memorandum. 99._____

100. Sent a check to a customer whose account had been overpaid in error. 100._____

101. The proprietor invested additional cash in the business. 101._____

102. Received a bank draft from a customer in payment of a note. 102._____

103. Sent our 90-day interest-bearing note to a creditor in settlement of account. 103._____

104. Honored a sight draft drawn on us by one of our creditors. 104._____

105. Sold goods to a customer, terms 60 days. 105._____

106. A customer's note, which we had discounted two months ago, was collected by our bank. 106._____

107. Purchased merchandise, terms 2/10 E.O.M. 107._____

108. Paid our note today. 108.____

109. A customer notifies us that he failed to deduct a discount on his last remittance. Sent him a check for the discount. 109.____

110. Last month's total of the Accounts Receivable column in the Cash Receipts book was posted in error to Notes Receivable Account. Make the correction entry. 110.____

Questions 111-112

DIRECTIONS: Questions 111 and 112 are to be answered based on the following:

    T. Lawson uses controlling accounts and a card system for the individual accounts with his customers and creditors.
    The card containing the account with G. White, to whom he sells goods, has been lost. Reference to monthly schedules of Accounts Receivable shows that White owed $3500 on April 1; $2900 on May 1; and $4300 on June 1.
    The cash book shows that Lawson received the following payments from White: $2500 on April 7; $3400 on April 14; and $3800 on May 25.
    The journal shows that damaged goods were returned by White on April 15, $250, and that White received an allowance of $50 for shortages on May 16. White gave Lawson a note for $3200 on May 30.

111. What were the Sales to White during April? 111.____

112. What were the Sales to White during May? 112.____

Questions 113-114

DIRECTIONS: Questions 113 and 114 are to be answered on the basis of the following:

    Your cash book balance on July 31 was $9242.18.
    The bank statement sent to you on August 1 shows a credit for interest of $16.20 and a deduction of $4.50 for collection expenses.
    You discover that one check paid by the bank was made out for $78.29 and you had entered it in the cash book as $72.89.
    The checks outstanding are #235 for $409.08; #240 for $279; #241 for $42.10; and #247 for $913.56.

113. What balance did the bank report? 113.____

114. What was your true cash balance on August 1? 114.____

115. You received an invoice dated Sept. 5, terms 2/10, n/30, f.o.b. destination, amounting to $350. The shipper paid $25 freight. On Sept. 8 you received a credit memorandum for $15 worth of goods returned. What was the amount of the check required to pay the invoice on Sept. 14? 115.____

9 (#2)

116. On March 3 you drew a check to pay an invoice of $750, terms 2/10, E.O.M., dated Feb. 3. What was the amount of the check?

116.____

117. On March 14 you drew a check to pay an invoice of $460, which included $30 freight prepaid by shipper. Invoice dated March 6 carried items 5/10, n/60. What was the amount of the check?

117.____

118. March 15 – Your employer borrowed from his bank on his own 90-day note for $1400. Rate of discount 6%. What amount should you enter in your net cash column in your cash receipts book?

118.____

119. May 9 – You discounted a customer's 60-day note at your bank. Face of note was $480. Date of note was May 3rd. Discount rate was 6%. What was the amount of the net proceeds?

119.____

120. Your Dec. 31 trial balance contained an item for Interest Income $165. On that date you discovered that you had collected $15 interest in advance, and that there was $22 interest accrued on customers' notes not yet due. What amount should be listed on the year's Profit and Loss Statement as interest income?

120.____

KEY (CORRECT ANSWERS)

1.	4135	26.	D	51.	A	76.	P	101.	3-12
2.	2260	27.	D	52.	B	77.	P	102.	3-9
3.	4327	28.	C	53.	A	78.	A	103.	1-8
4.	875	29.	C	54.	A	79.	P	104.	1-3
5.	2850	30.	D	55.	P	80.	P	105.	2-17
6.	4663	31.	D	56.	P	81.	P	106.	10-9
7.	127	32.	C	57.	F	82.	P	107.	13-1
8.	445	33.	C	58.	P	83.	D	108.	8-3
9.	700	34.	D	59.	D	84.	D	109.	18-3
10.	94	35.	C	60.	P	85.	B	110.	9-2
11.	88	36.	C	61.	B	86.	D	111.	5550
12.	282	37.	C	62.	A	87.	P	112.	8450
13.	91	38.	C	63.	P	88.	D	113.	10892.41
14.	5179	39.	C	64.	P	89.	F	114.	9248.48
15.	2506	40.	C	65.	A	90.	F	115.	328.30
16.	24	41.	D	66.	A	91.	11-3	116.	735
17.	800	42.	D	67.	P	92.	9-2	117.	438.50
18.	12200	43.	C	68.	P	93.	19-2	118.	1379
19.	95	44.	C	69.	E	94.	2-3	119.	475.68
20.	57	45.	C	70.	P	95.	1-8	120.	172
21.	64	46.	C	71.	F	96.	3-2		
22.	7	47.	D	72.	B	97.	16-3		
23.	10	48.	D	73.	P	98.	8-3		
24.	125	49.	C	74.	A	99.	1-15		
25.	8	50.	D	75.	A	100.	2-3		

EXAMINATION SECTION
TEST 1

DIRECTIONS: Each question or incomplete statement is followed by several suggested answers or completions. Select the one that BEST answers the question or completes the statement. *PRINT THE LETTER OF THE CORRECT ANSWER IN THE SPACE AT THE RIGHT.*

Questions 1-20.

DIRECTIONS: Listed below in T accounts are the five MAJOR classifications of accounts. Consider carefully each of the following statements and indicate the change by writing the appropriate letter from the T accounts in the space at the right.

ASSETS	LIABILITIES	PROPRIETORSHIP	INCOME	EXPENSES
A | B	C | D	E | F	G | H	I | J

<u>Sample Question</u>:
A decrease in cash
The CORRECT answer is B.

1. An increase in equipment   1._____
2. An increase in the proprietorship   2._____
3. An increase in office salaries   3._____
4. A decrease in accounts payable   4._____
5. An increase in merchandise inventory   5._____
6. A decrease in office equipment   6._____
7. A decrease in office supplies   7._____
8. An increase in the proprietor's drawing account   8._____
9. A withdrawal of capital by the proprietor   9._____
10. An increase in sales   10._____
11. An increase in salaries payable   11._____
12. An increase in the net profit for the period   12._____
13. An increase in the sales returns and allowances   13._____

14. A decrease in purchases   14._____

15. A decrease in the accounts receivable   15._____

16. An increase in the mortgage payable   16._____

17. An increase in delivery expense   17._____

18. An increase in notes payable   18._____

19. An increase in purchases returns and allowances   19._____

20. A decrease in delivery equipment   20._____

Questions 21-40.

DIRECTIONS: Indicate the title of the accounts to be debited and credited in journalizing, adjusting, and closing the transactions given below by writing in the space at the right the letters that correspond to the accounts listed at the right.

Sample Question:
Paid the rent for the month, $100

	Debit	Credit
	K	C

			Debit	Credit
21. C.M. Smith invested $10,000 in the business	A. Accounts Payable B. Accounts Receivable C. Cash		21._____	_____
22. Purchased merchandise on account from A.D. Hall, $875	D. Income & Expense Summary E. Insurance		22._____	_____
23. Sold merchandise on account to L.S. Brook, $500	F. Insurance Expense G. Merchandise Inventory		23._____	_____
24. Received $250 from cash sales	H. Office Supplies I. Office Supplies Used		24._____	_____
25. Purchased office supplies for cash, $90	J. Purchases K. Rent Expense		25._____	_____
26. Paid A.D. Hall $500 to apply on account	L. Salaries M. Salaries Payable N. Sales		26._____	_____
27. Paid insurance premium for the year, $360	O. C.M. Smith, Capital P. C.M. Smith, Drawing		27._____	_____
28. Paid C.M. Smith $100 for personal use			28._____	_____
29. Received $300 from L.S. Brooks, to apply on account			29._____	_____

3 (#1)

30. Paid salaries for the month $500   30.____ ____

Adjusting Entries

31. The supplies used during the month
    were $60   31.____ ____

32. The salaries owed at the close of
    the month were $40   32.____ ____

33. The prepaid insurance expired was $30   33.____ ____

34. The beginning merchandise inventory
    was $1200   34.____ ____

35. The closing merchandise inventory
    was $750   35.____ ____

Closing Entries

36. The sales account has a balance
    of $4500   36.____ ____

37. The salaries for the month were $540   37.____ ____

38. The purchase account balance is $3600   38.____ ____

39. The office supplies used were $75   39.____ ____

40. The income and expense summary has
    a net profit of $350   40.____ ____

4 (#1)

KEY (CORRECT ANSWERS)

					DEBIT	CREDIT		DEBIT	CREDIT
1.	A	11.	D	21.	C	O	31.	I	H
2.	F	12.	F	22.	J	A	32.	L	M
3.	I	13.	G	23.	B	N	33.	F	E
4.	C	14.	J	24.	C	N	34.	D	G
5.	A	15.	B	25.	H	C	35.	G	D
6.	B	16.	D	26.	A	C	36.	N	D
7.	B	17.	I	27.	E	C	37.	D	L
8.	E	18.	D	28.	P	C	38.	D	J
9.	E	19.	J	29.	C	B	39.	D	I
10.	H	20.	B	30.	L	C	40.	D	O

TEST 2

DIRECTIONS: Each question or incomplete statement is followed by several suggested answers or completions. Select the one that BEST answers the question or completes the statement. *PRINT THE LETTER OF THE CORRECT ANSWER IN THE SPACE AT THE RIGHT.*

Questions 1-16.

DIRECTIONS: Read each statement carefully. If you believe that the account should be debited, place a D for DEBIT in the space at the right. If you think it should be credited, place a C for CREDIT in the space at the right.

1. When sales are made for cash, the sales account is (debited or credited).   1.____

2. When sales are made on account, the customer's account is (debited or credited).   2.____

3. When merchandise is purchased for cash, the purchases account is (debited or credited).   3.____

4. The creditor's account is (debited or credited) when payment is made on account.   4.____

5. The sales account is (debited or credited) for the total of the amount column in the Sales Journal.   5.____

6. The cash account is (debited or credited) for the total of the cash column in the Cash Receipts Journal.   6.____

7. The purchases account is (debited or credited) for the total amount of the purchases column in the Purchases Journal.   7.____

8. The accounts receivable account is (debited or credited) for the total amount of the Sales Journal.   8.____

9. Each account in the Sales Journal is posted to the (debit or credit) of the customer's account.   9.____

10. The total of the accounts payable column in the Cash Payments Journal is posted to the (debit or credit) of the accounts payable account.   10.____

11. The total of the cash column in the Cash Payments Journal is posted to the (debit or credit) of the cash account.   11.____

12. Each account with an amount entered in the General column of the Cash Receipts Journal is (debited or credited).   12.____

103

13. credited
14. debited
15. credited
16. credited

17. A = 5,000
18. B = 7,000
19. C = 3,000
20. D = 50,000
21. E = 10,000
22. F = 12,000
23. G = 3,000
24. H = 400
25. I = 8,000
26. J = 6,500

27. K   27._____

28. L   28._____

29. M   29._____

30. N   30._____

KEY (CORRECT ANSWERS)

1.	C	11.	C	21.	10,000
2.	D	12.	C	22.	12,000
3.	D	13.	C	23.	3,000
4.	D	14.	D	24.	400
5.	C	15.	C	25.	8,000
6.	D	16.	C	26.	6,500
7.	D	17.	5,000	27.	200
8.	D	18.	7,000	28.	8,000
9.	D	19.	3,000	29.	2,000
10.	D	20.	50,000	30.	500

TEST 3

Questions 1-25

DIRECTIONS: Each of Questions 1 through 25 consists of a statement. You are to indicate whether the statement is TRUE (T) or FALSE (F). *PRINT THE LETTER OF THE CORRECT ANSWER IN THE SPACE AT THE RIGHT.*

1. One of the primary objectives of the proprietor of a business is to increase his proprietorship by earning a profit. 1.____

2. The length of time covered by the Income and Expense Statement is of no importance or significance. 2.____

3. The length of time covered by the Balance Sheet is of no importance or significance. 3.____

4. When a customer takes advantage of a cash discount, the amount of cash received is more than the amount of the invoice for which payment is received. 4.____

5. Posting of column totals from the Cash Receipts Journal to the General Ledger is done each day. 5.____

6. After the adjustments have been entered in their appropriate column in the worksheet, their equality is proved by adding the columns. 6.____

7. The amount of unsold merchandise is found by subtracting the merchandise sales from the merchandise purchased. 7.____

8. In the Income and Expense Statement, the sales minus the cost of goods sold equals the gross profit. 8.____

9. If the operating expenses exceed the gross profit, a net loss results. 9.____

10. Only asset, liability, and capital accounts appear in the post-closing trial balance. 10.____

11. The earning of a net profit by a business results in an increase in the net worth of the business. 11.____

12. If the assets of a business are less than the liabilities, the business is solvent. 12.____

13. Small business can use accounting and data processing machines to a better advantage than large businesses. 13.____

14. The adjusting entries can be prepared from the adjustment columns of the worksheet. 14._____

15. The amount of the supplies used during the fiscal period is credited to the supplies account at the close of the fiscal period. 15._____

16. If the credit side of the income and expense summary account is larger than the debit side, the difference is a net loss to the business. 16._____

17. The discount on sales is considered to be a part of the regular operating expenses of the business. 17._____

18. In writing off a customer's uncollectible amount, the allowance for bad debts in the General Ledger is credited. 18._____

19. The amount credited to the allowance for bad debts account is an estimated amount. 19._____

20. The allowance for depreciation account usually has a credit balance. 20._____

21. The time received for a fixed asset at the time it is replaced is always equal to its book value. 21._____

22. Prepaid expenses are sometimes called deferred credits to income. 22._____

23. Expenses that are incurred but not paid are termed accrued expenses. 23._____

24. Prepaid expenses may be shown on the balance sheet as a current asset. 24._____

25. Equipment is listed on the balance sheet as a fixed asset. 25._____

Questions 26-30.

DIRECTIONS: Questions 26 through 30 are to be answered by writing the CORRECT amount in the space at the right.

26. The office supplies account has a balance of $150 at the close of the fiscal period. The actual inventory of supplies is $60. What is the amount of supplies used during the period? 26._____

27. A company receives $490 in cash from a customer for the prompt payment of an invoice. Two percent was the discount. What was the original amount of the invoice? 27._____

28. The balance of the store supplies before adjustment is $400. The total cost of the store supplies on hand at the end of the period is $150. What is the amount of the adjusting entry? 28._____

29. What is the amount necessary to pay a $300 invoice, terms 3/10, 2/20, n/30, twelve days after date? 29.____

30. If equipment costing $1,500, with an estimated life of ten years, was purchased, what is the annual rate of depreciation? 30.____

KEY (CORRECT ANSWERS)

1.	T	11.	T	21.	F
2.	F	12.	F	22.	F
3.	T	13.	F	23.	T
4.	F	14.	T	24.	T
5.	F	15.	T	25.	T
6.	T	16.	F	26.	$90
7.	F	17.	F	27.	$500
8.	T	18.	F	28.	$250
9.	T	19.	T	29.	$294
10.	T	20.	T	30.	10%

TEST 4

DIRECTIONS: Each question or incomplete statement is followed by several suggested answers or completions. Select the one that BEST answers the question or completes the statement. *PRINT THE LETTER OF THE CORRECT ANSWER IN THE SPACE AT THE RIGHT.*

Questions 1-12.

DIRECTIONS: Each of Questions 1 through 12 consists of a statement. You are to indicate whether the statement is TRUE (T) or FALSE (F). *PRINT THE LETTER OF THE CORRECT ANSWER IN THE SPACE AT THE RIGHT.*

1. The supplies used during a fiscal period are shown on the balance sheet as a current asset.   1.____

2. If the assets and liabilities increase equally, the proprietorship also increases.   2.____

3. The Income and Expense Statement shows the results of business operations over a period of time.   3.____

4. An exchange of one asset for another asset of different value causes a change in the proprietorship.   4.____

5. The recording of allowance for depreciation actually results in writing down the asset values.   5.____

6. If the closing merchandise inventory is understated, the profit for the period will be understated.   6.____

7. If accrued salaries during a period are not recorded, the profit for the period will be overstated.   7.____

8. If sales returns are understated during a fiscal period, the profit for that period will be understated.   8.____

9. Unpaid salaries should be added to the salaries for the period before the profit for the period is figured.   9.____

10. When posting the Sales Journal, each item is posted separately to the accounts receivable controlling account in the General Ledger.   10.____

11. A business is said to be solvent when it has a net profit for the period.   11.____

12. Accrued income is income earned but not received during a fiscal period.   12.____

Questions 13-30.

DIRECTIONS: Below is a list of terms with an accompanying list of definitions or explanations. In the space at the right, put the letter of the term in Column II which BEST explains the definition or explanation in Column I.

COLUMN I

13. Entries needed to bring accounts up to date at the end of an accounting period

14. An entry in a book of original entry that has more than one debit or credit

15. An account used to summarize the income and expense data at the close of the fiscal period

16. An account with a balance that is partly a balance sheet amount and partly an income statement amount

17. Discount granted to a customer for early payment of his account

18. A journal designed for recording a particular type of transaction only

19. A ledger used for recording the details of a single account

20. An account in the general ledger that is supported by a subsidiary ledger

21. A list of individual account balances in a subsidiary ledger

22. Expense items bought and paid for, but not entirely consumed during the fiscal period

23. Expenses incurred but not paid during a fiscal period

24. The decrease in the value of a fixed asset due to wear and tear

25. The amount of unsold merchandise on hand

COLUMN II

A. Abstract
B. Accrued expenses
C. Adjusting entries
D. Allowance for bad debts
E. Book value
F. Cash discount
G. Compound entry
H. Controlling account
I. Current asset
J. Depreciation
K. Fixed asset
L. General ledger
M. Income & expense summary
N. Merchandise inventory
O. Mixed account
P. Petty cash
Q. Prepaid expenses
R. Retail method
S. Special journal
T. Straight-line method
U. Subsidiary ledger
V. Voucher

13.____
14.____
15.____
16.____
17.____
18.____
19.____
20.____
21.____
22.____
23.____
24.____
25.____

26. Assets of a more or less permanent nature used in the business   26.____

27. The amount of estimated uncollectible accounts receivable.   27.____

28. The most commonly used method of computing depreciation   28.____

29. The difference between the original cost of an asset and its valuation amount   29.____

30. A written authorization required for each expenditure   30.____

KEY (CORRECT ANSWERS)

1. F	11. F	21. A
2. F	12. T	22. Q
3. T	13. C	23. B
4. T	14. G	24. J
5. F	15. M	25. N
6. T	16. O	26. K
7. T	17. F	27. D
8. F	18. S	28. T
9. T	19. U	29. E
10. F	20. H	30. V

TEST 5

Questions 1-12.

DIRECTIONS: Questions 1 through 12 are to be answered by writing the CORRECT amount in the space at the right.

1. If the purchases for the month were $500, the beginning inventory was $1,500, the ending inventory was $1,000, and the gross profit was $2,000, what were the sales?   1.____

2. If the gross profit for the period was $750 and the net profit was $250, what was the amount of the expenses?   2.____

3. Determine the amount of the cost of goods sold if the purchases for the month were $10,000, the beginning inventory was $3,000, and the ending inventory was $5,000.   3.____

4. A typewriter was purchased for $300 with an estimated life of five years. What is the book value at the end of the third year?   4.____

5. A delivery truck costs $3,000. Its book value at the end of the third year was $2,100. What is the amount of depreciation each year?   5.____

6. The assets on a Balance Sheet are $7,500. The liabilities are $4,500. What is the capital?   6.____

7. A check was received for $242.50 in payment of a sale amounting to $250 less discount. What is the percent of discount allowed?   7.____

8. The capital at the close of the fiscal period was $10,000. The liabilities were $12,000. What are the TOTAL assets?   8.____

9. A note is dated March 1 and is due in 60 days. What is its due date?   9.____

10. A note is dated January 30. It is due in one month. What is its due date?   10.____

11. What is the interest on a note for $500 with interest at 6% for sixty days?   11.____

12. What is the interest on a note for $800 with interest at 6% for 45 days?   12.____

Questions 13-15

DIRECTIONS: Each of Questions 13 through 25 consists of a statement. You are to indicate whether the statement is TRUE (T) or FALSE (F). *PRINT THE LETTER OF THE CORRECT ANSWER IN THE SPACE AT THE RIGHT.*

13. To determine the value of the merchandise available for sale, the purchases are added to the beginning merchandise inventory.   13.____

14. The closing merchandise inventory is shown on both the Balance Sheet and   14.____
    the Income and Expense Statement.

15. The allowance for bad debts account is closed into the income and expense   15.____
    summary account at the close of the fiscal period.

16. The accounts payable account shows the total amount owed to creditors   16.____
    and also shows how much is owed to each creditor.

17. Sales discount is usually subtracted from the sales in the Income and   17.____
    Expense Statement.

18. The use of controlling accounts increases the possibility of errors in   18.____
    preparing the trial balance.

19. The use of controlling accounts results in fewer accounts in the General   19.____
    Ledger.

20. The total of the schedule of accounts receivable should equal the balance of   20.____
    the accounts receivable account in the General Ledger.

21. Closing entries summarize in the income and expense summary account   21.____
    the income costs and expense for the fiscal period.

22. The post-closing trial balance is made before the Balance Sheet has been   22.____
    made.

23. The closing entries are recorded in the General Journal.   23.____

24. The debit balance of the equipment account should show the book value   24.____
    of the equipment on hand.

25. The balance of the allowance for depreciation of equipment account is   25.____
    shown on the Balance Sheet.

KEY (CORRECT ANSWERS)

1.	$3,000	11.	$5.00
2.	$500	12.	$6.00
3.	$8,000	13.	T
4.	$120	14.	T
5.	$300	15.	F
6.	$3,000	16.	F
7.	3%	17.	T
8.	$22,000	18.	F
9.	April 30	19.	T
10.	Feb. 28	20.	T

21. T
22. F
23. T
24. F
25. T

ARITHMETICAL COMPUTATION AND REASONING
EXAMINATION SECTION
TEST 1

DIRECTIONS: Each question or incomplete statement is followed by several suggested answers or completions. Select the one that BEST answers the question or completes the statement. *PRINT THE LETTER OF THE CORRECT ANSWER IN THE SPACE AT THE RIGHT.*

1. 3/8 less than $40 is
    A. $25 B. $65 C. $15 D. $55

2. 27/64 expressed as a percent is
    A. 40.625% B. 42.188% C. 43.750% D. 45.313%

3. 1/6 more than 36 gross is _____ gross.
    A. 6 B. 48 C. 30 D. 42

4. 15 is 20% of

5. The number which when increased by 1/3 of itself equals 96 is
    A. 128 B. 72 C. 64 D. 32

6. 0.16 3/4 written as percent is
    A. 16 3/4% B. 16.3/4% C. .016 3/4% D. .0016 3/4%

7. 55% of 15 is
    A. 82.5 B. 0.825 C. 0.0825 D. 8.25

8. The number which when decreased by 1/3 of itself equals 96 is
    A. 64 B. 32 C. 128 D. 144

9. A carpenter used a board 15 3/4 ft. long from which 3 footstools were made with sufficient lumber left over for half of another footstool.
    If the lumber cost 24 1/2¢ per foot, the cost of EACH footstool was
    A. $1.54 B. $3.86 C. $1.10 D. $1.08

10. In one year, a luncheonette purchased 1231 gallons of milk for $907.99.
    The AVERAGE cost per half pint was
    A. $0.046 B. $0.045 C. $0.047 D. $0.044

11. The product of 23 and 9 3/4 is
    A. 191 2/3 B. 224 1/4 C. 213 3/4 D. 32 3/4

12. An order for 345 machine bolts at $4.15 per hundred will cost
    A. $0.1432 B. $1.1432 C. $14.32 D. $143.20

13. The fractional equivalent of .0625 is

    A. 1/16   B. 1/15   C. 1/14   D. 1/13

14. The number 0.03125 equals

    A. 3/64   B. 1/16   C. 1/64   D. 1/32

15. 21.70 divided by 1.75 equals

    A. 124   B. 12.4   C. 1.24   D. .124

16. The average cost of school lunches for 100 children varied as follows: Monday, $0.285; Tuesday, $0.237; Wednesday, $0.264; Thursday, $0.276; Friday, $0.292. The AVERAGE lunch cost

    A. $0.136   B. $0.270   C. $0.135   D. $0.271

17. The cost of 5 dozen eggs at $8.52 per gross is

    A. $3.50   B. $42.60   C. $3.55   D. $3.74

18. 410.07 less 38.49 equals

    A. 372.58   B. 371.58   C. 381.58   D. 382.68

19. The cost of 7 3/4 tons of coal at $20.16 per ton is

    A. $15.12   B. $151.20   C. $141.12   D. $156.24

20. The sum of 90.79, 79.09, 97.90, and 9.97 is

    A. 277.75   B. 278.56   C. 276.94   D. 277.93

KEY (CORRECT ANSWERS)

1. A
2. B
3. D
4. C
5. B

6. A
7. D
8. D
9. C
10. A

11. B
12. C
13. A
14. D
15. B

16. D
17. C
18. B
19. D
20. A

SOLUTIONS TO PROBLEMS

1. ($40)(5/8) = $25

2. 27/64 = .421875 ≈ 42.188%

3. (36)(1 1/6) = 42

4. Let x = missing number. Then, 15 = .20x. Solving, x = 75

5. Let x = missing number. Then, x + 1/3 x = 96. Simplifying, 4/3 x = 96. Solving, x = 96 ÷ 4/3 = 72

6. .16 3/4 = 16 3/4% by simply moving the decimal point two places to the right.

7. (.55)(15) = 8.25

8. Let x = missing number. Then, x - 1/3 x = 96. Simplifying, 2/3 x = 96. Solving, x = 96 ÷ 2/3 = 144

9. 15 3/4 ÷ 3 1/2 = 4.5 feet per footstool. The cost of one footstool is ($.245)(4.5) = $1.1025 ≈ $1.10

10. $907.99 ÷ 1231 = $.7376 per gallon. Since there are 16 half-pints in a gallon, the average cost per half-pint is $.7376 ÷ 16 ≈ $.046

11. (23)(9 3/4) = (23)(9.75) = 224.25 or 224 1/4

12. ($4.15)(3.45) = $14.3175 = $14.32

13. .0625 = 625/10,000 = 1/16

14. .03125 = 3125/100,000 = 1/32

15. 21.70 ÷ 1.75 = 12.4

16. The sum of these lunches is $1.354. Then, $1.354 ÷ 5 = $.2708 = $.271

17. $8.52 ÷ 12 = $.71 per dozen. Then, the cost of 5 dozen is ($.71)(5) = $3.55

18. 410.07 - 38.49 = 371.58

19. ($20.16)(7.75) = $156.24

20. 90.79 + 79.09 + 97.90 + 9.97 = 277.75

TEST 2

DIRECTIONS: Each question or incomplete statement is followed by several suggested answers or completions. Select the one that BEST answers the question or completes the statement. *PRINT THE LETTER OF THE CORRECT ANSWER IN THE SPACE AT THE RIGHT.*

1. 1600 is 40% of what number? 1._____
   A. 6400   B. 3200   C. 4000   D. 5600

2. An executive's time card reads: Arrived 9:15 A.M., Left 2:05 P.M. How many hours was he in the office? _____ hours _____ minutes. 2._____
   A. 5; 10   B. 4; 50   C. 4; 10   D. 5; 50

3. .4266 times .3333 will have the following number of decimals in the product: 3._____
   A. 8   B. 4   C. 1   D. None of these

4. An office floor is 25 ft. wide by 36 ft. long. To cover this floor with carpet will require _____ square yards. 4._____
   A. 100   B. 300   C. 900   D. 25

5. 1/8 of 1% expressed as a decimal is 5._____
   A. .125   B. .0125   C. 1.25   D. .00125

6. $\dfrac{6 \div 4}{6 \times 4}$ equals 6x4 6._____
   A. 1/16   B. 1   C. 1/6   D. 1/4

7. 1/25 of 230 equals 7._____
   A. 92.0   B. 9.20   C. .920   D. 920

8. 4 times 3/8 equals 8._____
   A. 1 3/8   B. 3/32   C. 12.125   D. 1.5

9. 3/4 divided by 4 equals 9._____
   A. 3   B. 3/16   C. 16/3   D. 16

10. 6/7 divided by 2/7 equals 10._____
    A. 6   B. 12/49   C. 3   D. 21

11. The interest on $240 for 90 days ' 6% is 11._____
    A. $4.80   B. $3.40   C. $4.20   D. $3.60

12. 16 2/3% of 1728 is 12._____
    A. 91   B. 288   C. 282   D. 280

13. 6 1/4% of 6400 is 13.____
   A. 2500   B. 410   C. 108   D. 400

14. 12 1/2% of 560 is 14.____
   A. 65   B. 40   C. 50   D. 70

15. 2 yards divided by 3 equals 15.____
   A. 2 feet   B. 1/2 yard   C. 3 yards   D. 3 feet

16. A school has 540 pupils. 45% are boys. How many girls are there in this school? 16.____
   A. 243   B. 297   C. 493   D. 394

17. .1875 is equivalent to 17.____
   A. 18 3/4   B. 75/18   C. 18/75   D. 3/16

18. A kitchen cabinet listed at $42 is sold for $33.60. The discount allowed is 18.____
   A. 10%   B. 15%   C. 20%   D. 30%

19. 3 6/8 divided by 8 1/4 equals 19.____
   A. 9 1/8   B. 12   C. 5/11   D. 243.16

20. An agent sold goods to the amount of $1480. His commission at 5 1/2% was 20.____
   A. $37.50   B. $81.40   C. 76.70   D. $81.10

KEY (CORRECT ANSWERS

1. C   11. D
2. B   12. B
3. A   13. D
4. A   14. D
5. D   15. A

6. A   16. B
7. B   17. D
8. D   18. C
9. B   19. C
10. C   20. B

SOLUTIONS TO PROBLEMS

1. Let x = missing number. Then, 1600 = .40x. Solving, x = 4000

2. 2:05 PM - 9:15 AM = 4 hours 50 minutes

3. The product of two 4-decimal numbers is an 8-decimal number.

4. (25 ft)(36 ft) = 900 sq.ft. = 100 sq.yds.

5. (1/8)(1%) = (.125)(.01) = .00125

6. (6 ÷ 4) ÷ (6 x 4) = 3/2 ÷ 24 = (3/2)(1/24) = (1/16)

7. (1/25)(230) = 9.20

8. (4)(3/8) = 12/8 = 1.5

9. 3/4 ÷ 4 = (3/4)(1/4) = 3/16

10. 6/7 / 2/7 = (6/7)(7/2) = 3

11. ($240)(.06)(90/360) = $3.60

12. (16 2/3%)(1728) = (1/6)(1728) = 288

13. (6 1/4%)(6400) = (1/16)(6400) = 400

14. (12 1/2%)(560) = (1/8)(560) = 70

15. 2 yds ÷ 3 = 2/3 yds = (2/3)(3) = 2 ft.

16. If 45% are boys, then 55% are girls. Thus, (540)(.55) = 297

17. .1875 = 1875/10,000 = 3/16

18. $42 - $33.60 = $8.40.
    The discount is $8.40 ÷ $42 = .20 = 20%

19. 3 6/8 - 8 1/4 = (30/8)(4/33) = 5/11

20. ($1480)(.055) = $81.40

TEST 3

DIRECTIONS: Each question or incomplete statement is followed by several suggested answers or completions. Select the one that BEST answers the question or completes the statement. *PRINT THE LETTER OF THE CORRECT ANSWER IN THE SPACE AT THE RIGHT.*

1. 93.648 divided by 0.4 is 1.____
   A. 23.412 B. 234.12 C. 2.3412 D. 2341.2

2. Add 4.3682, .0028, 34., 9.92, and from the sum subtract 1.992. The remainder is 2.____
   A. .46299 B. 4.6299 C. 462.99 D. 46.299

3. At $2.88 per gross, three dozen will cost 3.____
   A. $8.64 B. $0.96 C. $0.72 D. $11.52

4. 13 times 2.39 times 0.024 equals 4.____
   A. 745.68 B. 74.568 C. 7.4568 D. .74568

5. A living room suite is marked $64 less 25 percent. A cash discount of 10 percent is allowed. The cash price is 5.____
   A. $53.20 B. $47.80 C. $36.00 D. $43.20

6. 1/8 of 1 percent expressed as a decimal is 6.____
   A. .125 B. .0125 C. 1.25 D. .00125

7. 16 percent of 482.11 equals 7.____
   A. 77.1376 B. 771.4240 C. 7714.2400 D. 7.71424

8. A merchant sold a chair for $60. This was at a profit of 25 percent of what it cost him. The chair cost him 8.____
   A. $48 B. $45 C. $15 D. $75

9. Add 5 hours 13 minutes, 3 hours 49 minutes, and 14 minutes. The sum is _____ hours _____ minutes. 9.____
   A. 9; 16 B. 9; 76 C. 8; 16 D. 8; 6

10. 89 percent of $482 is 10.____
    A. $428.98 B. $472.36 C. $42.90 D. $47.24

11. 200 percent of 800 is 11.____
    A. 16 B. 1600 C. 2500 D. 4

12. Add 2 feet 3 inches, 4 feet 11 inches, 8 inches, 6 feet 6 inches. The sum is _____ feet _____ inches. 12.____
    A. 12; 4 B. 12; 14 C. 14; 4 D. 14; 28

13. A merchant bought dresses at $15 each and sold them at $20 each. His overhead expenses are 20 percent of cost. His net profit on each dress is   13._____

   A. $1   B. $2   C. $3   D. $4

14. 0.0325 expressed as a percent is   14._____

   A. 325%   B. 3 1/4%   C. 32 1/2%   D. 32.5%

15. Add 3/4, 1/8, 1/32, 1/2; and from the sum subtract 4/8. The remainder is   15._____

   A. 2/32   B. 7/8   C. 29/32   D. 3/4

16. A salesman gets a commission of 4 percent on his sales. If he wants his commission to amount to $40, he will have to sell merchandise totaling   16._____

   A. $160   B. $10   C. $1,000   D. $100

17. Jones borrowed $225,000 for five years at 3 1/2 percent. The annual interest charge was   17._____

   A. $1,575   B. $1,555   C. $7,875   D. $39,375

18. A kitchen cabinet listed at $42 is sold for $33.60. The discount allowed is _____ percent.   18._____

   A. 10   B. 15   C. 20   D. 30

19. The exact number of days from May 5, 2007 to July 1, 2007 is _____ days.   19._____

   A. 59   B. 58   C. 56   D. 57

20. A dealer sells an article at a loss of 50% of the cost. Based on the selling price, the loss is   20._____

   A. 25%   B. 50%   C. 100%   D. none of these

KEY (CORRECT ANSWERS)

1. B
2. D
3. C
4. D
5. D
6. D
7. A
8. A
9. A
10. A
11. B
12. C
13. B
14. B
15. C
16. C
17. C
18. C
19. D
20. C

SOLUTIONS TO PROBLEMS

1. $93.648 \div .4 = 234.12$

2. $4.368 + .0028 + 34 + 9.92 - 1.992 = 48.291 - 1.992 = 46.299$

3. $2.88 for 12 dozen means $.24 per dozen. Three dozen will cost $(3)($.24) = $.72$

4. $(13)(2.39)(.024) = .74568$

5. $($64)(.75)(.90) = 43.20

6. $(1/8)(1\%) = (.125)(.01) = .00125$

7. $(.16)(482.11) = 77.1376$

8. Let $x = $ cost. Then, $1.25x = 60. Solving, $x = 48

9. 5 hrs. 13 min. + 3 hrs. 49 min. + 14 min = 8 hrs. 76 min.

10. $(.89)($482) = 428.98

11. $200\% = 2$. So, $(200\%)(800) = (2)(800) = 1600$

12. 2 ft. 3 in. + 4 ft. 11 in. + 8 in. + 6 ft. 6 in. + 12 ft. 28 in. = 14 ft. 4 in.

13. Overhead is $(.20)($15) = 3. The net profit is $$20 - $15 - $3 = 2

14. $.0325 = 3.25\% = 3\ 1/4\%$

15. $3/4 + 1/8 + 1/32 + 1/2 - 4/8 = 45/32 - 4/8 = 29/32$

16. Let $x = $ sales. Then, $$40 = .04x$. Solving, $x = 1000

17. Annual interest is $($225,000)(.035) \times 1 = 7875$

18. $$42 - $33.60 = 8.40. Then, $$8.40 \div $42 = .20 = 20\%$

19. The number of days left for May, June, July is 26, 30, and 1. Thus, $26 + 30 + 1 = 57$

20. Let $x = $ cost, so that $.50x = $ selling price. The loss is represented by $.50x \div .50x = 1 = 100\%$ on the selling price. (Note: The loss in dollars is $x - .50x = .50x$)

ARITHMETIC
EXAMINATION SECTION
TEST 1

DIRECTIONS: Each question or incomplete statement is followed by several suggested answers or completions. Select the one that *BEST* answers the question or completes the statement. *PRINT THE LETTER OF TEE CORRECT ANSWER IN THE SPACE AT THE RIGHT.*

1. Add $4.34, $34.50, $6.00, $101.76, $90.67. From the result, subtract $60.54 and $10,56. 1.____
   A. $76.17   B. $156.37   C. $166.17   D. $300.37

2. Add 2,200, 2,600, 252 and 47.96. From the result, subtract 202.70, 1,200, 2,150 and 434.43. 2.____
   A. 1,112.83   B. 1,213.46   C. 1,341.51   D. 1,348.91

3. Multiply 1850 by .05 and multiply 3300 by .08 and, then, add both results, 3.____
   A. 242.50   B. 264,00   C. 333.25   D. 356.50

4. Multiply 312.77 by .04. Round off the result to the nearest hundredth. 4.____
   A. 12.52   B. 12.511   C. 12.518   D. 12.51

5. Add 362.05, 91.13, 347.81 and 17.46 and then divide the result by 6. The answer, rounded off to the nearest hundredth, is: 5.____
   A. 138.409   B. 137.409   C. 136.41   D. 136.40

6. Add 66.25 and 15.06 and, then, multiply the result by 2 1/6. The answer is, most nearly, 6.____
   A. 176.18   B. 176.17   C. 162.66   D. 162.62

7. Each of the following items contains three decimals. In which case do *all* three decimals have the *SAME* value? 7.____
   A. .3; .30; .03   B. .25; .250; .2500
   C. 1.9; 1.90;1.09   D. .35; .350; .035

8. Add 1/2 the sum of (539.84 and 479.26) to 1/3 the sum of (1461.93 and 927.27). Round off the result to the nearest whole number. 8.____
   A. 3408   B. 2899   C. 1816   D. 1306

9. Multiply $5,906.09 by 15% and, then, divide the result by 3 and round off to the nearest cent. 9.____
   A. $295.30   B. $885.91   C. $2,657.74   D. $29,530.45

10. Multiply 630 by 517. 10.____
    A. 325,710   B. 345,720   C. 362,425   D. 385,660

11. Multiply 35 by 846.

    A. 4050   B. 9450   C. 18740   D. 29610

12. Multiply 823 by 0.05.

    A. 0.4115   B. 4.115   C. 41.15   D. 411.50

13. Multiply 1690 by 0.10.

    A. 0.169   B. .1.69   C. 16.90   D. 169.0

14. Divide 2765 by 35.

    A. 71   B. 79   C. 87   D. 93

15. From $18.55 subtract $6.80.

    A. $9.75   B. $10.95   C. $11.75   D. $25.35

16. The sum of 2.75 + 4.50 + 3.60 is:

    A. 9.75   B. 10.85   C. 11.15   D. 11.95

17. The sum of 9.63 + 11.21 + 17.25 is:

    A. 36.09   B. 38.09   C. 39.92   D. 41.22

18. The sum of 112.0 + 16.9 + 3.84 is:

    A. 129.3   B. 132.74   C. 136.48   D. 167.3

19. When 65 is added to the result of 14 multiplied by 13, the answer is:

    A. 92   B. 182   C. 247   D. 16055

20. From $391.55 subtract $273.45.

    A. $118.10   B. $128.20   C. $178.10   D. $218.20

KEY (CORRECT ANSWERS)

1.	C	11.	D
2.	A	12.	C
3.	D	13.	D
4.	D	14.	B
5.	C	15.	C
6.	B	16.	B
7.	B	17.	B
8.	D	18.	B
9.	C	19.	C
10.	A	20.	A

SOLUTIONS TO PROBLEMS

1. ($4.34 + $34.50 + $6.00 + $101.76 + $90.67) - ($60.54 + $10.56) = $237.27 - $71.10 = $166.17.

2. (2200 + 2600 + 252 + 47.96) - (202.70 + 1200 + 2150 + 434.43) = 5099.96 - 3987.13 = 1112.83

3. (1850)(.05) + (3300)(.08) = 92.5 + 264 = 356.50

4. (312.77)(.04) = 12.5108 = 12.51 to nearest hundredth

5. $(362.05 + 91.13 + 347.81 + 17.46) \div 6 = 136.40\overline{83} = 136.41$ to nearest hundredth

6. $(66.25 + 15.06)(2\frac{1}{6}) = 176.171\overline{6} \approx 176.17$

7. .25 = .250 = .2500

8. $(\frac{1}{2})(539.84 + 479.26) + \frac{1}{3}(1461.93 + 927.27) = 509.55 + 796.4 = 1305.95 = 1306$ nearest whole number

9. ($5906.09)(.15) ÷ 3 = ($885.9135)/3 = 295.3045 = $295.30 to nearest cent

10. (630)(517) = 325,710

11. (35)(846) = 29,610

12. (823)(.05) = 41.15

13. (1690)(10) = 169.0

14. 2765 ÷ 3.5 = 79

15. $18.55 - $6.80 = $11.75

16. 2.75 + 4.50 + 3.60 = 10.85

17. 9.63 + 11.21 + 17.25 = 38.09

18. 112.0 + 16.9 + 3.84 = 132.74

19. 65 + (14)(13) = 65 + 182 = 247

20. $391.55 - $273.45 = $118.10

TEST 2

DIRECTIONS   Each question or incomplete statement is followed by several suggested answers or completions. Select the one that *BEST* answers the question or completes the statement. *PRINT THE LETTER OF TEE CORRECT ANSWER IN THE SPACE AT THE RIGHT.*

1. The sum of $29.61 + $101.53 + $943.64 is: 1._____
   A. $983.88   B. $1074.78   C. $1174.98   D. $1341.42

2. The sum of $132.25 + $85.63 + $7056,44 is: 2._____
   A. $1694.19   B. $7274.32   C. $8464.57   D. $9346.22

3. The sum of 4010 + 1271 + 838 + 23 is: 3._____
   A. 6142   B. 6162   C. 6242   D. 6362

4. The sum of 53632 + 27403 + 98765 + 75424 is: 4._____
   A. 19214   B. 215214   C. 235224   D. 255224

5. The sum of 76342 + 49050 + 21206 + 59989 is: 5._____
   A. 196586   B. 206087   C. 206587   D. 234487

6. The sum of $452.13 + $963.45 + $621.25 is: 6._____
   A. $1936.83   B. $2036.83   C. $2095.73   D. $2135.73

7. The sum of 36392 + 42156 + 98765 is: 7._____
   A. 167214   B. 177203   C. 177313   D. 178213

8. The sum of 40125 + 87123 + 24689 is: 8._____
   A. 141827   B. 151827   C. 151937   D. 161947

9. The sum of 2379 + 4015 + 6521 + 9986 is: 9._____
   A. 22901   B. 22819   C. 21801   D. 21791

10. From 50962 subtract 36197.   10._____
    A. 14675   B. 14765   C. 14865   D. 24765

11. From 90000 subtract 31928.   11._____
    A. 58072   B. 59062   C. 68172   D. 69182

12. From 63764 subtract 21548.   12._____
    A. 42216   B. 43122   C. 45126   D. 85312

13. From $9605.13 subtract $2715.96.   13._____
    A. $12,321.09   B. $8,690.16   C. $6,990.07   D. $6,889.17

14. From 76421 subtract 73101.   14._____
    A. 3642   B. 3540   C. 3320   D. 3242

15. From $8.25 subtract $6.50.   15._____
    A. $1.25   B. $1.50   C. $1.75   D. $2.25

16. Multiply 583 by 0.50.   16._____
    A. $291.50 B. 28.15   C. 2.815   D. 0.2815

17. Multiply 0.35 by 1045.   17._____
    A. 0.36575 B. 3.6575 C. 36.575 D. 365.75

18. Multiply 25 by 2513.   18._____
    A. 62825   B. 62725   C. 60825   D. 52825

19. Multiply 423 by 0.01.   19._____
    A. 0.0423 B. 0.423   C. 4.23   D. 42.3

20. Multiply 6.70 by 3.2.   20._____
    A. 2.1440 B. 21.440 C. 214.40 D. 2144.0

KEY (CORRECT ANSWERS)

1.	B	11.	A
2.	B	12.	A
3.	A	13.	D
4.	D	14.	C
5.	C	15.	C
6.	B	16.	A
7.	C	17.	D
8.	C	18.	A
9.	A	19.	C
10.	B	20.	B

---

3 (#2)

SOLUTIONS TO PROBLEMS

1. $29.61 + $101.53 + $943.64 = $1074.78

2. $132.25 + $85.63 + $7056.44 = $7274.32

3. 4010 + 1271 + 838 + 23 = 6142

4. 53,632 + 27,403 + 98,765 + 75,424 = 255,224

5. 76,342 + 49,050 + 21,206 + 59,989 = 206,587

6. $452.13 + $963.45 + $621.25 = $2036.83

7. 36,392 + 42,156 + 98,765 = 177,313

8. 40,125 + 87,123 + 24,689 = 151,937

9. 2379 + 4015 + 6521 + 9986 = 22,901

10. 50962 - 36197 = 14,765

11. 90,000 - 31,928 = 58,072

12. 63,764 - 21,548 = 42,216

13. $9605.13 - $2715.96 = $6889.17

14. 76,421 - 73,101 = 3320

15. $8.25 - $6.50 = $1.75

16. (583)(.50) = 291.50

17. (.35)(1045) = 365.75

18. (25)(2513) = 62,825

19. (423)(.01) = 4.23

20. (6.70)(3.2) = 21.44

TEST 3

DIRECTIONS: Each question or incomplete statement is followed by several suggested answers or completions. Select the one that BEST answers the question or completes the statement. *PRINT THE LETTER OF TEE CORRECT ANSWER IN THE SPACE AT THE RIGHT.*

Questions 1-4.

DIRECTIONS: For each of Questions 1-4, perform the indicated arithmetic and choose the correct answer from among the four choices given.

1. 12.485
   + 347

   A. 12,038   B. 12,128   C. 12,782   D. 12,832

   1._____

2. 74,137
   + 711

   A. 74,326   B. 74,848   C. 78,028   D. .D. 78,926

   2._____

3. 3,749
   - 671

   A. 3,078   B. 3,168   C. 4,028   D. 4,420

   3._____

4. 19,805
   -18904

   A. 109   B. 901   C. 1,109   D. 1,901

   4._____

5. When 119 is subtracted from the sum of 2016 + 1634, the remainder is:

   A. 2460   B. 3531   C. 3650   D. 3769

   5._____

6. Multiply 35 X 65 X 15.

   A. 2275   B. 24265   C. 31145   D. 34125

   6._____

7. 90% expressed as a decimal is:

   A. .009   B. .09   C. .9   D. 9.0

   7._____

8. Seven-tenths of a foot expressed in inches is:

   A. 5.5   B. 6.5   C. 7   D. 8.4

   8._____

9. If 95 men were divided into crews of five men each, the *number* of crews that will be formed is:

   A. 16   B. 17   C. 18   D. 19

   9._____

10. If a man earns $19.50 an hour, the *number* of working hours it will take him to earn $4,875 is, most nearly,

    A. 225 B. 250 C. 275 D. 300

11. If 5 1/2 loads of gravel cost $55.00, then 6 1/2 loads will cost:

    A. $60. B. $62.50 C. $65. D. $66.00

12. At $2.50 a yard, 27 yards of concrete will cost:

    A. $36. B. $41.80 C. $54. D. $67.50

13. A distance is measured and found to be 52.23 feet. In feet and inches, this distance is, most nearly, 52 feet *and*

    A. 2 3/4" B. 3 1/4" C. 3 3/4" D. 4 1/4"

14. If a maintainer gets $5.20 per hour and time and one-half for working over 40 hours, his *gross* salary for a week in which he worked 43 hours would be

    A. $208.00 B. $223.60 C. $231.40 D. $335.40

15. The circumference of a circle is given by the formula $C = \Pi D$, where C is the circumference, D is the diameter, and Π is about 3 1/7.
    If a coil is 15 turns of steel cable has an average diameter of 20 inches, the *total* length of cable on the coil is nearest to

    A. 5 feet B. 78 feet C. 550 feet D. 943 feet

16. The measurements of a poured concrete foundation show that 54 cubic feet of concrete have been placed.
    If payment for this concrete is to be on the basis of cubic yards, the 54 cubic feet must be

    A. multiplied by 27   B. multiplied by 3
    C. divided by 27   D. divided by 3

17. If the cost of 4 1/2 tons of structural steel is $1,800, then the cost of 12 tons is, most nearly,

    A. $4,800 B. $5,400 C. $7,200 D. $216,000

18. An hourly-paid employee working 12:00 midnight to 8:00 a.m. is directed to report to the medical staff for a physical examination at 11:00 a.m. of the same day.
    The pay allowed him for reporting will be an extra

    A. 1 hour B. 2 hours C. 3 hours D. 4 hours

19. The *total* length of four pieces of 2" pipe, whose lengths are 7' 3 1/2", 4' 2 3/16", 5' 7 5/16", and 8' 5 7/8", respectively, is:

    A. 24' 6 3/4"   B. 24' 7 15/16"
    C. 25' 5 13/16"   D. 25' 6 7/8"

20. As a senior mortuary caretaker, you are preparing a monthly report, using the following figures: 20.____

    No. of bodies received   983
    No. of bodies claimed   720
    No. of bodies sent to city cemetery   14
    No. of bodies sent to medical schools   9

How many bodies remained at the end of the monthly reporting period?

    A. 230   B. 240   C. 250   D. 260

KEY (CORRECT ANSWERS)

1.	D	11.	C
2.	B	12.	D
3.	A	13.	A
4.	B	14.	C
5.	B	15.	B
6.	D	16.	C
7.	C	17.	A
8.	D	18.	C
9.	D	19.	D
10.	B	20.	B

SOLUTIONS TO PROBLEMS

1. $12{,}485 + 347 = 12{,}832$

2. $74{,}137 + 711 = 74{,}848$

3. $3749 - 671 = 3078$

4. $19{,}805 - 18{,}904 = 901$

5. $(2016 + 1634) - 119 = 3650 - 119 = 3531$

6. $(35)(65)(15) = 34{,}125$

7. $90\% = .90$ or $.9$

8. $(\frac{7}{10})(12) = 8.4$ inches

9. $95 \div 5 = 19$ crews

10. $\$4875 \div \$19.50 = 250$ days

11. Let x = cost. Then, $\dfrac{5\frac{1}{2}}{6\frac{1}{2}} = \dfrac{\$55.00}{x}$. $5\frac{1}{2} = 357.50$. Solving, $x = \$65$

12. $(\$2.50)(27) = \$67.50$

13. $.23$-ft. $= 2.76$ in., so 52.23 ft ≈ 52 ft. $2\frac{3}{4}$ in. $(.76 \approx \frac{3}{4})$

14. Salary $= (\$5.20)(40) + (\$7.80)(3) = \$231.40$

15. Length $\approx (15)(3\frac{1}{7})(20) \approx 943$ in. ≈ 78 ft.

16. There are 27 cu.ft. in 1 cu.yd. To change from 54 cu.ft. to cu.yds., divide by 27.

17. $\$1800 \div 4\frac{1}{2} = \$400$ per ton. Then, 12 tons cost $(\$400)(12) = \$4800$

18. Instead of working 12 to 8, he will be staying until 11 AM, an extra 3 hours.

19. $7'3\frac{1}{2}" + 4'2\frac{3}{16}" + 5'7\frac{5}{16}" + 8'5\frac{7}{8}" = 24'17\frac{30}{16}" = 24'18\frac{7}{8}"$

20. $983 - 720 - 14 - 9 = 240$ bodies left.

ARITHMETICAL REASONING

EXAMINATION SECTION

TEST 1

DIRECTIONS: Each question or incomplete statement is followed by several suggested answers or completions. Select the one that BEST answers the question or completes the statement. *PRINT THE LETTER OF THE CORRECT ANSWER IN THE SPACE AT THE RIGHT.*

1. The ABC Corporation had a gross income of $125,500.00 in 2019. Of this, it paid 60% for overhead.
   If the gross income for 2020 increased by $6,500 and the cost of overhead increased to 61% of gross income, how much MORE did it pay for overhead in 2020 than in 2019?
   A. $1,320   B. $5,220   C. $7,530   D. $8,052

2. After one year, Mr. Richards paid back a total of $16,950 as payment for a $15,000 loan. All the money paid over $15,000 was simple interest.
   The interest charge was MOST NEARLY
   A. 13%   B. 11%   C. 9%   D. 7%

3. A checking account has a balance of $253.36.
   If deposits of $36.95, $210.23, and $7.34 and withdrawals of $117.35, $23.37, and $15.98 are made, what is the NEW balance of the account?
   A. $155.54   B. $351.18   C. $364.58   D. $664.58

4. In 2020, the W Realty Company spent 27% of its income on rent.
   If it earned $97,254 in 2020, the amount it paid for rent was
   A. $26,258.58   B. 26,348.58   C. $27,248.58   D. $27,358.58

5. Six percent simple annual interest on $2,436.18 is MOST NEARLY
   A. $145.08   B. $145.17   C. $146.08   D. $146.17

6. H. Partridge receives a weekly gross salary (before deductions) of $397.50. Through weekly payroll deductions of $13.18, he is paying back a loan he took from his pension fund.
   If other fixed weekly deductions amount to $122.76, how much pay would Mr. Partridge take home over a period of 33 weeks?
   A. $7,631.28   B. $8,250.46   C. $8,631.48   D. $13,117.50

7. Mr. Robertson is a city employee enrolled in a city retirement system. He has taken out a loan from the retirement fund and is paying it back at the rate of $14.90 every two weeks.
   In eighteen weeks, how much money will he have paid back on the loan?
   A. $268.20   B. $152.80   C. $134.10   D. $67.05

2 (#1)

8. In 2019, The Iridor Book Company had the following expenses: rent, $6,500; overhead, $52,585; inventory, $35,700; and miscellaneous, $1,275.
If all of these expenses went up 18% in 2020, what would they TOTAL in 2020?
A. $17,290.80   B. $78,769.20   C. $96,060.00   D. $113,350.80

9. Ms. Ranier had a gross salary of $710.72 paid once every two weeks.
If the deductions from each paycheck are $125.44, $50.26, $12.58, and $2.54, how much money would Ms. Ranier take home in eight weeks?
A. $2,079.60   B. $2,842.88   C. $4,159.20   D. $5,685.76

10. Mr. Martin had a net income of $95,500 in 2019.
If he spent 34% on rent and household expenses, 3% on house furnishings, 25% on clothes, and 36% on food, how much was left for savings and other expenses?
A. $980   B. $1,910   C. $3,247   D. $9,800

11. Mr. Elsberg can pay back a loan of $1,800 from the city employees' retirement system if he pays back $36.69 every two weeks for two full years.
At the end of the two years, how much more than the original $1,800 he borrowed will Mr. Elsberg have paid back?
A. $53.94   B. $107.88   C. $190.79   D. $214.76

12. Mr. Nusbaum is a city employee receiving a gross salary (salary before deductions) of $20,800. Every two weeks, the following deductions are taken out of his salary: Federal Income Tax, $162.84; FICA, $44.26; State Tax, $29.2; City Tax, $13.94; Health Insurance, $3.14.
If Mr. Nusbaum's salary and deductions remained the same for a full calendar year, what would his net salary (gross salary less deductions) be in that year?
A. $6,596.20   B. $14,198.60   C. $18,745.50   D. $20,546.30

13. Add: 8936, 7821, 8953, 4297, 9785, 6579.
A. 45,371   B. 45,381   C. 46,371   D. 46,381

14. Multiply: 987
              867
A. 854,609   B. 854,729   C. 855,709   D. 855,729

15. Divide: 59)321439.0
A. 5438.1   B. 5447.1   C. 5448.1   D. 5457.1

16. Divide: .052)721
A. 12,648.0   B. 12,648.1   C. 12,649.0   D. 12,649.1

17. If the total number of employees in one city agency increased from 1,927 to 2,006 during a certain year, the percentage increase in the number of employees for that year is MOST NEARLY
A. 4%   B. 5%   C. 6%   D. 7%

18. During a single fiscal year, which totaled 248 workdays, one account clerk verified 1,488 purchase vouchers.
    Assuming a normal work week of five days, what is the AVERAGE number of vouchers verified by the account clerk in a one-week period during this fiscal year?
    A. 25   B. 30   C. 35   D. 40

    18.____

19. Multiplying a number by .75 is the same as
    A. multiplying it by ²/₃
    B. dividing it by ²/₃
    C. multiplying it by ¾
    D. dividing it by ¾

    19.____

20. In City Agency A, ²/₃ of the employees are enrolled in a retirement system. City Agency B has the same number of employees as Agency A and 60% of these are enrolled in a retirement system.
    If Agency A has a total of 660 employees, how many MORE employees does it have enrolled in a retirement system than does Agency B?
    A. 36   B. 44   C. 56   D. 66

    20.____

21. Net worth is equal to assets minus liabilities.
    If, at the end of 2019, a textile company had assets of $98,695.83 and liabilities of $59,238.29, what was its net worth?
    A. $38,478.54   B. $38,488.64   C. $39,457.54   D. $48,557.54

    21.____

22. Mr. Martin's assets consist of the following: Cash on hand, $5,233.74, Automobile, $3,206.09; Furniture, $4,925.00; Government Bonds, $5,500.00; and House, $36,69.85.
    What are his TOTAL assets?
    A. $54,545.68   B. $54,455.68   C. $55,455.68   D. $55,555.68

    22.____

23. If Mr. Mitchell has $627.04 in his checking account and then writes three checks for $241.75, $13.24, and $102.97, what will be his new balance?
    A. $257.88   B. $269.08   C. $357.96   D. $369.96

    23.____

24. An employee's net pay is equal to his total earnings less all deductions.
    If an employee's total earnings in a pay period are $497.05, what is his net pay if he has the following deductions: Federal Income Tax, $18.79; City Tax, $7.25; Pension, $1.88?
    A. $351.17   B. $351.07   C. $350.17   D. $350.07

    24.____

25. A petty cash fund had an opening balance of $85.75 on December 1. Expenditures of $23.00, $15.65, $5.23, $14.75, and $26.38 were made out of this fund during the first 14 days of the month. Then, on December 17, another $38.50 was added to the fund.
    If additional expenditures of $17.18, $3.29, and $11.64 were made during the remainder of the month, what was the FINAL balance of the petty cash fund at the end of December?
    A. $6.93   B. $7.13   C. $46.51   D. $91.40

    25.____

KEY (CORRECT ANSWERS)

1.	B	11.	B
2.	A	12.	B
3.	B	13.	C
4.	A	14.	D
5.	D	15.	C
6.	C	16.	D
7.	C	17.	A
8.	D	18.	B
9.	A	19.	C
10.	B	20.	B

21. C
22. D
23. B
24. D
25. B

SOLUTIONS TO PROBLEMS

1. ($132,000)(.61) − ($125,500)(.60) = $5,220

2. Interest = $1,950. As a percent, $1950 ÷ 15,000 = 13%

3. New balance = $253.36 + $36.95 + $210.23 + $7.34 - $117.35 - $23.37 - $15.98 = $351.18

4. Rent = ($97,254)(.27) = $26,258.58

5. ($2,436.18)(.06) ≈ $146.17

6. ($397.50 - $13.18 - $122.76) = $8,631.48

7. ($14.90)$(\frac{18}{2})$ = $134.10

8. ($6,500 + $52,585 + $35,700 + $1,275)(1.18) = $113,350.80

9. ($710.72 - $125.44 - $50.26 - $12.58 - $2.54)$(\frac{8}{2})$ = $2,079.60

10. (1 - .34 - .03 - .25 - .36) - $1,800 = $107.88

11. (36.69)(52) - $1,800 = $107.88

12. $20,800 − (26)($162.84+$44.26+$29.72+$13.94+$3.14) = $14,198.60

13. 8,936 + 7,821 + 8,953 + 4,297 + 9,785 + 6,579 = 46,371

14. (987)(867) − 855,729

15. 321,439 ÷ 59 ≈ 5,448.1

16. 721 ÷ .057 ≈ 12,649.1

17. (2,006-1,927) ÷ 1,927 ≈ 4%

18. Let x = number of vouchers. Then, $\frac{x}{5} = \frac{1488}{248}$. Solving, x = 30

19. Multiplying by .75 is equivalent to multiplying by $\frac{3}{4}$

20. (660)$(\frac{2}{3})$ − (660)(.60) = 44

21. Net worth = $98,695.83 - $59,238.29 = $39,457.54

22. Total Assets = $5,233.74 + $3,206.09 + $4,925.00 + $5,500.00) + $36,690.85 = $55,555.68.

23. New balance = $627.04 - $241.75 - $13.24 - $102.97 = $269.08

24. Net pay = $497.05 - $90.32 - $28.74 - $18.79 - $7.25 - $1.88 = $350.07

25. Final balance = $85.75 - $23.00 - $15.65 - $5.23 - $14.75 - $26.38 + $38.50 - $17.18 - $3.29 - $11.64 = $7.13

TEST 2

DIRECTIONS: Each question or incomplete statement is followed by several suggested answers or completions. Select the one that BEST answers the question or completes the statement. *PRINT THE LETTER OF THE CORRECT ANSWER IN THE SPACE AT THE RIGHT.*

1. The formula for computing base salary is: Earnings equals base gross plus additional gross.
   If an employee's earnings during a particular period are in the amounts of $597.45, $535.92, $639.91, and $552.83, and his base gross salary is $525.50 per paycheck, what is the TOTAL of the additional gross earned by the employee during that period?
   A. $224.11   B. $224.21   C. $224.51   D. $244.11

   1.____

2. If a lump sum death benefit is paid by the retirement system in an amount equal to 3/7 of an employee's last yearly salary of $13,486.50, the amount of the death benefit paid is MOST NEARLY
   A. $5,749.29   B. $5,759.92   C. $5,779.92   D. $5,977.29

   2.____

3. Suppose that a member has paid 15 installments on a 28-installment loan. The percentage of the number of installments paid to the retirement system is
   A. 53.57%   B. 53.97%   C. 54.57%   D. 55.37%

   3.____

4. If an employee takes a 1-month vacation during a calendar year, the percentage of the year during which he works is MOST NEARLY
   A. 90.9%   B. 91.3%   C. 91.6%   D. 92.1%

   4.____

5. Suppose that an employee took a leave of absence totaling 7 months during a calendar year.
   Assuming the employee did not take any vacation time during the remainder of that year, the percentage of the year in which he worked is MOST NEARLY
   A. 41.7%   B. 43.3%   C. 46.5%   D. 47.1%

   5.____

6. A member has borrowed $4,725 from her funds in the retirement system. If $3,213 has been repaid, the percentage of the loan which is still outstanding is MOST NEARLY
   A. 16%   B. 32%   C. 48%   D. 68%

   6.____

7. If an employee worked only 24 weeks during the year because of illness, the portion of the year he was out of work was MOST NEARLY
   A. 46%   B. 48%   C. 51%   D. 54%

   7.____

8. If an employee purchased credit for a 16-week period of service which he had prior to rejoining the retirement system, the percentage of a year he purchased credit for was MOST NEARLY
   A. 27.9%   B. 28.8%   C. 30.7%   D. 33.3%

   8.____

2 (#2)

9. If an employee contributes 2/11 of his yearly salary to his pension fund account, the percentage of his yearly salary which he contributes is MOST NEARLY
   A. 17.9%   B. 18.2%   C. 18.4%   D. 19.0%

9.____

10. In 2018, the maximum amount of income from which social security tax could be withheld (base salary) was $70,500. In 2020, the base salary was $82,500. The 2020 base salary represents a percentage increase over the 2018 base salary of APPROXIMATELY
    A. 15%   B. 16%   C. 17%   D. 18%

10.____

11. If 17.5% of an employee's salary is withheld for taxes, the one of the following which is the fraction of the salary withheld is
    A. 3/20   B. 8/35   C. 7/40   D. 4/25

11.____

12. If a person withdraws 42% of the funds from his account with the retirement system, the remaining balance represents a fraction of MOST NEARLY
    A. 7/13   B. 5/9   C. 7/12   D. 4/7

12.____

13. A property decreases in value from $45,000 to $35,000. The percent of decrease is MOST NEARLY
    A. 20.5%   B. 22.2%   C. 25.0%   D. 28.6%

13.____

14. The fraction $\frac{487}{101326}$ expressed as a decimal is MOST NEARLY
    A. .0482   B. .00481   C. .0049   D. .00392

14.____

15. The reciprocal of the sum of 2/3 and 1/6 can be expressed as
    A. 0.83   B. 1.20   C. 1.25   D. 1.50

15.____

16. Total land and building costs for a new commercial property equal $50 per square foot.
    If the investors expect a 10 percent return on their costs, and if total operating expenses average 5 percent of total costs, annual gross rentals per square foot must be AT LEAST
    A. $7.50   B. $8.50   C. $10.00   D. $12.00

16.____

17. The formula for computing the amount of annual deposit in a compound interest bearing account to provide a lump sum at the end of a period of years is
    $X = \frac{r \cdot L}{(1+r)^{n-1}}$ (X is the amount of annual deposit, r is the rate of interest, and n is the number of years and L = lump sum).
    Using the formula, the annual amount of the deposit at the end of each year to accumulate $20,000 at the end of 3 years with interest at 2 percent on annual balances is
    A. $6,120.00   B. $6,203.33   C. $6,535.09   D. $6,666.66

17.____

18. An investor sold two properties at $150,000 each. On one he made a 2.5 percent profit. On the other, he suffered a 25 percent loss.
The NET result of his sales was
A. neither a gain nor a loss
B. a $20,000 loss
C. a $75,000 gain
D. a $75,000 loss

18.____

19. A contractor decides to install a chain fence covering the perimeter of a parcel 75 feet wide and 112 feet in depth.
Which one of the following represents the number of feet to be covered?
A. 187   B. 364   C. 374   D. 8,400

19.____

20. A builder estimates he can build an average of 4½ one-family homes to an acre. There are 640 acres to one square mile.
Which one of the following CORRECTLY represents the number of one-family homes the builder would estimate he can build on one square mile?
A. 1,280   B. 1,920   C. 2,560   D. 2,880

20.____

21. $.01059 deposit at 7 percent interest will yield $1.00 in 30 years.
If a person deposited $1,059 at 7 percent interest on April 4, 1991, which one of the following amounts would represent the worth of this deposit on March 31, 2021?
A. $100   B. $1,000   C. $10,000   D. $100,000

21.____

22. A building has an economic life of forty years.
Assuming the building depreciates at a constant annual rate, which one of the following CORRECTLY represents the yearly percentage of depreciation?
A. 2.0%   B. 2.5%   C. 5.0%   D. 7.0%

22.____

23. A building produces a gross income of $200,000 with a net income of $20,000, before mortgage charges and capital recapture. The owner is able to increase the gross income 5 percent without a corresponding increase in operating costs.
The effect upon the net income will be an INCREASE of
A. 5%   B. 10%   C. 12.5%   D. 50%

23.____

24. The present value of $1.00 not payable for 8 years, and at 10 percent interest, is $.4665.
Which of the following amounts represents the PRESENT value of $1,000 payable 8 years hence at 10 percent interest?
A. $46.65   B. $466.50   C. $4,665.00   D. $46,650.00

24.____

25. The amount of real property taxes to be levied by a city is $100 million. The assessment roll subject to taxation shows an assessed valuation of $2 billion.
Which one of the following tax rates CORRECTLY represents the tax rate to be levied per $100 of assessed valuation?
A. $.50   B. $5.00   C. $50.00   D. $500.00

25.____

KEY (CORRECT ANSWERS)

1.	A		11.	C
2.	C		12.	C
3.	A		13.	B
4.	C		14.	B
5.	A		15.	B
6.	B		16.	A
7.	D		17.	C
8.	C		18.	B
9.	B		19.	C
10.	C		20.	D

21. D
22. B
23. D
24. B
25. B

5 (#2)

SOLUTIONS TO PROBLEMS

1. $597.45 + $535.91 + $639.91 + $552.83 = $2,326.11. Then, $2,326.11 − (4)($525.50) = $224.11

2. Death benefit = ($13,486.50)$(\frac{3}{7})$ ≈ $5,779.92

3. $\frac{15}{28}$ ≈ 53.57%

4. $\frac{11}{12}$ ≈ 91.6% (closer to 91.7%)

5. $\frac{5}{12}$ ≈ 41.7%

6. ($4,725-$3,213) ÷ $4,725 = 32%

7. $\frac{28}{52}$ ≈ 54%

8. $\frac{16}{52}$ ≈ 30.7% (closer to 30.8%)

9. $\frac{2}{11}$ ≈ 18.2%

10. ($82,500 - $70,500) ÷ $70,500 = 17%

11. 17.5% = $\frac{175}{1000}$ = $\frac{7}{40}$

12. 100% - 42% = 58% = $\frac{58}{100}$ = $\frac{29}{50}$, closest to $\frac{7}{12}$ in selections

13. $\frac{\$10,000}{\$45,000}$ ≈ 22.2%

14. 487/101,216 ≈ .00481

15. $\frac{2}{3} + \frac{1}{6} = \frac{5}{6}$ Then, $1 \div \frac{5}{6} = \frac{6}{5}$ = 1.20

16. (.15)($50) = $7.50

17. x = (.02)($20,000)/[(1+.02)³ − 1] = 400 ÷ .061208 ≈ $6,535.09

18. Sold 150,000, 25% loss = paid 200,000, loss of $50,000 Sold 150,000, 25% profit = paid 120,000, profit of 30,000 − 50,000 + 30,000 = 20,000 (loss)

19. Perimeter = (2)(75) + (2)(112) = 374 ft.

20. (640)(4½) = 2,880 homes

21. (1÷.01059)(1059) = $100,000

22. 1÷4 = .025 = 2.5%

23. New gross income = ($200,000)(X1.05) = $210,000
    Then, ($210,000-$200,000) ÷ $20,000 = 50%

24. Let x = present value of $1,000. Then, $\dfrac{\$1.00}{\$.4665} = \dfrac{\$1000}{x}$
    Solving, x = $466.50

25. Let x = tax rate. Then, $\dfrac{\$100,000,000}{\$2,000,000,000} = \dfrac{x}{\$100}$
    Solving, x = $5.00

TEST 3

DIRECTIONS: Each question or incomplete statement is followed by several suggested answers or completions. Select the one that BEST answers the question or completes the statement. *PRINT THE LETTER OF THE CORRECT ANSWER IN THE SPACE AT THE RIGHT.*

1. It is found that for the past three years the average weekly number of inspections per inspector ranged from 20 inspections to 40 inspections.
   On the basis of this information, it is MOST reasonable to conclude that
   A. on the average, 30 inspections per week were made
   B. the average weekly number of inspections never fell below 20
   C. the performance of inspectors deteriorated over the three-year period
   D. the range in average weekly inspections was 60

   1.____

Questions 2-4.

DIRECTIONS: Questions 2 through 4 are to be answered on the basis of the following information.

The number of students admitted to University X in 2019 from High School Y was 268 students. This represented 13.7 percent of University X's entering freshman classes. In 2020, it is expected that University X will admit 591 students from High School Y, which is expected to represent 19.4 percent of the 2020 entering freshman classes of University X.

2. Which of the following is CLOSEST estimate of the size of University's expected 2020 entering freshman classes?
   _____ students
   A. 2,000   B. 2,500   C. 3,000   D. 3,500

   2.____

3. Of the following, the expected percentage of increase from 2019 to 2020 in the number of students graduating from High School Y and entering University X as freshmen is MOST NEARLY
   A. 5.7%   B. 20%   C. 45%   D. 120%

   3.____

4. Assume that the cost of processing admission to University X from High School Y in 2019 was an average of $28. Also, that this was 1/3 more than the average cost of processing each of the other 2019 freshmen admissions to University X.
   Then, the one of the following that MOST closely shows the total processing cost of all 2019 freshman admissions to University X is
   A. $6,500   B. $20,000   C. $30,000   D. $40,000

   4.____

5. Assume that during the fiscal year 2019-2020, a bureau produced 20% more work units than it produced in the fiscal year 2018-2019. Also assume that during the fiscal year 2019-2020 that bureau's staff was 20% smaller than it was in the fiscal year 2018-2019.

   5.____

147

On the basis of this information, it would be MOST proper to conclude that the number of work units produced per staff member in that bureau in the fiscal year 2019-2020 exceeded the number of work units produced per staff member in that bureau in the fiscal year 2018-2019 by which one of the following percentages?
   A. 20%   B. 25%   C. 40%   D. 50%

6. Assume that during the following fiscal years (FY), a bureau has received the following appropriations:
    FY 2015-2016 - $200,000
    FY 2016-2017 - $240,000
    FY 2017-2018 - $280,000
    FY 2018-2019 - $390,000
    FY 2019-2020 - $505,000

The bureau's appropriation for which one of the following fiscal years showed the LARGEST percentage of increase over the bureau's appropriation for the immediately previous fiscal year?
   A. FY 2016-2017   B. FY 2017-2018
   C. FY 2018-2019   D. FY 2010-2020

7. Assume that the number of buses (U_t) required for a given line-haul system serving the Central Business District depends upon roundtrip time (t), capacity of bus (c), and the total number of people to be moved in a peak hour (P) in the major direction, i.e., in the morning and out in the evening.
The formula for the number of buses required is $U_t =$
   A. Ptc   B. $\frac{tP}{c}$ C. $\frac{cP}{t}$ D. $\frac{ct}{P}$

8. The area, in blocks, that can be served by a single stop for any maximum walking distance is given by the following formula: $a = 2w^2$. In this formula, a = the area served by a stop and w = maximum walking distance.
If people will tolerate a walk of up to three blocks, how many stops would be needed to service an area of 288 square blocks?
   A. 9   B. 16   C. 18   D. 27

Questions 9-11.

DIRECTIONS: Questions 9 through 11 are to be answered on the basis of the following information.

In 2019, a police precinct records 456 cases of car thefts, which is 22.6 percent of all grand larcenies. In 2020, there were 560 such cases, which constituted 35% of the broader category.

9. The number of crimes in the broader category in 2020 was MOST NEARLY
   A. 1,600   B. 1,700   C. 1,960   D. 2,800

3 (#3)

10. The change from 2019 to 2020 in the number of crimes in the broader category represented MOST NEARLY a
    A. 2.5% decrease
    B. 10.1% increase
    C. 12.5% increase
    D. 20% decrease

    10.____

11. In 2020, one out of every 6 of these crimes was solved. This represents MOST NEARLY what percentage of the total number of crimes in the broader category that year?
    A. 5.8
    B. 6
    C. 9.3
    D. 12

    11.____

12. Assume that a maintenance shop does 5 brake jobs to every 3 front-end jobs. It does 8,000 jobs altogether in a 240-day year. In one day, one worker can do 3 front-end jobs or 4 brake jobs.
    About how many workers will be needed in the shop?
    A. 3
    B. 5
    C. 10
    D. 18

    12.____

13. Assume that the price of a certain item declines by 6% one year, and then increases by 5 and 10 percent, respectively, during the next two years.
    What is the OVERALL increase in price over the three-year period?
    A. 4.2
    B. 6
    C. 8.6
    D. 10.1

    13.____

14. After finding the total percent change in a price (TO) over a three-year period, as in the preceding question, one could compute the average annual percent change in the price by using the formula
    A. $(1+TC)^{1/3}$
    B. $\frac{(1+TC)}{3}$
    C. $(1+TC)^{1/3-1}$
    D. $\frac{1}{(1+TC)^{1/3}-1}$

    14.____

15. 357 is 6% of
    A. 2,142
    B. 5,950
    C. 4,140
    D. 5,900

    15.____

16. In 2019, a department bought n pieces of a certain supply item for a total of $x. In 2020, the department bought k percent fewer of the item but had to pay a total of g percent more for it.
    Which of the following formulas is CORRECT for determining the average price per item in 2020?
    A. $100\frac{xg}{nk}$
    B. $\frac{x(100+g)}{n(100-k)}$
    C. $\frac{x(100-g)}{n(100+k)}$
    D. $\frac{x}{n} - 100\frac{g}{k}$

    16.____

17. A sample of 18 income tax returns, each with 4 personal exemptions, is taken for 2019 and 2020. The breakdown is as follows in terms of income:

Average Gross Income (in thousands)	Number of Returns	
	2019	2020
40	6	2
80	10	11
120	2	5

    There is a personal deduction per exemption of $500.
    There are no other expense deductions. In addition, there is an exclusion of $3,000 for incomes less than $50,000 and $2,000 for incomes from $50,000 to $99,999.99. From $100,000 upward there is no exclusion.

    17.____

The average net taxable income for the samples in thousands for 2019 is MOST NEARLY
A. $67   B. $85   C. $10   D. $128

18. In the preceding question, the increase in average net taxable income for the sample (in thousands) between 2019 and 2020 is
A. 16   B. 20   C. 24   D. 34

19. Assume that supervisor S has four subordinates—A, B, C, and D.
The MAXIMUM number of relationships, assuming that all combinations are included, that can exist between S and his subordinates is
A. 28   B. 15   C. 7   D. 4

20. If the workmen's compensation insurance rate for clerical workers is 93 cents per $100 of wages, the total premium paid by a city whose clerical staff earns $8,765,000 is MOST NEARLY
A. $8,150   B. $81,515   C. $87,650   D. $93,765

21. Assume that a budget of $3,240,000,000 for the fiscal year beginning July 1, 2020 has been approved. A city sales tax is expected to provide $1,100,000,000; licenses, fees and sundry revenues ae expected to yield $121,600,000; the balance is to be raised from property taxes. A tax equalization board has appraised all property in the city at a fair value of $42,500,000,000. The council wishes to assess property at 60% of its fair value.
The tax rate would need to be MOST NEARLY _____ per $100 of assessed value.
A. $12.70   B. $10.65   C. $7.90   D. $4.00

22. Men's white linen handkerchiefs cost $12.90 for 3.
The cost per dozen handkerchiefs is
A. $77.40   B. $38.70   C. $144.80   D. $51.60

23. Assume that it is necessary to partition a room measuring 40 feet by 20 feet into eight smaller rooms of equal size.
Allowing no room for aisles, the MINIMUM amount of partitioning that would be needed is _____ feet.
A. 90   B. 100   C. 110   D. 140

24. Assume that two types of files have been ordered: 200 of type A and 100 of type B. When the files are delivered, the buyer discovers that 25% of each type is damaged. Of the remaining files, 20% of type A and 40% of type B are the wrong color.
The total number of files that are the WRONG COLOR is
A. 30   B. 40   C. 50   D. 60

25. In a unit of five inspectors, one inspector makes an average of 12 inspections a day, two inspectors make an average of 10 inspections a day, and two inspectors make an average of 9 inspections a day.
If in a certain week one of the inspectors who makes an average of nine inspections a day is out of work on Monday and Tuesday because of illness and all the inspectors do no inspections for half a day on Wednesday because of a special meeting, the number of inspections this unit can be expected to make in that week is MOST NEARLY

25.____

 A. 215 B. 225 C. 230 D. 250

KEY (CORRECT ANSWERS)

1. B
2. C
3. D
4. D
5. D

6. C
7. B
8. B
9. A
10. D

11. A
12. C
13. C
14. C
15. B

16. B
17. A
18. A
19. B
20. B

21. C
22. D
23. B
24. D
25. A

SOLUTIONS TO PROBLEMS

1. Since the number of weekly inspections ranged from 20 to 40, this implies that the average weekly number of inspections never fell below 20.

2. 591 ÷ 194 ≈ 3046, closest to 3,000 students

3. (591-268) ÷ 268 = 120%

4. Total processing cost = (268)(28) + (1,688)($21) = $42,952, closest to $40,000. [Note: Since 268 represents 13.7%, total freshman population = 268 ÷ .137 ≈ 1,956. Then, 1,956 − 268 = 1,688]

5. Let x = staff size in 2018-2019. Then, .80x = staff size in 2019-2020. Since the 2019-2020 staff produced 20% more work, this is represented by 1.20. However, to measure the productivity per staff member, the factor 1/.80 = 1.25 must also be used to equate the 2 staffs. Then, (1.20)(1.25) = 1.50. Thus, the 2019-2020 staff produced 50% more than the 2018-2019 staff.

6. The respective percent increases are ≈ 20%, 17%, 39%, 29%. The largest would be, over the previous fiscal year, for the current fiscal year 2018-2019

7. $\frac{P}{c}$ = number of buses needed per hour. If t = time (in hrs.), then U_t = tP.c

8. a = (2)(9) = 18 for 1 stop. Then, 288 ÷ 18 = 15 stops.

9. 560 ÷ .35 = 1600 grand larcenies.

10. 456 ÷ .226 = 2018; 560 ÷ .35 = 1600. Then, (1,600-2,018) ÷ 2,018 = -20% or a 20% decrease.

11. $(\frac{1}{6})(560) = 93\frac{1}{3}$. Then, $93\frac{1}{3}$ ÷ 1,600 = 5.8%

12. There are 5,000 brake jobs and 3,000 front-end jobs in one year.
5,000 ÷ 4 = 1,250 days, and 1,250 ÷ 240 ≈ 5.2. Also, 3,000 ÷ 3 = 1,000 days, and 1,000 ÷ 240 ≈ 4.2. Total number of workers needed ≈ 5.2 + 4.2 ≈ 10.

13. (.94)(1.05)(1.10) = 1.0857, which represents an overall increase by about 8.6%.

14. Average annual % change = $(1+TC)^{1/3} - 1 = (1.0857)^{1/3} - 1 \approx 2.8\%$.

15. 357 ÷ .06 = 5,950

16. In 2020, $(h)(1-\frac{k}{100})$ pieces cost $(x)(1 + \frac{g}{100})$ dollars. To calculate the cost for 1 piece (average cost), find the value of $[(x)(1 + \frac{G}{100})] \div [(n)(1 - \frac{K}{100})] = [(x)(100+g)/100]$. $[100/\{n(100-k)\}] = [x(100+g)]/[n(100-k)]$

17.

	#	Deductions Up to 50,000		
40,000	6	2000	3000	40,000-3,000-2,000 = 35,000 x 6
80,000	10	2000	2000	80,000-2,000-2,000 = 76,000 x 10
20,000	2	2000		= 118000 x 2

35,000 x 6 = 210,000 = 210
76,000 x 10 = 760,000 = 760
118,800 x 2 = 236,000 = 236
                        1206

1206 ÷ 18 = 67

18. 2020

		Deductions		
40,000	2	2000	3000	35,000 x 2 = 70,000
80,000	11	2000	2000	76,000 x 11 = 836,000
120,000	5	2000		118,000 x 5 = 590,000
				1,496,000

1,496,000/18 = 83,111
83,111 − 67,000 = 16,111 = most nearly 16 (in thousands)

19. We are actually looking for the number of different groups of different sizes involving S. This reduces to $_4C_1 + {_4C_2} + {_4C_2} + {_4C_4}$ = 4 + 6 + 4 + 1 = 15. The notation $_nC_r$ means combinations of n things taken R at a time = [(n)(n-1)(n-2)(…)(n-R+1)]/[(R)(R-1)(…)(1)]. The 15 groups are: SA, SB, SC, SD, SAB, SAC, SAD, SBC, SBD, SCD, SABC, SABD, SACD, SBCD, SABCD.

20. Let x = total premiums. Then, $\frac{.93}{100} = \frac{X}{8,765,000}$ Solving, x = $81,515

21. The balance, raised from property taxes, = $3,240,000,000 - $1,100,000,000 − $121,600,000 = $2,018,400,000. Now, (.60)($42,500,000,000) = $25,500,000. The tax rate per $100 of assessed value = ($2,018,400,000)($100)(/$25,500,000,00 = $7.90.

22. A dozen costs ($12.90)($\frac{12}{3}$) = $51.60.

23. (40(20) ÷ 8 = 100 ft.

24. Total number of wrong-color files = (200)(.75)(.20)+(100)(.75)(.40) = 60

25. Weekly number of inspections = (12×5) + (10×5) + (10×5) + (9×5) + 9×5) = 250
Subtract: 9 Monday, 9 Tuesday, 25 Wednesday
Total: 250 − 9 − 9 − 25 = 207
Closest entry is choice A.

BASIC FUNDAMENTALS OF BOOKKEEPING

CONTENTS

		Page
I.	INTRODUCTION	1
II.	REQUIREMENTS OF A GOOD RECORD SYSTEM	1
III.	IMPORTANT BOOKKEEPING RECORDS	2
	A. Bookkeeping Books	2
	B. Financial Reports	2
	C. The Balance Sheet	3
	1. Assets	3
	a. Current Assets	4
	b. Fixed Assets	4
	c. Other Assets	5
	2. Liabilities	5
	a. Current Liabilities	5
	b. Long-Term Liabilities	6
	D. The Income Statement	6
	1. Sales	7
	2. Cost of Goods Sold	7
	3. Gross Margin	7
	4. Net Profit	8
IV.	OTHER RECORDS	9
	A. Daily Summary of Sales and Cash Receipts	9
	R. Petty Cash and Charge Funds	10
	C. Record of Cash Disbursement	11
	D. Accounts Receivable Records	12
	E. Property Records and Depreciation	12
	F. Schedule of Insurance Coverage	13
V.	CONCLUSION	13

BASIC FUNDAMENTALS OF BOOKKEEPING

I. INTRODUCTION

Why keep records? If you are a typical small-business man, your answer to this question is probably, "Because the Government requires it!" And if the question comes in the middle of a busy day, you may add a few heartfelt words about the amount of time you have to spend on records--just for the Government.

Is it "just for the Government," though? True, regulations of various governmental agencies have greatly increased the record-keeping requirements of business. But this may be a good thing for the small-business man, overburdened though he is.

Many small-business managers don't recognize their bookkeeping records for what they can really do. Their attitudes concerning these records are typified by one businessman who said, "Records only tell you what you have done in the past. It's too late to do anything about the past; I need to know what is going to happen in the future. "However, the past can tell us much about what may happen in the future; and, certainly we can profit in the future from knowledge of our past mistakes.

These same managers may recognize that records are necessary in filing their tax returns, or that a banker requires financial information before he will lend money, but often their appreciation of their bookkeeping systems ends at this point. However, there are many ways in which the use of such information can help an owner manage his business more easily and profitably.

The small-businessman is confronted with an endless array of problems and decisions every day. Sound decisions require an informed manager; and many management problems can be solved with the aid of the right bookkeeping information.

II. REQUIREMENTS OF A GOOD RECORD SYSTEM

Of course, to get information that is really valuable to you--to get the right information--requires a good bookkeeping system. What are the characteristics of a good system? You want one that is simple and easy to understand, reliable, accurate, consistent, and one that will get the information to you promptly.

A simple, well-organized system of records, regularly kept up, can actually be a timesaver--by bringing order out of disorder. Furthermore, competition is very strong in today's business areas. A businessman needs to know almost on a day-to-day basis where his business stands profit wise, which lines of merchandise or services are the most or the least profitable, what his working-capital needs are, and many other details. He can get this information with reasonable certainty only if he has a good recordkeeping system—one that gives him all the information he needs.

In setting up a recordkeeping system that is tailored to your business, you will probably need the professional help of a competent accountant. And you may want to retain the services of an accountant or bookkeeper to maintain these records. But it is your job to learn to interpret this information and to use it effectively.

One of the reasons that many managers have misgivings about keeping records is that they don't understand them or know how they can be used. The owner or manager of a small business may be an expert in his line of business; however, he generally does not have a background in keeping records. So he is usually confused. What we will try to do in this discussion is to highlight the "why and what of bookkeeping." In so-doing, we aim to eliminate that confusion.

III. IMPORTANT BOOKKEEPING RECORDS

Today's managers should be familiar with the following bookkeeping records:

- Journal
- Ledgers
- Balance sheet
- Income statement
- Funds flow statement

We will discuss each of them in turn. In addition, a brief discussion of other supporting records will be made.

A. Bookkeeping Books

The journal, which accountants call "the book of original entry," is a chronological record of all business transactions engaged in by the firm. It is simply a financial diary. The ledgers, or "books of account," are more specialized records used to classify the journal entries according to like elements. For example, there would be a separate ledger account for cash entries, another for all sales, and still others for items such as accounts receivable, inventory, and loans. All transactions are first entered in the journal, and then posted in the appropriate ledger. The journal and ledgers are of minor importance to the manager in making decisions, but they play a vital role for the accountant or bookkeeper because the more important accounting statements such as the balance sheet and the income statement are derived from the journal and ledger entries.

B. Financial Reports

The two principal financial reports in most businesses are the balance sheet and the income statement. Up to about 25 or 30 years ago, the balance sheet was generally considered to be the most important financial statement. Until that time, it was generally used only as a basis for the extension of credit and bank loans, and very little thought was given to the information it offered that might be important in „the operation and management of the business. Starting about 30 years ago, emphasis has gradually shifted to the income statement. Today the balance sheet and income statements are of equal importance, both to the accountant in financial reporting and to the manager faced with a multitude of administrative problems.

Essentially, the balance sheet shows what a business has, what it owes, and the investment of the owners in the business. It can be likened to a snapshot, showing the financial condition of the business *at a certain point in time*. The income statement, on the other hand, is a summary of business operations for a certain period--usually between two balance sheet dates. The income statement can be compared to a moving picture; it indicates the activity of a business *over a certain period of time*. In very general terms, the balance sheet tells you where you are, and the income statement tells you how you got there since the last time you had a balance sheet prepared.

Both the balance sheet and income statement can be long and complicated documents. Both accountants and management need some device that can highlight the critical financial information contained in these complex documents. Certain standard ratios or relationships between items on the financial statements have been developed that allow the interested parties to quickly determine important characteristics of the firm's activities. There are many relationships that might be important in a specific business that would not be as significant in another.

Other devices of the bookkeeper, such as funds flow statements, daily summaries of sales and cash receipts, the checkbook, account receivable records, property depreciation records, and insurance scheduling have also been found useful to management.

C. The Balance Sheet

As stated earlier, the balance sheet represents what a business has, what it owes, and the investment of the owners. The things of value that the business has or owns are called *assets*. The claims of creditors against these assets are called liabilities. The value of the assets over and above the *liabilities* can be justifiably called the owner's claim. This amount is usually called the owner's equity (or net worth).

This brings us to the *dual-aspect concept* of bookkeeping. The balance sheet is set up to portray two aspects of each entry or event recorded on it. For each thing of value, or asset, there is a claim against that asset. The recognition of this concept leads to the balance sheet formula: ASSETS = LIABILITIES + OWNER'S EQUITY. Let's take an example to clarify this concept. Suppose Joe Smith decides to start a business. He has $2,000 cash in the bank. He got this sum by investing $1,000 of his own money and by borrowing $1,000 from the bank. If he were to draw up a balance sheet at this time, he would have assets of $2 000 cash balanced against a liability claim of $1,000 and an owner's claim of $1,000. Using the balance sheet formula: $2,000 = $1,000 + $1,000. This formula means there will always be a balance between assets and claims against them. The balance sheet *always* balances unless there has been a clerical error.

The balance sheet is usually, constructed in a two-column format. The assets appear in the left hand column and the claims against the assets (the liabilities and owner's equity) are in the right hand column. Other formats are sometimes used; but, in any case, the balance sheet is-an itemized or detailed account of the basic formula: as sets = liabilities + owner's equity.

1. Assets

I have been speaking of assets belonging to the business. Of course, the business does not legally own anything unless it is organized as a corporation. But regardless of whether the business is organized as a proprietorship, a partnership, or a corporation, all business bookkeeping should be reckoned and accounted apart from the accounting of the personal funds and assets of, its owners.

Assets are typically classified into three categories:

- Current assets
- Fixed assets
- Other assets

a. Current Assets

For bookkeeping purposes, the term "current assets" is used to designate cash and other assets which can be converted to cash during the normal operating cycle of the business (usually one year). The distinction between current assets and noncurrent assets is important since lenders and others pay much attention to the total amount of current assets. The size of current assets has a significant relationship to the stability of the business because it represents, to some degree, the amount of cash that might be raised quickly to meet current obligations. Here are some of the major current asset items.

> **Cash** consists of funds that are immediately available to use without restrictions. These funds are usually in the form of checking-account deposits in banks, cash-register money, and petty cash. Cash should be large enough to meet obligations that are immediately due.
>
> **Accounts, receivable** are Arricnint8 'Owed to the company by its customers as a result of sales. Essentially, these accounts are the result of granting credit to customers. They may take the form of charge accounts where no interest or service charge is made, or they may be of an interest-bearing nature. In either case they are a drain on working capital. The more that is outstanding on accounts receivable, the less money that is available to meet current needs. The trick with accounts receivable is to keep them small enough so as not to endanger working capital, but large enough to keep from losing sales to credit-minded customers.
>
> **Inventory** is defined as those items which are held for sale in the ordinary course of business, or which are to be consumed in the production of goods and services that are to be sold. Since accountants are conservative by nature, they include in inventory only items that are salable, and these items are valued at cost or market value, whichever is lower? Control of inventory and inventory expenses is one of management's most important jobs-particularly for retailers-- and good bookkeeping records in this area are particularly useful.
>
> **Prepaid expenses** represent assets, paid for in advance, but whose usefulness will usually expire in a short time. A good example of this is prepaid insurance. A business pays for insurance protection in advance--usually three to five years in advance. The right to this protection is a thing of value--an asset--and the unused portion can be refunded or converted to cash.

b. Fixed Assets

"Fixed assets" are items owned by the business that have relatively long life. These assets are used in the production or sale of other goods and services. If they were held for resale, they would be classified as inventory, even though they might be long-lived assets.

Normally these assets are composed of land, buildings, and equipment. Some companies lump their fixed assets into one entry on their balance sheets, but you gain more information and can exercise more control over these assets if they are listed separately on the balance sheet. You may even want to list various types of equipment separately.

There is one other aspect of fixed-asset bookkeeping that we should discuss--and this is depreciation. Generally fixed assets-with the exception of land-depreciate, or decrease in value with the passing of time. That is, a building or piece of equipment that is five years old is not worth as much as it was when it was new. For a balance sheet to show the true value of these assets, it must reflect this loss in value. For both tax and other accounting purposes, the businessman is allowed to deduct this loss in value each year over the useful life of the assets, until, over a period of time, he has deducted the total cost of the asset. There are several accepted ways to calculate how much of an asset's value can be deducted for depreciation in a given year. Depreciation is allowed as an expense item on the income statement, and we will discuss this fact later.

c. Other Assets

"Other assets" is a miscellaneous category. It accounts for any investments of the firm in securities, such as stock in other private companies or government bonds. It also includes intangible assets such as goodwill, patents, and franchise costs. Items in the "other-assets" category have a longer life than current-asset items.

2. Liabilities

"Liabilities" are the amounts of money owed by the business to people other than the owners. They are claims against the company's total assets, although they are not claims against any specific asset, except in the cases of some mortgages and equipment liens. Essentially, liabilities are divided into two classes:

Current liabilities

Long-term Liabilities

a. Current Liabilities

The term "current liabilities" is used to describe those claims of outsiders on the business that will fall, due within one year. Here are some of the more important current-liabilities entries on the balance sheet:

Accounts payable represent the amounts owed to vendors, wholesalers, and other suppliers from whom the business has bought items on account. This includes any items of inventory, supply, or capital equipment which have been purchased on credit and for which payment is expected in less than one year. For example, a retail butcher purchased 500 pounds of meat for $250, a quantity of fish that cost $50, and a new air-conditioning unit for his store for $450. He bought all of these items on 60-day terms. His accounts payable were increased by $750. Of course, at the same time his inventory increased by $300 and his fixed assets rose by $450. If he had paid cash for these items, his accounts payable would not have been affected, but his cash account would have decreased by $750, thus keeping the accounting equation in balance.

Short-term loans, which are sometimes called notes payable, are loans from individuals, banks, or other lending institutions which fall due within a year. Also included in this category is the portion of any long-term debt that will come due within a year.

Accrued expenses are obligations which the company has incurred, but for 'which there has been no formal bill or invoice as yet. An example of this is accrued taxes. The owner knows the business has the obligation to pay taxes; and they are accruing or accumulating each day. The

fact that the taxes do not have to be paid until a later date does not diminish the obligation. Another example of accrued expenses is wages. Although wages are paid weekly or monthly, they are being earned hourly or daily and constitute a valid claim against the company.
An accurate balance sheet will reflect these obligations.

b. Long-Term Liabilities

Claims of outsiders on the business that do not come due within one year are called "long-term liabilities" or, simply, "other liabilities." Included in this category are bonded indebtedness, mortgages, and long-term loans from individuals, banks, and others from whom the business may borrow money, such as the SBA. As was stated before, any part of a long-term debt that falls due within one year from the date of the balance sheet would be recorded as part of the current liabilities of the business.

Owner's Equity

The owner's equity section of the balance sheet is located on the right-hand side underneath the listing of the liabilities. It shows the claims of the owners on the company. Essentially, this is a balancing figure--that is, the owners get what's left of the assets after the liability claims have been recognized. This is an obvious definition, if you will remember the balance sheet formula. Transposing the formula as we learned it a few minutes ago, it becomes Assets - Liabilities = Owner's Equity. In the case where the business is a sole proprietorship, it is customary to show owner's equity as one entry with no distinction being made between the owner's initial investment and the accumulated retained earnings of the business. However, in the case of an incorporated business, there are entries for stockholders' claims as well as for earnings that have been accumulated and retained in the business. Of course, if the business has been consistently operating at a loss, the proprietor's claim may be less than his initial investment. And, in the case of a corporation, the balancing account could be operating deficit rather than retained earnings.

If we put together the entries we have been talking about, we have a complete balance sheet. There is a lot of information in this statement. It tells you just what you have and where it is. It also tells you what you owe. You need this information to help you decide what actions you should take in running your business. If you need to borrow money, the banker or anyone else from whom you borrow will want to look at your balance sheet.

D. THE INCOME STATEMENT

In recent years the income statement has become as important as the balance sheet as a financial and management record. It is also called the profit and loss statement, or simply the P and L statement. This financial record summarizes the activities of the company over a period of time, listing those that can be expressed in dollars. That is, it reports the revenues of the company and the expenses incurred in. obtaining the revenues, and it shows the profit or loss resulting from these activities. The income statement complements the balance sheet. While balance sheet analysis shows the change in position of the company at the end of accounting periods, the income statement shows how the change took place during the accounting period. Both reports 'are necessary for a full understanding of the operation of the business.

The income statement for particular company should be tailored to fit the activities of that company, and there is no rigid format that must be followed in constructing this report. But the following categories are found in most income statements.

1. Sales

The major activity of most businesses is the sales of products and services, and the bulk of revenue comes from sales. In recording sales, the figure used is net sales-that is, sales after discounts, allowances, and returned goods have been accounted for.

2. Cost of Goods Sold

Another important item, in calculating profit or loss, is the cost of the goods that the company has sold. This item is difficult to calculate accurately. Since the goods sold come from inventory, and since the company may have bought parts of its inventory at several prices, it is hard to determine exactly what is the cost of the particular part of the inventory that was sold. In large companies, and particularly in companies using cost accounting, there are some rather complicated methods of determining "cost of goods sold, " but they are beyond the scope of this presentation. However, there is a simple, generally accepted way of calculating cost of goods sold. In this method you simply add the net amount of purchases during the accounting period to your beginning inventory, and subtract from this your ending inventory. The result can be considered cost-of-goods sold.

3. Gross Margin

The difference between sales and cost of goods sold is called the "gross margin" or gross profit. This item is often expressed as a percentage of sales, as well as in dollar figures. The percentage gross margin is a very significant figure because it indicates what the average markup is on the merchandise sold. So, if a manager knows his expenses as a percentage of sales, he can calculate the mark up necessary to obtain the gross margin he needs for a profitable operation. It is surprising how many small-business men do not know what basis to use in setting markups. In fact, with the various, allowances, discounts, and markdowns that a business may offer, many managers do not know what their markup actually is. The gross margin calculation on the income statement can help the manager with this problem.

There are other costs of running a business besides the cost of the goods sold. When you use the simple method of determining costs of goods sold, these costs are called "expenses."

For example, here are some typical expenses: salaries and wages, utilities, depreciation, interest, administrative expenses, supplies, bad debts, advertising, and taxes--Federal, State, and local. These are typical expenses, but there are many other kinds of expenses that may be experienced by other businesses. For example, we have shown in the Blank Company's balance sheet that he owns his own land and building--with a mortgage, of course. These accounts for part of his depreciation and interest expenses, but for a company that rents its quarters, rent would appear as the expense item. Other common expenses are traveling expense, commissions, and advertising.

Most of these expense items are self-explanatory, but there are a few that merit further comment. For one thing, the salary or draw of the owner should be recorded among the expenses--either as a part of salaries and wages or as part of administrative expenses. To exclude the owner's compensation from expenses distorts the actual profitability of the business. And, if the company is incorporated, it would reduce the allowable tax deductions of the business. Of course, for tax purposes, the owner's salary or draw in a proprietorship or partnership is considered as part of the net profit.

We discussed depreciation when we examined the balance sheet, and we mentioned that it was an item of expense. Although no money is actually paid out for depreciation, it is a real expense because it represents reduction in the value of the assets.

The most important thing about expenses is to be sure to include all of the expenses that the business incurs. This not only helps the owner get a more accurate picture of his operation but it allows him to take full advantage of the tax deductions that legitimate expenses offer.

4. Net Profit

In a typical company when expenses are subtracted from gross margin, the remainder is profit. However, if the business receives revenue from sources other than sales, such as rents, dividends on securities held by the company, or interest on money loaned by the company, it is added to profit at this point. For bookkeeping purposes, the resulting profit is labeled "profit before taxes." This is the figure from which Federal income taxes are figured. If the business is a proprietorship, the profit is taxed as part of the owner's income. If the business is a corporation, the profits may be taxed on the basis of the corporate income tax schedule. When income taxes have been accounted for, the resultant entry is called "net profit after taxes," or simply "net profit." This is usually the final entry on the income statement.

Another financial record which managers can use to advantage is the funds flow statement. This statement is also called statement of sources and uses of funds and sometimes the "where got--where gone" statement. Whatever you call it, a record of sources and uses of past funds is useful to the manager. He can use it to evaluate past performance, and as a guide in determining future uses and sources of money.

When we speak of "funds" we do not necessarily mean actual "dollars" or "cash." Although accounting records are all written in monetary terms, they do not always involve an exchange of money. Many times in business transactions, it is credit rather than dollars that changes hands. Therefore, when we speak of funds flow, we are speaking of exchanges of *economic values* rather than merely the physical flow of dollars.

Basically, funds are used to: increase assets and reduce liabilities. They are also sometimes used to reduce owner's equity. An example of this would be the use of company funds to buy up outstanding stock or to buy out a partner. Where do funds come from? The three basic sources of funds are a reduction in assets, increases in liabilities, and increased owner's equity. All balance sheet items can be affected by the obtaining and spending of company fund's.

To examine the construction and use of a funds flow statement, let's take another look at the Blank Company. Here we show comparative balance sheets for two one-year periods. For the sake of simplicity, we have included only selected items from the balance sheets for analysis. Notice that the company gained funds by:

reducing cash $300,

increasing accounts payable $400,

putting $500 more owner's equity in the business, and

plowing back $800 of the profit into the business.

These funds were used to:

increase accounts receivable $300,
increase inventory $200,

buy $500 worth of equipment, and

pay off $1,000 worth of long-term debt.

This funds flow statement has indicated to Mr. Blank where he has gotten his funds and how he has spent them. He can analyze these figures in the light of his plans and objectives and take appropriate action.

For example, if Mr. Blank wants to answer the question "Should I buy new capital equipment?" a look at his funds flow statement would show him his previous sources of funds, and it would give him a clue as to whether he could obtain funds for any new equipment.

IV. OTHER RECORDS

Up to this point, we have been talking about the basic types of bookkeeping records. In addition, we have discussed the two basic financial statements of a business: the balance sheet and the profit and loss statement. Now let us give our attention briefly to some other records which are very helpful to running a business successfully.

One element that appears on the balance sheet which I believe we can agree is important is cash. Because it is the lifeblood of all business, cash should be controlled and safeguarded at all times. The daily summary of sales and cash receipts and the checkbook are used by many manager s of small businesses to help provide that control.

A. Daily Summary of Sales and Cash. Receipts

Not all businesses summarize their daily transactions. However, a daily summary of sales and cash receipts is a very useful tool for checking how your business is doing on a day-to-day basis. At the close of each day's business, the actual cash on hand is counted and "balanced" against the total of the receipts recorded for the day. This balancing is done by means of the Daily Summary of Sales and Cash Receipts. This is a recording of every cash 'receipt and every charge sale, whether you use a cash register or sales checks or both. If you have more than one cash register, a daily summary should be prepared for each; the individual cash-register summaries can then be combined into one overall summary for convenience in handling.

In the daily summary form used for purposes of illustration, (see Handout), the first section, "Cash Receipts," records the total of all cash taken in during the day from whatever source. This is the cash that must be accounted for over and above, the amount in the change and/ or petty cash funds. We shall touch upon these two funds later. The three components of cash receipts are (1) cash sales, (2) collections on accounts, and (3) miscellaneous receipts.

The daily total of cash sales is obtained from a cash-register tape reading or, if no cash register is used, by totaling the cash-sales checks.

For collections on accounts, an individual record of each customer payment on account should be kept, whether or not these collections are rung up on a cash register. The amount to be entered on the daily summary is obtained by totaling these individual records.

Miscellaneous receipts are daily cash transactions that cannot be classified as sales or collections. They might include refunds from suppliers for overpayment, advertising rebates or allowances, . collections of rent from sub-leases or concessions, etc. Like collections on account, a sales check or memo should be made out each time such cash is taken in.

The total of daily cash receipts to be accounted for on the daily summary is obtained by adding cash sales, collections on account, and miscellaneous receipts.

The second section, "Cash on Hand," of a daily summary is a count of the cash actually on hand plus the cash that is represented by petty cash slips. The daily summary provides for counts of your total coins, bills, and checks as well as the amount expended for petty cash. The latter is determined by adding the amounts on the individual petty cash slips. By totaling all four of these counts, you obtain the total cash accounted for. To determine the amount of your daily cash deposit, you deduct from the "total cash accounted for" the total of the petty cash and change funds.

Cash to be deposited on the daily summary should always equal the total receipts to be accounted for minus the fixed amount of your petty cash and change funds. If it does not, all the work in preparing the daily summary should be carefully checked. Obviously, an error in giving change, in ringing up a sale, or neglecting to do so, will result in a cash shortage or overage. The daily summary provides spaces for such errors so that the proper entries can be made in your bookkeeping records. The last section of your daily summary, "Sales," records the total daily sales broken down into (1) cash sales and (2) charge sales.

As soon as possible after the daily summary has been completed, all cash for deposit should be taken to the bank. A duplicate deposit slip, stamped by the bank, should be kept with the daily summary as evidence that the deposit was made.

B. Petty Cash and Charge Funds

The record of, daily, sales and cash. Receipts which we have just described. is designed. on the assumption that a petty cash fund and a change cash fund, or a combination change and petty cash fund, are used. All businesses, small and large, have day-to-day expenses that are so small they do not warrant the drawing of a check. Good management practice calls for careful control of such expenses. The petty cash fund provides such control. It is a sum of money which is obtained by drawing a check to provide several days, a week's, or a month's need of cash for small purchases. The type of business will determine the amount of the petty cash fund.

Each time a payment is made from the petty cash, a slip should be made out. If an invoice or receipt is available, it should be attached to the petty- cash slip. The slips and the money ordinarily, but not necessarily, are kept separate from other currency in your cash till, drawer, or register. At all times, the total of unspent petty cash and petty cash slips should equal the fixed amount of the fund. When the total of the slips approaches the fixed amount of the petty cash fund, a check is drawn for the total amount of the slips. The money from this check is used to bring the fund back to its fixed amount.

In addition to a petty cash fund, some businesses that receive cash in over-the-counter transactions have a change fund. The amount needed for making change varies with the size and type of business, and, in some cases, with the days of the week. Control of the money in your change fund will be made-easier, however, if you set a fixed amount large enough to meet all the ordinary change-making needs of your business. Each day, when the day's receipts are balanced and prepared for a bank deposit, you will retain bills and coins totaling the fixed amount of the fund for use the following day. Since you had that amount on hand before you made the day's first sale, the entire amount of the day's receipts will still be available for your bank deposit.

In some cases, the petty cash fund is kept in a petty cash box or safe, apart from the change fund. However, the same fund can serve for both petty cash and change. For example, if you decide that you need $50 for making change and $25 for petty cash, one $75 fund can be used. Whenever, in balancing the day's operations, you see that the petty cash slips total more than $25, you can write a petty cash check for the amount of the slips.

C. Record of Cash Disbursement

To safeguard your cash, it is recommended that all receipts be deposited in a bank account and that all disbursements, except those made from the petty cash fund, are made by drawing a check on that account. Your bank account should be used exclusively for business transactions. If your business is typical, you will have to write checks for merchandise purchases, employee's salaries, rent, utilities, payroll taxes, petty cash, and various other expenses. Your check stubs will serve as a record of cash disbursements.

The checkbook stub should contain all the details of the disbursement including the date, payee, amount and purpose of the payment. In addition, a running balance of the amount you have in your bank account should be maintained by subtracting the amount of each check from the existing balance after the previous check was drawn. If the checks of your checkbook are prenumbered, it is important to mark plainly in the stub when a check is voided for one reason or another.

Each check should have some sort of written document to support it--an invoice, petty-cash voucher, payroll summary and so on. Supporting documents should be approved by you or someone you have authorized before a check is drawn. They should be marked paid and filed after the check is drawn.

Periodically, your bank will send you a statement of your account and return cancelled checks for which money has been withdrawn from your account. It is important that you reconcile your records with those of the bank. This means that the balances in your checkbook and on the bank statement should agree. Uncashed checks must be deducted from your checkbook balance and deposits not recorded on the bank statement must be added to its balance in order to get both balances to agree.

D. Accounts Receivable Records

If you extend credit to your customers, you must keep an accurate account of your credit sales not only in total as you have done on the daily summary but also by the amount that each individual customer owes you. Moreover, you must be systematic about billings and collections. This is important. It results in better relations with your charge customers and in fewer losses from bad debts.

The simplest method of handling accounts receivable--other than just keeping a file of sales-slip carbons--is to have an account sheet for each credit customer. Charge sales and payments on charge sales are posted to each customer sheet. Monthly billing to each of your charge customers should be made from their individual account sheets.

At least two or three times a year, your accounts receivable should be aged. You do this by posting each customer's account and his unpaid charges in columns according to age. These columns are labeled: not due; 1 to 30 days past due; 31 to 60 days past due; 61 to 90 days past due; etc. This analysis will indicate those customers who are not complying with your credit terms.

E. Property Records and Depreciation

In every type of business, it is necessary to purchase property and equipment from time to time. This property usually will last for several years, so it would be unrealistic to show the total amount of the purchase as an expense in any one year. Therefore, when this property is set up in the books as an asset, records must be kept to decrease its value over its life. This decrease is known as depreciation. I have mentioned this before during this talk. The amount of the decrease in value in one year, that is, the depreciation, is charged as an expense for the year.

I am talking about this expense, particularly, because no cash is paid out for it. It is a non-cash, not-out-of-pocket expense. You don't have to hand over actual money at the end of the month.

Records should be kept of this because, otherwise, there is a danger that this expense will be overlooked. Yet it is impossible to figure true profit or loss without considering it. When you deduct the depreciation expense from your firm's income, you reduce your tax liabilities. When you put this depreciation expense into a depreciation allowance account, you are keeping score on your "debt" to depreciation.

In a barber shop, to take a simple example, depreciation of its chairs, dryers, and clippers at the end of the year amounts to $136. You deduct this $136 from the shop's income, in this case, to pay the debt credited to your depreciation allowance account. Since this equipment has the same depreciation value each year, the depreciation allowance account at the end of 3 years will show that a total of $408 worth of equipment has been used up. The books of the barbershop therefore show an expense of $408 which actually has not been spent. It is in the business to replace the depreciated equipment. If replacement will not take place in the immediate future, the money can be used in inventory, or in some other way to generate more sales or profits.

How you handle this money depends on many things. You can set it aside at a low interest rate and have that much less operating money. Or you can put it to work in your business where it will help to keep your finances healthy.

Remember, however, that you must be prepared financially when it is time to buy replacement equipment. A depreciation allowance account on your books can help to keep you aware of this. It helps you keep score on how much depreciation or replacement money you are using in your business.

Keeping score with a depreciation allowance account helps you to know when you need to convert some of your assets into replacement cash. If, for example, you know on January 1 that Your delivery truck will be totally depreciated by June 30, you can review the situation objectively. You can decide whether you ought to use the truck longer or replace it. If you decide to replace it, then you can plan to accumulate the cash, and time the purchase in order to make the best deal.

F. Schedule of Insurance Coverage

The schedule of insurance coverage is prepared to indicate the type of coverage and the amount presently in force. This schedule should list all the insurance carried by your business-- fire and extended coverage, theft, liability, life, business interruption and so forth.

This schedule should be prepared to present the following: name of insurance company, annual premium, expiration date, type of coverage, amount of coverage, asset insured, and estimated current value of asset insured.

An analysis of this schedule should indicate the adequacy of insurance coverage. A review of this schedule with your insurance agent is suggested.

V. CONCLUSION

During the brief time allotted to this subject of the basic fundamentals of bookkeeping, we have just scratched its surface. What we have tried to do is to inform you, as small-business managers, of the importance of good records. We have described the components of the important records that you must have if you are going to manage your business efficiently and profitably. In addition, we have brought to your attention some of the subsidiary records that will aid you in managing your business.

There are other records such as breakeven charts, budgets, cost accounting systems, to mention a few, which can also benefit the progressive manager. However, we do not have the time even to give you the highlights of those management tools. Your accountant can assist you in learning to understand and use them. Moreover, he can help you to develop and use the records we have discussed. For further information about them, you also can read the publications of the Small Business Administration, some of which are available to you free of charge.

By reading and using the accounting advice available to you, you can make sure that you have the right records to improve your managing skill and thereby increase your profits.

BASIC FUNDAMENTALS OF A FINANCIAL STATEMENT

TABLE OF CONTENTS

	PAGE
Commentary	1
Financial Reports	1
Balance Sheet	1
Assets	1
The ABC Manufacturing Co., Inc.	
Consolidated Balance Sheet – December 31	2
Fixed Assets	3
Depreciation	4
Intangibles	4
Liabilities	5
Reserves	6
Capital Stock	6
Surplus	6
What Does the Balance Sheet Show?	7
Net Working Capital	7
Inventory and Inventory Turnover	8
Net Book Value of Securities	8
Proportion of Bonds, Preferred and Common Stock	9
The Income Account	10
Cost of Sales	11
The ABC Manufacturing Co., Inc.	
Consolidated Income and Earned Surplus – December 31	11
Maintenance	12
Interest Charges	13
Net Income	13
Analyzing the Income Account	14
Interest Coverage	15
Earnings Per Common Share	15
Stock Prices	16
Important Terms and Concepts	17

BASIC FUNDAMENTALS OF A FINANCIAL STATEMENT

COMMENTARY

The ability to read and understand a financial statement is a basic requirement for the accountant, auditor, account clerk, bookkeeper, bank examiner, budget examiner, and, of course, for the executive who must manage and administer departmental affairs.

FINANCIAL REPORTS

Are financial reports really as difficult as all that? Well, if you know they are not so difficult because you have worked with them before, this section will be of auxiliary help for you. However, if you find financial statements a bit murky, but realize their great importance to you, we ought to get along fine together. For "mathematics," all we'll use is fourth-grade arithmetic.

Accountants, like all other professionals, have developed a specialized vocabulary. Sometimes this is helpful and sometimes plain confusing (like their practice of calling the income account, "Statement of Profit and Loss," when it is bound to be one or the other). But there are really only a score or so technical terms that you will have to get straight in mind. After that is done, the whole foggy business will begin to clear and in no time at all you'll be able to talk as wisely as the next fellow.

BALANCE SHEET

Look at the sample balance sheet printed on Page 2, and we'll have an insight into how it is put together. This particular report is neither the simplest that could be issued, nor the most complicated. It is a good average sample of the kind of report issues by an up-to-date manufacturing company.

Note particularly that the balance sheet represents the situation as it stood on one particular day, December 31, not the record of a year's operation. This balance sheet is broken into two parts on the left are shown *ASSETS* and on the right *LIABILITIES*. Under the asset column, you will find listed the value of things the company owns or are owed to the company. Under liabilities are listed the things the company owes to others, plus reserves, surplus, and the stated value of the stockholders' interest in the company.

One frequently hears the comment, "Well, I don't see what a good balance sheet is anyway, because the assets and liabilities are always the same whether the company is successful or not."

It is true that they always balance and, by itself, a balance sheet doesn't tell much until it is analyzed. Fortunately, we can make a balance sheet tell its story without too much effort—often an extremely revealing story, particularly, if we compare the records of several years.

ASSETS

The first notation on the asset side of the balance sheet is *CURRENT ASSETS* (Item 1). In general, current assets include cash and things that can be turned into cash in a hurry, or that, in the normal course of business, will be turned into cash in the reasonably near future, usually within a year.

Item 2 on our sample sheet is *CASH*. Cash is just what you would expect—bills and silver in the till and money on deposit in the bank.

UNITED STATES GOVERNMENT SECURITIES is Item 3. The general practice is to show securities listed as current assets at cost or market value, whichever is lower. The figure, for all reasonable purposes, represents the amount by which total cash could be easily increased if the company wanted to sell these securities.

The next entry is *ACCOUNTS RECEIVABLE* (Item 4). Here we find the total amount of money owed to the company by its regular business creditors and collectable within the next year. Most of the money is owed to the company by its customers for goods that the company delivered on credit. If this were a department store instead of a manufacturer, what you owed the store on our charge account would be included here. Because some people fail to pay their bills, the company sets up a reserve for doubtful accounts, which it subtracts from all the money owed.

THE ABC MANUFACTURING COMPANY, INC.
CONSOLIDATED BALANCE SHEET – DECEMBER 31

Item			Item		
1. CURRENT ASSETS			16. CURRENT LIABILITIES		
2. Cash			17. Accts. Payable		$300,000
3. U.S. Government Securities			18. Accrued Taxes		800,000
4. Accounts Receivable (less reserves)		2,000,000	19. Accrued Wages, interest and Other Expenses		370,000
5. Inventories (at lower of cost or market)		2,000,000	20. Total Current Liabilities		$1,470,000
6. Total Current Assets		$7,000,000	21. FIRST MORTGAGE SINKING FUND BONDS, 3½ % DUE 2020		$2,000,000
7. INVESTMENT IN AFFILIATED COMPANY Not consolidated (at cost, not in excess of net assets)		200,000	22. RESERVE FOR CONTINGENCIES		200,000
8. OTHER INVESTMENTS At cost, less than market		100,000	23. CAPITAL STOCK: 24. 5% Preferred Stock (authorized and issued 10,000 shares of $100 par shares of $100 (par value)	$1,000,000	
9. PLANT IMPROVEMENT FUND		550,000			
10. PROPERTY, PLANT AND EQUIPMENT: Cost	$8,000,000		25. Common stock (authorized and issued 400,000 shares of no par value)	1,000,000	
11. Less Reserve for Depreciation	5,000,000				
12. NET PROPERTY		3,000,000			2,000,000
13. PREPAYMENTS		50,000	26. SURPLUS:		
14. DEFERRED CHARGES		100,000	27. Earned	3,530,000	
15. PATENTS AND GOODWILL		100,000	28. Capital (arising from sale of common capital stock at price in excess of stated value)	1,900,000	
					5,430,000
TOTAL		$11,000,000	TOTAL		$11,100,000

Item 5, *INVENTORIES*, is the value the company places on the supplies it owns. The inventory of a manufacturer may contain raw materials that it uses in making the things it sells, partially finished goods in process of manufacture, and, finally, completed merchandise that it is ready to sell. Several methods are used to arrive at the value placed on these various items. The most common is to value them at their cost or present market value, whichever is lower.

You can be reasonably confident, however, that the figure given is an honest and significant one for the particular industry if the report is certified by a reputable firm of public accountants.

Next on the asset side is *TOTAL CURRENT ASSETS* (Item 6). This is an extremely important figure when used in connection with other items in the report, which we will come to presently. Then we will discover how to make total current assets tell their story.

INVESTMENT IN AFFILIATED COMPANY Item 7) represents the cost to our parent company of the capital stock of its subsidiary or affiliated company. A subsidiary is simply one company that is controlled by another. Most corporations that own other companies outright lump the figures in a CONSOLIDATED BALANCE SHEET. This means that, under cash, for example, one would find a total figure that represented all of the cash of the parent company and of its wholly owned subsidiary. This is a perfectly reasonable procedure because, in the last analysis, all of the money is controlled by the same persons.

Our typical company shows that it has *OTHER INVESTMENTS* (Item 8), in addition to its affiliated company. Sometimes good marketable securities other than Government bonds are carried as current assets, but the more conservative practice is to list these other security holdings separately. If they have been bought as a permanent investment, they would always be shown by themselves. "At cost, less than market" means that our company paid $100,000 for these other investments, but they are now worth more.

Among our assets is a *PLANT IMPROVEMENT FUND* (Item 9). Of course, this item does not appear in all company balance sheets, but is typical of special funds that companies set up for one purpose or another. For example, money set aside to pay off part of the bonded debt of a company might be segregated into a special fund. The money our directors have put aside to improve the plant would often be invested in Government bonds,

FIXED ASSETS

The next item (10) is *PROPERTY, PLANT, AND EQUIPMENT*, but it might just as well be labeled Fixed Assets as these items are used more or less interchangeably, Under Item 10, the report gives the value of land, buildings, and machinery and such movable things as trucks, furniture, and hand tools. Historically, probably more sins were committed against this balance sheet item than any other.

In olden days, cattlemen used to drive their stock to market in the city. It was a common trick to stop outside of town, spread out some salt for the cattle to make them thirsty and then let them drink all the water they could hold. When they were weighed for sale, the cattlemen would collect cash for the water the stock had drunk. Business buccaneers, taking the cue from their farmer friends, would often "write up" the value of their fixed assets. In other words, they would increase the value shown on the balance sheet, making the capital stock appear to be worth a lot more than it was. *Watered stock* proved a bad investment for most stockholders. The practice has, fortunately, been stopped, though it took major financial reorganizations to squeeze the water out of some securities.

The most common practice today is to list fixed assets at cost. Often, there is no ready market for most of the things that fall under this heading, so it is not possible to give market value. A good report will tell what is included under fixed assets and how it has been valued. If the value has been increased by *write-up* or decreased by *write-down*, a footnote explanation is usually given. A *write-up* might occur, for instance, if the value of real estate increased substantially. A *write-down* might follow the invention of a new machine that put an important part of the company's equipment out of date.

DEPRECIATION

Naturally, all of the fixed property of a company will wear out in time (except, of course, non-agricultural land). In recognition of this fact, companies set up a *RESERVE FOR APPRECIATION* (Item 11). If a truck costs $4,000 and is expected to last four years, it will be depreciated at the rate of $1,000 a year.

Two other items also frequently occur in connection with depreciation—*depletion* and *obsolescence*. Companies may lump depreciation, depletion, and obsolescence under a single title, or list them separately.

Depletion is a term used primarily by mining and oil companies (or any of the so-called extractive industries). Depletion means exhaust or use up. As the oil or other natural resource is used up, a reserve is set up, to compensate for the natural wealth the company no longer owns. This reserve is set up in recognition of the fact that, as the company sells its natural product, it must get back not only the cost of extracting but also the original cost of the natural resource.

Obsolescence represents the loss in value because a piece of property has gone out of date before it wore out. Airplanes are modern examples of assets that tend to get behind the times long before the parts wear out. (Women and husbands will be familiar with the speed at which ladies' hats "obsolesce.")

In our sample balance sheet we have placed the reserve for depreciation under fixed assets and then subtracted, giving us *NET PROPERTY* (Item 12), which we add into the asset column. Sometimes, companies put the reserve for depreciation in the liability column. As you can see, the effect is just the same whether it is *subtracted* from assets or *added* to liabilities.

The manufacturer, whose balance sheet we use, rents a New York showroom and pays his rent yearly, in advance. Consequently, he has listed under assets *PREPAYMENTS* (Item 13). This is listed as an asset because he has paid for the use of the showroom, but has not yet received the benefit from its use. The use is something coming to the firm in the following year and, hence, is an asset. The dollar value of this asset will decrease by one-twelfth each month during the coming year.

DEFERRED CHARGES (Item 14) represents a type of expenditure similar to prepayment. For example, our manufacturer brought out a new product last year, spending $100,000 introducing it to the market. As the benefit from this expenditure will be returned over months or even years to come, the manufacturer did not think it reasonable to charge the full expenditure against costs during the year. He has *deferred* the charges and will write them off gradually.

INTANGIBLES

The last entry in our asset column is *PATENTS AND GOODWILL* (Item 15). If our company were a young one, set up to manufacturer some new patented product, it would probably carry its patents at a substantial figure. In fact, *intangibles* of both old and new companies are often of great but generally unmeasurable worth.

Company practice varies considerably in assigning value to intangibles. Proctor & Gamble, despite the tremendous goodwill that has been built up for *Ivory Soap*, has reduced all of its intangibles to the nominal $1. Some of the big cigarette companies, on the contrary, place a high dollar value on the goodwill their brand names enjoy. Companies that spend a good deal for research and the development of new products are more inclined than others to reflect this fact in the value assigned to patents, license agreements, etc.

LIABILITIES

The liability side of the balance sheet appears a little deceptive at first glance. Several of the entries simply don't sound like liabilities by any ordinary definition of the term.

The first term on the liability side of any balance sheet is usually CURRENT LIABILITIES (Item 16). This is a companion to the Current Assets item across the page and includes all debts that fall due within the next year. The relation between current assets and current liabilities is one of the most revealing things to be gotten from the balance sheet, but we will go into that quite thoroughly later on.

ACCOUNTS PAYABLE (Item 17) represents the money that the company owes to its ordinary business creditors—unpaid bills for materials, supplies, insurance, and the like. Many companies itemize the money they owe in a much more detailed fashion than we have done, but, as you will see, the totals are the most interesting thing to us.

Item 18, *ACCRUED TAXES*, is the tax bill that the company estimates it still owes for the past year. We have lumped all taxes in our balance sheet, as many companies do. However, sometimes you will find each type of tax given separately. If the detailed procedure is followed, the description of the tax is usually quite sufficient to identify the separate items.

Accounts Payable was defined as the money the company owed to its regular business creditors. The company also owes, on any given day, wages to its own employees; interest to its bondholders and to banks from which it may have borrowed money; fees to its attorneys; pensions, etc. These are all totaled under *ACCRUED WAGES, INTEREST AND OTHER EXPENSES* (Item 19).

TOTAL CURRENT LIABILITIES (Item 20) is just the sum of everything that the company owed on December 31 and which must be paid sometime in the next twelve months.

It is quite clear that all of the things discussed above are liabilities. The rest of the entries on the liability side of the balance sheet, however, do not seem at first glance to be liabilities.

Our balance sheet shows that the company, on December 31, had $2,000,000 of 3½ percent First Mortgage BONDS outstanding (Item 21). Legally, the money received by a company when it sells bonds is considered a loan to the company. Therefore, it is obvious that the company owes to the bondholders an amount equal to the face value or the *call price* of the bonds it has outstanding. The call price is a figure usually larger than the face value of the bonds at which price the company can *call* the bonds in from the bondholders and pay them off before they ordinarily fall due. The date that often occurs as part of the name of a bond is the date at which the company has promised to pay off the loan from the bondholders.

RESERVES

The next heading, *RESERVE FOR CONTINGENCIES* (Item 22) sounds more like an asset than a liability. "My reserves," you might say, "are dollars in the bank, and dollars in the bank are assets.

No one would deny that you have something there. In fact, the corporation treasurer also has his reserve for contingencies balanced by either cash or some kind of unspecified investment on the asset side of the ledger. His reason for setting up a reserve on the liability side of the balance sheet is a precaution against making his financial position seem better than it is. He decided that the company might have to pay out this money during the coming year if certain things happened. If he did not set up the "reserve," his surplus would appear larger by an amount equal to his reserve.

A very large reserve for contingencies or a sharp increase in this figure from the previous year should be examined closely by the investor. Often, in the past, companies tried to hide their true earnings by transferring funds into a contingency reserve. As a reserve looks somewhat like a true liability, stockholders were confused about the real value of their securities. When a reserve is not set up for protection against some very probable loss or expenditure, it should be considered by the investor as part of surplus.

CAPITAL STOCK

Below reserves there is a major heading, CAPITAL STOCK (Item 23). Companies may have one type of security outstanding, or they may have a dozen. All of the issues that represent shares of ownership are capital, regardless of what they are called on the balance sheet—preferred stock, preference stock, common stock, founders' shares, capital stock, or something else.

Our typical company has one issue of 5 percent PREFERRED STOCK (Item 24). It is called *preferred* because those who own it have a right to dividends and assets before the *common* stockholders—that is, the holders are in a preferred position as owners. Usually, preferred stockholders do not have a voice in company affairs unless the company fails to pay them dividends at the promised rate. Their rights to dividends are almost always *cumulative*. This simply means that all past dividends must be paid before the other stockholders can receive anything. Preferred stockholders are not creditors of the company so it cannot properly be said that the company *owes* them the value of their holdings. However, in case the company decided to go out of business, preferred stockholders would have a prior claim on anything that was left in the company treasury after all of the creditors, including the bondholders, were paid off. In practice, this right does not always mean much, but it does explain why the book value of their holdings is carried as a liability.

COMMON STOCK (Item 25) is simple enough as far as definition is concerned. It represents the rights of the ordinary owner of the company. Each company has as many owners as it has stockholders. The proportion of the company that each stockholder owns is determined by the number of shares he has. However, neither the book value of a no-par common stock, nor the par value of an issue that has a given par, can be considered as representing either the original sale price, the market value, or what would be left for the stockholders if the company were liquidated.

A profitable company will seldom be dissolved. Once things have taken such a turn that dissolution appears desirable, the stated value of the stock is generally nothing but a fiction. Even if the company is profitable as a going institution, once it ceases to function even its tangible assets drop in value because there is not usually a ready market for its inventory of raw materials and semi-finished goods, or its plant and machinery.

SURPLUS

The last major heading on the liability side of the balance sheet is SURPLUS (Item 26). The surplus, of course, is not a liability in the popular sense at all. It represents, on our balance sheet, the difference between the stated value of our common stock and the net assets behind the stock.

Two different kinds of surplus frequently appear on company balance sheets, and our company has both kinds. The first type listed is EARNED surplus (Item 27). Earned surplus is roughly similar to your own savings. To the corporation, earned surplus is that part of net income which has not been paid to stockholders as dividends. It still belongs to you, but the directors have decided that it is best for the company and the stockholders to keep it in the business. The surplus may be invested in the plant just as you might invest part of your savings in your home. It may also be in cash or securities.

In addition to the earned surplus, our company also has a *CAPITAL* surplus (Item 28) of $1,900.00, which the balance sheet explains arose from selling the stock at a higher cost per share than is given as its stated value. A little arithmetic shows that the stock is carried on the books at $2.50 a share while the capital surplus amounts to $4.75 a share. From this we know that the company actually received an average of $7.25 net a share for the stock when it was sold.

WHAT DOES THE BALANCE SHEET SHOW?

Before we undertake to analyze the balance sheet figures, a word on just what an investor can expect to learn is in order. A generation or more ago, before present accounting standards had gained wide acceptance, considerable imagination went into the preparation of balance sheets. This, naturally, made the public skeptical of financial reports. Today, there is no substantial ground for skepticism. The certified public accountant, the listing requirements of the national stock exchanges, and the regulations of the Securities and Exchange Commission have, for all practical purposes, removed the grounds for doubting the good faith of financial reports.

The investor, however, is still faced with the task of determining the significance of the figures. As we have already seen, a number of items are based, to a large degree, upon estimates, while others are, of necessity, somewhat arbitrary.

NET WORKING CAPITAL

There is one very important thing that we can find from the balance sheet and accept with the full confidence that we know what we are dealing with. That is net working capital, sometimes simply called working capital.

On the asset side of our balance sheet, we have added up all of the current assets and show the total as Item 6. On the liability side, Item 20 gives the total of current liabilities. *Net working capital* or *net current assets* is the difference left after subtracting current liabilities from current assets. If you consider yourself an investor rather than a speculator, you should always insist that any company in which you invest have a comfortable amount of working capital. The ability of a company to meet its obligations with ease, expand its volume as business expands and take advantage of opportunities as they present themselves, is, to an important degree, determined by its working capital.

Probably the question in your mind is: "*Just what does 'comfortable amount' of working capital mean?*" Well, there are several methods used by analysts to judge whether a particular company has a sound working capital position. The first rough test for an industrial company is to compare the working capital figure with the current liability total. Most analysts say that minimum safety requires that net working capital at least equal current liabilities. Or, put another way, current assets should be at least twice as large as current liabilities.

There are so many different kinds of companies, however, that this test requires a great deal of modification if it is to be really helpful in analyzing companies in different industries. To help you interpret the current position of a company in which you are considering investing, the *current ratio* is more helpful than the dollar total of working capital. The current ratio is current assets divided by current liabilities.

In addition to working capital and current ratio, there are two other ways of testing the adequacy of the current position. *Net quick assets* provide a rigorous and important test of a company's ability to meet its current obligations. Net quick assets are found by taking total current assets (Item 6) and subtracting the value of inventories (Item 5). A well-fixed industrial company should show a reasonable excess of quick assets over current liabilities.

Finally, many analysts say that a good industrial company should have at least as much working capital (current assets less current liabilities) as the total book value of its bonds and preferred stock. In other words, current liabilities, bonded debt, and preferred stock *altogether* should not exceed the current assets.

INVENTORY AND INVENTORY TURNOVER

In the recent past, there has been much talk of inventories. Many commentators have said that these carry a serious danger to company earnings if management allows them to increase too much. Of course, this has always been true, but present high prices have made everyone more inventory-conscious than usual.

There are several dangers in a large inventory position. In the first place, sharp drop in price may cause serious losses; also, a large inventory may indicate that the company has accumulated a big supply of unsalable merchandise. The question still remains, however: "What do we mean by large inventory?"

As you certainly realize, an inventory is large or small only in terms of the yearly turnover and the type of business. We can discover the annual turnover of our sample company by dividing inventories (Item 5) into total annual sales (item "a" on the income account).

It is also interesting to compare the value of the inventory of a company being studied with total current assets. Again, however, there is considerable variation between different types of companies, so that the relationship becomes significant only when compared with similar companies.

NET BOOK VALUE OF SECURITIES

There is one other very important thing that can be gotten from the balance sheet, and that is the net book or equity value of the company's securities. We can calculate the net book value of each of the three types of securities our company has outstanding by a little very simple arithmetic. *Book value* means *the value at which something is carried on the books of the company.*

The full rights of the bondholders come before any of the rights of the stockholders, so, to find the net book value or net tangible assets backing up the bonds we add together the balance sheet value of the bonds, preferred stock, common stock, reserve, and surplus. This gives us a total of $9,630,000, (We would not include contingency reserve if we were reasonably sure the contingency was going to arise, but, as general reserves are often equivalent to surplus, it is, usually, best to treat the reserve just as though it were surplus.) However, part of this value represents the goodwill and patents carried at $100,000, which is not a tangible item, so, to be conservative, we subtract this amount, leaving $9,530,000 as the total net book value of the bonds. This is equivalent to $4,765 for each $1,000 bond, a generous figure. To calculate the net book value of the preferred stock, we must eliminate the face value of the bonds, and then, following the same procedure, add the value of the preferred stock, common stock, reserve, and surplus, and subtract goodwill. This gives us a total net book value for the preferred stock of $7,530 or $753 for each share of $100 par value preferred. This is also very good coverage for the preferred stock, but we must examine current earnings before becoming too enthusiastic about the value of any security.

The net book value of the common stock, while an interesting figure, is not so important as the coverage on the senior securities. In case of liquidation, there is seldom much left for the common stockholders because of the normal loss in value of company assets when they are put up for sale, as mentioned before. The book value figure, however, does give us a basis for comparison with other companies. Comparisons of net book value over a period of years also show us if the company is a soundly growing one or, on the other hand, is losing ground. Earnings, however, are our important measure of common stock values, as we will see shortly.

The net book value of the common stock is found by adding the stated value of the common stock, reserves, and surplus and then subtracting patents and goodwill. This gives us a total net book value of $6,530,000. As there are 400,000 shares of common outstanding, each share has a net book value of $16.32. You must be careful not to be misled by book value figures, particularly of common stock. Profitable companies (Coca-Cola, for example) often show a very low net book value and very substantial earnings. Railroads, on the other hand, may show a high book value for their common stock but have such low or irregular earnings that the market price of the stock is much less than its apparent book value. Banks, insurance companies, and investment trusts are exceptions to what we have said about common stock net book value. As their assets are largely liquid (i.e., cash, accounts receivable, and marketable securities), the book value of their common stock sometimes indicates its value very accurately.

PROPORTION OF BONDS, PREFERRED AND COMMON STOCK

Before investing, you will want to know the proportion of each kind of security issued by the company you are considering. A high proportion of bonds reduces the attractiveness of both the preferred and common stock, while too large an amount of preferred detracts from the value of the common.

The *bond ratio* is found by dividing the face value of the bonds (Item 21), or $2,000,000, by the total value of the bonds, preferred stock, common stock, reserve, and surplus, or $9,630,000. This shows that bonds amount to about 20 percent of the total of bonds, capital, and surplus.

The *preferred stock ratio* is found in the same way, only we divide the stated value of the preferred stock by the total of the other five items. Since we have half as much preferred stock as we have bonds, the preferred ratio is roughly 10.

Naturally, the *common stock ratio* will be the difference between 100 percent and the totals of the bonds and preferred, or 70 percent in our sample company. You will want to remember that the most valuable method of determining the common stock ratio is in combination with reserve and surplus. The surplus, as we have noted, is additional backing for the common stock and usually represents either original funds paid in to the company in excess of the stated value of the common stock (capital surplus), or undistributed earnings (earned surplus).

Most investment analysts carefully examine industrial companies that have more than about a quarter of their capitalization represented by bonds, while common stock should total at least as much as all senior securities (bonds and preferred issues). When this is not the case, companies often find it difficult to raise new capital. Banks don't like to lend them money because of the already large debt, and it is sometimes difficult to sell common stock because of all the bond interest or preferred dividends that must be paid before anything is available for the common stockholder.

Railroads and public utility companies are exceptions to most of the rules of thumb that we use in discussing The ABC Manufacturing Company, Inc. Their situation is different because of the tremendous amounts of money they have invested in their fixed assets, their small inventories and he ease with which they can collect their receivables. Senior securities of railroads and utility companies frequently amount to more than half of their capitalization, Speculators often interest themselves in companies that have a high proportion of debt or preferred stock because of the *leverage factor*. A simple illustration will show why. Let us take, for example, a company with $10,000,000 of 4 percent bonds outstanding. If the company is earning $440,000 before bond interest, there will be only $40,000 left for the common stock ($10,000,000 at 4% equals $400,000). However, an increase of only 10 percent in earnings (to $484,000) will leave $84,000 for common stock dividends, or an increase of more than 100 percent. If there is only a small common issue, the increase in earnings per share would appear very impressive.

You have probably already noticed that a decline of 10 percent in earnings would not only wipe out everything available for the common stock, but result in the company being unable to cover its full interest on its bonds without dipping into surplus. This is the great danger of so-called high leverage stocks and also illustrates the fundamental weakness of companies that have a disproportionate amount of debt or preferred stock. Investors would do well to steer clear of them. Speculators, however, will continue to be fascinated by the market opportunities they offer.

THE INCOME ACCOUNT

The fundamental soundness of a company, as shown by its balance sheet, is important to investors, but of even greater interest is the record of its operation. Its financial structure shows much of its ability to weather storms and pick up speed when times are good. It is the income record, however, that shows us how a company is actually doing and gives us our best guide to the future.

The *Consolidated Income and Earned Surplus* account of our company is stated on the next page. Follow the items given there and we will find out just how our company earned its money, what it did with its earnings, and what it all means in terms of our three classes of securities. We have used a combined income and surplus account because it is the form most frequently followed by industrial companies. However, sometimes the two statements are given separately. Also, a variety of names are used to describe this same part of the financial report. Sometimes it is called profit and loss account, sometimes *record of earnings*, and, often, simply *income account*. They are all the same thing.

The details that you will find on different income statements also vary a great deal. Some companies show only eight or ten separate items, while others will give a page or more of closely spaced entries that break down each individual type of revenue or cost. We have tried to strike a balance between extremes; give the major items that are in most income statements, omitting details that are only interesting to the expert analyst.

The most important source of revenue always makes up the first item on the income statement. In our company, it is *Net Sales* (Item "a"). If it were a railroad or a utility instead of a manufacturer, this item would be called *gross revenues*. In any case, it represents the money paid into the company by its customers. Net sales are given to show that the figure represents the amount of money actually received after allowing for discounts and returned goods.

Net sales or gross revenues, you will note, is given before any kind of miscellaneous revenue that might have been received from investments, the sale of company property, tax refunds, or the like. A well-prepared income statement is always set up this way so that the stockholder can estimate the success of the company in fulfilling its major job of selling goods or service. If this were not so, you could not tell whether the company was really losing or making money on its operations, particularly over the last few years when tax rebates and other unusual things have often had great influence on final net income figures.

The ABC Manufacturing Company, Inc.
CONSOLIDATED INCOME AND EARNED SURPLUS
For the Year Ended December 31

Item		
a. Sales		$10,000,000
b. COST OF SALES, EXPENSES AND OTHER OPERATING CHARGES:		
c. Cost of Goods Sold	$7,000,000	
d. Selling, Administrative & Gen. Expenses	500,000	
e. Depreciation	200,000	
f. Maintenance and Repairs	400,000	
g. Taxes (Other than Federal Inc. Taxes)	300,000	8,400,000
h. NET PROFIT FROM OPERATIONS		$1,600,000
i. OTHER INCOME:		
j. Royalties and Dividends	$250,000	
k. Interest	25,000	
l. TOTAL		$1,875,000
m. INTEREST CHARGES:		
n. Interest on Funded Debt	$70,000	
o. Other Interest	20,000	90,000
p. NET INCOME BEFORE PROVISION FOR FED. INCOME TAXES		$1,785,000
q. PROVISION FOR FEDERAL INCOME TAXES		678,300
r. NET INCOME		$1,106,700
s. DIVIDENDS		
t. Preferred Stock - $5.00 Per Share	$50,000	
u. Common Stock - $1.00 Per Share	400,000	
v. PROVISION FOR CONTINGENCIES	200,000	650,000
w. BALANCE CARRIED TO EARNED SURPLUS		456,700
x. EARNED SURPLUS – JANUARY 1		3,073,000
y. EARNED SURPLUS – DECEMBER 31		$3,530,000

COST OF SALES

A general heading, *Cost of Sales, Expenses, and Other Operating Charges* (Item "b") is characteristic of a manufacturing company, but a utility company or railroad would call all of these things *operating expenses*.

The most important subdivision is *Cost of Goods Sold* (Item "c"). Included under cost of goods sold are all of the expenses that go directly into the manufacture of the products the company sells—raw materials, wages, freight, power, and rent. We have lumped these expenses together, as many companies do. Sometimes, however, you will find each item listed separately. Analyzing a detailed income account is a pretty technical operation and had best be left to the expert.

We have shown separately, opposite "d," the *Selling, Administrative and General Expenses* of the past year. Unfortunately, there is little uniformity among companies in their treatment of these important non-manufacturing costs. Our figure includes the expenses of management; that is, executive salaries and clerical costs; commissions and salaries paid to salesmen; advertising expenses, and the like.

Depreciation ("e") shows us the amount that the company transferred from income during the year to the depreciation reserve that we ran across before as Item "11" on the balance sheet (Page 2). Depreciation must be charged against income unless the company is going to live on its own fat, something that no company can do for long and stay out of bankruptcy.

MAINTENANCE

Maintenance and Repairs (Item "f") represents the money spent to keep the plant in good operating order. For example, the truck that we mentioned under depreciation must be kept running day by day. The cost of new tires, recharging the battery, painting and mechanical repairs are all maintenance costs. Despite this day-to-day work on the truck, the company must still provide for the time when it wears out—hence, the reserve for depreciation.

You can readily understand from your own experience the close connection between maintenance and depreciation. If you do not take good care of your own car, you will have to buy a new one sooner than you would had you maintained it well. Corporations face the same problem with all of their equipment. If they do not do a good job of maintenance, much more will have to be set aside for depreciation to replace the abused tools and property.

Taxes are always with us. A profitable company always pays at least two types of taxes. One group of taxes are paid without regard to profits, and include real estate taxes, excise taxes, social security, and the like (Item "g"). As these payments are a direct part of the cost of doing business, they must be included before we can determine the *Net Profit From Operations* (Item "h").

Net Profit From Operations (sometimes called *gross profit*) tells us what the company made from manufacturing and selling its products. It is an interesting figure to investors because it indicates how efficiently and successfully the company operates in its primary purpose as a creator of wealth. As a glance at the income account will tell you, there are still several other items to be deducted before the stockholder can hope to get anything. You can also easily imagine that for many companies these other items may spell the difference between profit and loss. For these reasons, we use net profit from operations as an indicator of progress in manufacturing and merchandising efficiency, not as a judge of the investment quality of securities.

Miscellaneous Income not connected with the major purpose of the company is generally listed after net profit from operations. There are quite a number of ways that corporations increase their income, including interest and dividends on securities they own, fees for special services performed, royalties on patents they allow others to use, and tax refunds. Our income statement shows *Other Income* as Item "i," under which is shown income from *Royalties* and *Dividends* (Item "j"), and as a separate entry, *Interest* (Item "k") which the company received from its bond investments. The *Total* of other income (Item "l") shows us how much The ABC Manufacturing Company received from so-called *outside activities*. Corporations with diversified interests often receive tremendous amounts of other income.

INTEREST CHARGES

There is one other class of expenses that must be deducted from our income before we can determine the base on which taxes are paid, and that is *Interest Charges* (Item "m"). As our company has $2,000,000 worth of 3 ½ percent bonds outstanding, it will pay *Interest* on Funded Debt of $70,000 (Item "n"). During the year, the company also borrowed money from the bank, on which it, of course, paid interest, shown as *Other Interest* (Item "o").

Net Income Before Provision for Federal Income Taxes ("Item "p") is an interesting figure for historical comparison. It shows us how profitable the company was in all of its various operations. A comparison of this entry over a period of years will enable you to see how well the company had been doing as a business institution before the government stepped in for its share of net earnings. Federal taxes have varied so much in recent years that earnings before taxes are often a real help in judging business progress.

A few paragraphs back we mentioned that a profitable corporation pays two general types of taxes. We have already discussed those that are paid without reference to profits. *Provision for Federal Income Taxes* (Item "q") is ordinarily figured on the total income of the company after normal business expenses, and so appears on our income account below these charges. Bond interest, for example, as it is payment on a loan, is deducted beforehand. Preferred and common stock dividends, which are profits that go to owners of the company, come after all charges and taxes.

NET INCOME

After we have deducted all of our expenses and income taxes from total income, we get *Net Income* (Item "r"). Net income is the most interesting figure of all to the investor. Net income is the amount available to pay dividends on the preferred and common stock. From the balance sheet, we have learned a good deal about the company's stability and soundness of structure; from net profit from operations, we judge whether the company is improving in industrial efficiency. Net income tells us whether the securities of the company are likely to be a profitable investment.

The figure given for a single year is not nearly all of the store, however. As we have noted before, the historical record is usually more important than the figure for any given year. This is just as true of net income as any other item. So many things change from year to year that care must be taken not to draw hasty conclusions. During the war, Excess Profits Taxes had a tremendous effect on the earnings of many companies. In the next few years, carryback tax credits allowed some companies to show a net profit despite the fact that they had operated at a loss. Even net income can be a misleading figure unless one examines it carefully. A rough and easy way of judging how sound a figure it is would be to compare it with previous years.

The investor in stocks has a vital interest in *Dividends* (Item "s"). The first dividend that our company must pay is that on its *Preferred Stock* (Item "t"). Some companies will even pay preferred dividends out of earned surplus accumulated in the past if the net income is not large enough, but such a company is skating on thin ice unless the situation is most unusual.

The directors of our company decided to pay dividends totaling ($400,000 on the *Common Stock*, or $1 a share (Item "u"). As we have noted before, the amount of dividends paid is not determined by net income, but by a decision of the stockholders' representatives—the company's directors. Common dividends, just like preferred dividends, can be paid out of surplus if there is little or no net income. Sometimes companies do this if they have a long history of regular payments and don't want to spoil the record because of some special temporary situation that caused them to lose money. This occurs even less frequently and is more dangerous than paying preferred dividends out of surplus.

It is much more common, on the contrary, to plough earnings back into the business—a phrase you frequently see on the financial pages and in company reports. The directors of our typical company have decided to pay only $1 on the common stock, though net income would have permitted them to pay much more. They decided that the company should save the difference.

The next entry on our income account, *Provision for Contingencies* (Item "v") shows us where our reserve for contingencies arose. The treasurer of our typical company has put the provision for contingencies after dividends. However, you will discover, if you look at very many financial reports, that it is sometimes placed above net income.

All of the net income that was not paid out as dividends, or set aside for contingencies, is shown as *Balance Carried to Earned Surplus* (Item "w"). In other words, it is kept in the business. In previous years, the company had also earned more than it paid out so it had already accumulated by the beginning of the year an earned surplus of $3,073,000 (Item "x"). When we total the earned surplus accumulated during the year to that which the company had at the first of the year, we get the total earned surplus at the end of the year (Item "y"). You will notice that the total here is the same as that which we ran across on the balance sheet as Item 27.

Not all companies combine their income and surplus account. When they do not, you will find that *balance carried to surplus* will be the last item on the income account. The statement of consolidated surplus would appear as a third section of the corporation's financial report. A separate surplus account might be used if the company shifted funds for reserves to surplus during the year or made any other major changes in its method of treating the surplus account.

ANALYZING THE INCOME ACCOUNT

The income account, like the balance sheet, will tell us a lot more if we make a few detailed comparisons. The size of the totals on an income account doesn't mean much by itself. A company can have hundreds of millions of dollars in net sales and be a very bad investment. On the other hand, even a very modest profit in round figure may make a security attractive if there are only a small number of shares outstanding.

Before you select a company for investment, you will want to know something of its *margin of profit*, and how this figure has changed over the years. Finding the margin of profit is very simple. We just divide the net profit from operations (Item "h") by net sales (Item "a"). The figure we get (0.16) shows us that the company made a profit of 16 percent from operations. By itself, though, this is not very helpful. We can make it significant in two ways.

In the first place, we can compare it with the margin of profit in previous years, and, from this comparison, learn if the company excels other companies that do a similar type of business. If the margin of profit of our company is very low in comparison with other companies in the same field, it is an unhealthy sign. Naturally, if it is high, we have grounds to be optimistic.

Analysts also frequently use *operating ratio* for the same purpose. The operating ratio is the complement of the margin of profit. The margin of profit of our typical company is 16. The operating ratio is 84. You can find the operating ratio either by subtracting the margin of profit from 100 or dividing the total of operating costs ($8,400,000) by net sales ($10,000,000).

The margin of profit figure and the operating ratio, like all of those ratios we examined in connection with the balance sheet, give us general information about the company, help us judge its prospects for the future. All of these comparisons have significance for the long term as they tell us about the fundamental economic condition of the company. But you still have the right to ask: "Are the securities good investments for me now?"

Investors, as opposed to speculators, are primarily interested in two things. The first is safety for their capital and the second, regularity of income. They are also interested in the rate of return on their investment but, as you will see, the rate of return will be affected by the importance placed on safety and regularity. High income implies risk. Safety must be bought by accepting a lower return.

The safety of any security is determined primarily by the earnings of the company that are available to pay interest or dividends on the particular issues. Again, though, round dollar figures aren't of much help to us. What we want to know is the relationship between the total money available and the requirements for each of the securities issued by the company.

INTEREST COVERAGE

As the bonds of our company represent part of its debt, the first thing we want to know is how easily the company can pay the interest. From the income account we see that the company had total income of $1,875,000 (Item "1"). The interest charge on our bonds each year is $70,000 (3½ percent of $2,000,000—Item 21 on the balance sheet). Dividing total income by bond interest charges ($1,875,000 by $70,000) shows us that the company earned its bond interest 26 times over. Even after income taxes, bond interest was earned 17 times, a method of testing employed by conservative analysts. Before an industrial bond should be considered a safe investment, so our company has a wide margin of safety.

To calculate the *preferred dividend coverage* (i.e., the number of times preferred dividends were earned), we must use net income as our base, as Federal Income Taxes and all interest charges must be paid before anything is available for stockholders. As we have 10,000 shares of $100 par value of preferred stock which pays a dividend of 5 percent, the total dividend requirement for the preferred stock is $50,000 (Items 24 on the balance sheet and "t" on the income account).

EARNINGS PER COMMON SHARE

The buyer of common stocks is often more concerned with the earnings per share of his stock than he is with the dividend. It is usually earnings per share or, rather, prospective earnings per share, that influence stock market prices. Our income account does not show the earnings available for the common stock, so we must calculate it ourselves. It is net income less preferred dividends (Items "r"- "t"), or $1,056,700. From the balance sheet, we know that there are 400,000 shares outstanding, so the company earned about $2.64 per share.

All of these ratios have been calculated for a single year. It cannot be emphasized too strongly, however, that the record is more important to the investor than the report of any single year. By all the tests we have employed, both the bonds and the preferred stock of our typical company appear to be very good investments, if their market prices were not too high. The investor would want to look back, however, to determine whether the operations were reasonably typical of the company.

Bonds and preferred stocks that are very safe usually sell at pretty high prices, so the yield to the investor is small. For example, if our company has been showing about the same coverage on its preferred dividends for many years and there is good reason to believe that the future will be equally kind, the company would probably replace the old 5 percent preferred with a new issue paying a lower rate, perhaps 4 percent.

STOCK PRICES

As the common stock does not receive a guaranteed dividend, its market value is determined by a great variety of influences in addition to the present yield of the stock measured by its dividends. The stock market, by bringing together buyers and sellers from all over the world, reflects their composite judgment of the present and future value of the stock. We cannot attempt here to write a treatise on the stock market. There is one important ratio, however, that every common stock buyer considers. That is the ratio of earnings to market price.

The so-called *price-earnings ratio* is simply the earnings per share on the common stock divided into the market price. Our typical company earned $2.64 a common share in the year. If the stock were selling at $30 a share, its price-earnings ratio would be about 11.4. This is the basis figure that you would want to use in comparing the common stock of this particular company with other similar stocks.

17
IMPORTANT TERMS AND CONCEPTS

LIABILITIES
 WHAT THE COMPANY OWES—+ RESERVES + SURPLUS + STOCKHOLDERS INTEREST IN THE COMPANY

ASSETS
 WHAT THE COMPANY OWNS— + WHAT IS OWED TO THE COMPANY

FIXED ASSETS
 MACHINERY, EQUIPMENT, BUILDINGS, ETC.

EXAMPLES OF FIXED ASSETS
 DESKS, TABLES, FILING CABINETS, BUILDINGS, LAND, TIMBERLAND, CARS AND TRUCKS, LOCOMOTIVES AND FREIGHT CARS, SHIPYARDS, OIL LANDS, ORE DEPOSITS, FOUNDRIES

EXAMPLES OF:
 PREPAID EXPENSES
  PREPAID INSURANCE, PREPAID RENT, PREPAIDD ROYALTIES AND PREPAID INTEREST

 DEFERRED CHARGES
  AMORTIZATION OF BOND DISCOUNT, ORGANIZATION EXPENSE, MOVING EXPENSES, DEVELOPMENT EXPENSES

ACCOUNTS PAYABLE
 BILLS THE COMPANY OWES TO OTHERS

BONDHOLDERS ARE CREDITORS
 BOND CERTIFICATES ARE IOU'S ISSUED BY A COMPANY BACKED BY A PLEDGE

BONDHOLDERS ARE OWNERS
 A STOCK CERTIFICATE IS EVIDENCE OF THE SHAREHOLDER'S OWNERSHIP

EARNED SURPLUS
 INCOME PLOWED BACK INTO THE BUSINESS

NET SALES
 GROSS SALES MINUS DISCOUNTS AND RETURNED GOODS

NET INCOME
 = TOTAL INCOME MINUS ALL EXPENSES AND INCOME TAXES

www.ingramcontent.com/pod-product-compliance
Lightning Source LLC
Chambersburg PA
CBHW081811300426
44116CB00014B/2321